THE UNITED NATIONS CONVENTION AGAINST TORTURE

INTERNATIONAL STUDIES IN HUMAN RIGHTS

Ramcharan, B.G. (ed.): International Law and Fact-Finding in the Field of Human Rights. 1982. ISBN 90-247-3042-2.

Ramcharan, B.G.: Humanitarian Good Offices in International Law. 1983. ISBN 90-247-2805-3.

Alston, P. and Tomaševski, K. (eds.): The Right to Food. 1984. ISBN 90-247-3087-2.

Bloed, A. and Van Dijk, P. (eds.): Essays on Human Rights in the Helsinki Process. 1985. ISBN 90-247-3211-5.

Ramcharan, B.G. (ed.): The Right to Life in International Law. 1985. ISBN 90-247-3074-0.

Törnudd, K.: Finland and the International Norms of Human Rights. 1986. ISBN 90-247-3257-3.

Thoolen, H. and Verstappen, B.: Human Rights Missions. A Study of the Fact-finding Practice of Non-governmental Organizations. 1986. ISBN 90-247-3364-2.

Hannum, H.: The Right to Leave and Return in International Law and Practice. 1987. ISBN 90-247-3445-2.

Burgers, J.H. and Danelius, H.: The United Nations Convention against Torture. 1988. ISBN 90-247-3609-9

The Martinus Nijhoff series 'International Studies in Human Rights' is designed to shed light on current legal and political aspects of process and organization in the field of human rights.

The United Nations Convention against Torture

A Handbook on the Convention against Torture and Other Cruel, Inhuman or Degrading Treatment or Punishment

by

J. Herman BURGERS and Hans DANELIUS

MARTINUS NIJHOFF PUBLISHERS
DORDRECHT / BOSTON / LONDON

Library of Congress Cataloging in Publication Data

Burgers, Herman, 1926-
The United Nations Convention against Torture.

(International studies in human rights ; 9)
1. Convention against Torture and Other Cruel,
Inhuman, or Degrading Treatment or Punishment (1984)
2. Torture (International law) 3. Human rights.
I. Danelius, Hans. II. Title. III. Series:
International studies in human rights ; v. 9.
K5410.T6B87 1988 341.4'81 87-24042

ISBN 90-247-3609-9

Published by Martinus Nijhoff Publishers,
P.O. Box 163, 3300 AD Dordrecht, The Netherlands

Sold and distributed in the U.S.A. and Canada
by Kluwer Academic Publishers,
101 Philip Drive, Norwell, MA 02061, U.S.A.

Sold in the U.K. and Ireland
by Kluwer Law, part of Kluwer Publishing Ltd.,
1 Harlequin Avenue, Brentford,
Middlesex TW 8 9EW, U.K.

In all other countries, sold and distributed
by Kluwer Academic Publishers Group,
P.O. Box 322, 3300 AH Dordrecht, The Netherlands

Printed in the Netherlands

Preface

The *Convention against Torture and Other Cruel, Inhuman or Degrading Treatment or Punishment*, adopted by the General Assembly of the United Nations on 10 December 1984, entered into force on 26 June 1987 for the first twenty States which ratified it. The present handbook is intended first of all for use by people who will have to work with the *Convention* in the exercise of their functions, such as diplomats, magistrates, law enforcement officials, military officers and lawyers. It has also been written for the benefit of all persons interested in the fight against torture and other inhuman acts inflicted upon people who are deprived of their liberty. Furthermore, it may be of some value for students of international law and international relations.

This treatise consists of, on the one hand, a description and analysis of the contents of the *Convention* and, on the other hand, a historical survey of the background and the genesis of the *Convention.*

The first chapter gives a summary account of what the *Convention* is about. The fourth chapter contains an article-by-article commentary on the provisions of the *Convention.* The second and third chapters provide mainly historical information.

The *Convention* was adopted on 10 December 1984 after preparatory work which stretched over a period of seven years. Most of this work was done in a Working Group established by the United Nations Commission on Human Rights. The *travaux préparatoires* of the *Convention* cannot be easily studied in UN documents. The principal source materials which have been published are the seven reports submitted by the Working Group to the Commission on Human Rights during the period 1978–1984. No records were made of the deliberations in the Working Group. Most of the proposals tabled in the course of these deliberations had the form of conference room papers that have not been published. Several interesting details of the elaboration of the *Convention* are registered only in the memories of those who took part in the drafting work.

The third chapter describes the essentials of the drafting history of the *Convention*, in the first place because some knowledge of this history is indispensable for a full understanding of the final text, in the second place because this history is important in itself as a case-study in international legislation. The historical account given in this chapter is based on both published and unpublished UN documents as well as on the personal recollections of the authors.

For a full appreciation of the *Convention* it is also necessary to understand its place in the context of a multitude of efforts undertaken during the past decades in order to combat the pestilence of torture. In particular the nineteen-seventies saw a series of initiatives for this purpose, both of a non-governmental and of an intergovernmental character. One of the first results was the adoption of a UN *Declaration* against torture in 1975. The second chapter sketches this general background of the *Convention*, including some activities carried out after the *Convention* had been finalized. The same chapter also explains some basic characteristics of international human rights law for the benefit of those readers who are not familiar with its terms and concepts.

The two authors were actively involved in the preparation of the *Convention.* Herman Burgers, at the time a member of the Netherlands delegation to the UN Commission on Human Rights, served during 1982–1984 as chairman-rapporteur of the Working Group set up by the Commission to draw up the text of the *Convention.* Hans Danelius, then Under-Secretary for Legal and Consular Affairs of the Swedish Ministry of Foreign Affairs and now Ambassador of Sweden in the Netherlands, wrote the initial drafts both of the *Declaration* and of the *Convention* and participated actively in all sessions of the Working Group.

Table of contents

Chapter I

The essentials of the Convention

a) *Principal aim of the Convention*

It is expedient to redress at the outset a widespread misunderstanding as to the objective of the *Convention against Torture and Other Cruel, Inhuman or Degrading Treatment or Punishment*, adopted by the General Assembly of the United Nations in 1984.[1] Many people assume that the *Convention's* principal aim is to *outlaw* torture and other cruel, inhuman or degrading treatment or punishment. This assumption is not correct insofar as it would imply that the prohibition of these practices is established under international law by the *Convention* only and that this prohibition will be binding as a rule of international law only for those States which have become parties to the *Convention*. On the contrary, the *Convention* is based upon the recognition that the above-mentioned practices are already outlawed under international law. The principal aim of the *Convention* is to *strengthen* the existing prohibition of such practices by a number of supportive measures.

A second aspect that has to be noted is that the *Convention* does not deal with cases of ill-treatment which occur in an exclusively non-governmental setting. It only relates to practices which occur under some sort of responsibility of public officials or other persons acting in an official capacity.

In aiming at the effective elimination of torture and other forms of cruel, inhuman or degrading treatment or punishment, the *Convention* pays particular attention to influencing the behaviour of persons who may become involved in situations in which such practices might occur.

In all these aspects the *Convention* has been inspired primarily by the *Declaration* on the same subject-matter, adopted by the General Assembly of the United Nations in 1975.[2]

b) *Structure of the Convention*

The articles of the *Convention* are divided in three parts. Part I (articles 1-16) contains the substantive provisions. Most of these provisions relate only to torture and not to other forms of cruel, inhuman or degrading treatment or punishment. However, a limited number of provisions apply to all categories. Part II (articles 17-24) contains the implementation provisions. These articles provide for several forms of international supervision with regard to the

[1] See Appendix 1.
[2] See Appendix 2.

observance by States Parties of their obligations under the substantive provisions. Part III (articles 25-32) contains the final clauses. These provisions deal with such matters as signature and ratification of the *Convention*, its entry into force, amendments, denunciation, settlement of disputes concerning the *Convention's* interpretation or application, and optional exclusion of one of the implementation provisions.

c) *Substantive provisions relating to all forms of cruel, inhuman or degrading treatment or punishment*

The substantive part contains a limited number of provisions which apply both to torture and to other acts of cruel, inhuman or degrading treatment or punishment, when such acts are committed by or at the instigation of or with the consent or acquiescence of a public official or other person acting in an official capacity.

Each State Party shall prevent any such acts in any territory under its jurisdiction (article 2, paragraph 1, and article 16, paragraph 1).

Each State Party shall include the prohibition of all such acts in the rules or instructions issued with regard to the duties and functions of both civil and military law enforcement personnel as well as medical personnel, public officials and other persons who may be involved in the custody, interrogation or treatment of any individual subjected to any form of arrest, detention or imprisonment (article 10, paragraph 2).

Each State Party shall ensure that education and information regarding this prohibition are fully included in the training of all such persons (article 10, paragraph 1).

Each State Party shall keep under systematic review interrogation rules, instructions, methods and practices as well as arrangements for the custody and treatment of persons under arrest, detention or imprisonment, with a view to preventing torture or any other acts of cruel, inhuman or degrading treatment or punishment (article 11).

Each State Party shall ensure that its competent authorities proceed to a prompt and impartial investigation, wherever there is reasonable ground to believe that any such act has been committed on its territory (article 12).

Any individual who alleges he has been subjected to any such act shall be entitled to have his case promptly and impartially examined by the competent authorities (article 13).

The text of articles 10, 11, 12 and 13 only refers to torture. Article 16, paragraph 1, provides that the obligations contained in these articles also apply to other forms of cruel, inhuman or degrading treatment or punishment.

d) *Substantive provisions relating specifically to torture*

The substantive part opens with an elaborate definition of torture for the purposes of the *Convention* (article 1, paragraph 1). The definition refers to any act by which severe pain or suffering, whether physical or mental, is intentionally inflicted on a person by – or at the instigation of or with the consent or acquiescence of – a public official or other person acting in an official capacity. The definition further explains that it refers to these acts when committed for such purposes as obtaining information or a confession from the direct victim or from a third person, punishing, intimidating or coercing him or a third person, or for any reason based on discrimination. Pain or suffering arising only from lawful sanctions are not included in the definition.

Each State Party shall take effective measures to prevent acts of torture on its territory (article 2, paragraph 1).

No exceptional circumstances whatsoever, whether a state of war, a threat of war, internal political instability or any other public emergency, may be invoked as a justification of torture (article 2, paragraph 2).

No order from a superior officer or a public authority may be invoked as a justification of torture (article 2, paragraph 3).

Any statement which has been made as a result of torture shall not be invoked as evidence in any proceedings (article 15).

Victims of torture shall have an enforceable right to fair and adequate compensation including the means for as full rehabilitation as possible (article 14).

No State Party shall expel, return or extradite a person to another State where there are substantial grounds for believing that he would be in danger of being subjected to torture (article 3).

Articles 4 to 9 contain provisions relating to the application of penal law with regard to persons who are guilty of torture.

Each State Party shall ensure that acts of torture, attempts to commit torture as well as acts constituting complicity or participation in torture are offences under its criminal law, punishable by appropriate penalties which take into account their grave nature (article 4).

In respect of those offences the *Convention* contains a system of universal jurisdiction, resulting from articles 5, 6 and 7. This means that there shall be no safe-haven for torturers or for their accomplices in the countries which are Parties to the *Convention*. Each State Party in whose territory a person alleged to have committed such an offence is found shall, even if the alleged offender is not its national and if the offence was committed abroad, be obliged to submit the case to its competent authorities for the purpose of prosecution unless it extradites the alleged offender to another State.

With regard to the offences referred to in article 4, the *Convention* further contains provisions concerning extradition to other States Parties (article 8) and concerning assistance to other States Parties in connection with criminal proceedings (article 9).

e) *Implementation provisions*

The implementation part provides first of all for the creation of an international supervisory body (articles 17 and 18). This body, the "Committee against Torture", consists of ten experts who are elected by the States Parties. The experts perform their functions not in the capacity of government representatives but in their personal capacity. Once a year, the Committee submits a report on its activities to the States Parties and to the United Nations General Assembly (article 24).

The States Parties are to submit to the Committee reports on the measures they have taken to give effect to their undertakings under the *Convention*; these reports are also transmitted to all States Parties (article 19, paragraphs 1 and 2).

The reports of the States Parties are considered by the Committee. The Committee may forward general comments on a particular report to the State Party concerned. It may also decide to include such general comments in its own annual report, together with the observations thereon received from the State Party (article 19, paragraphs 3 and 4).

The provisions of article 19 apply to all States Parties. The same does not hold for the provisions contained in articles 20 to 22.

According to article 20, the Committee may initiate a confidential inquiry if it receives reliable information which appears to it to contain well-founded indications that torture is being systematically practised in the territory of a State Party. The Committee transmits the findings of such an inquiry to the State Party concerned together with its comments or suggestions. These proceedings are confidential, but after they have been completed the Committee may, after consultation with the State Party concerned, decide to include a summary account of the results of the proceedings in its annual report.

According to article 28 each State Party may at the time of signature or ratification of the *Convention* or at the time of accession to the *Convention* declare that it does not recognize the competence of the Committee provided for in article 20.

Articles 21 and 22 contain two optional procedures enabling the Committee to consider complaints against States Parties. These procedures are optional because each of them applies only to those States Parties which have declared explicitly that they recognize the competence of the Committee under the procedure. Under the first procedure the Committee may consider communications from a State Party who claims that another State Party is not fulfilling its obligations under the *Convention* (article 21). Under the second procedure the Committee may consider communications from or on behalf of individuals who claim to be victims of a violation of the *Convention* by a State Party (article 22).

Chapter II

The Background of the Convention

1. Human rights and the United Nations

a) *The human rights idea*

Before the twentieth century States seldom entered into legal obligations towards other States in respect of the treatment of their own citizens; however, such obligations have become almost commonplace following the Second World War. This was due to the impact of the idea of human rights, an idea which in itself goes much further back in history.

The idea of human rights developed as a defence against despotism in the exercise of government power. It was based upon the recognition that the human being does not exist for the benefit of the State, but that the State exists for the benefit of the human being. The principal objective of human rights is to provide a set of rules for the relationship between the individual and the government, bearing in mind their fundamental inequality of power. These rules bring out the belief that this relationship must not only be characterized by rights of the government and corresponding duties of the individual, but must also be based upon rights of the individual which entail obligations on the part of the government.

Twice in the course of history the idea of human rights arose as a wave, exerting a powerful influence in the fields of politics, legislation and the administration of justice. The first wave had its beginnings in the seventeenth century and its culmination towards the end of the eighteenth century. English and French thinkers in particular argued that the human being was endowed by nature with inalienable fundamental rights which can be invoked against the government and which must be safeguarded by the government. This concept was given a prominent place in the American *Declaration of Independence* of 1776. In France the same idea was elaborated in the *Declaration of the Rights of Man and of the Citizen* of 1789. In the course of the nineteenth century human rights were incorporated into the constitutions of a considerable number of countries.

The second wave began its rise in the 1930s. This renewed interest in the old idea of human rights developed as a reaction against the ideologies and practices of the totalitarian régimes that had come to power in several countries. The idea received a tremendous stimulant after the collapse of the Third Reich when the full scale of the horrors perpetrated by the Nazis came to light. This prompted the founders of the United Nations at the Conference of San Francisco in 1945 to give the promotion of human rights an important place among the tasks of the new world organization.

b) *Human rights instruments of the UN and other intergovernmental organizations*

The Charter of the United Nations authorized one of the principal organs of the organization, the Economic and Social Council (ECOSOC), to establish a commission for the promotion of human rights. The ECOSOC set up the Commission on Human Rights in 1946. The first assignment of this Commission was to prepare an International Bill of Rights, after the example of the national Bills of Rights that had been proclaimed in previous centuries. The Commission conceived the establishment of such an International Bill of Rights as a three-step process. The first step would consist of describing the rights concerned, the second step of embedding these rights in legal obligations of States, and the third step of constructing an international system for ensuring the implementation of these obligations by the States.

The first step was completed in a surprisingly brief time. On the basis of a text prepared by the Commission, the General Assembly of the United Nations adopted on 10 December 1948 the *Universal Declaration of Human Rights*. This simple document of only thirty articles has remained until today the foundation for all further UN activities concerning human rights.

The Commission combined the second and the third step and submitted to the General Assembly in 1954 its drafts for two international treaties, each of which would cover one part of the rights set out in the *Universal Declaration* and contain a system for monitoring the implementation of those rights. However, a considerable delay intervened in the finalization of these treaties by the Assembly. It was not until 1966 that the General Assembly established the definitive text of these two basic treaties, which were named the *International Covenant on Civil and Political Rights* and the *International Covenant on Economic, Social and Cultural Rights*. And it was not until 1976 that the two *Covenants* entered into force. At present, over eighty States have become parties to the *Covenants*.

Whereas it took twenty years to complete the International Bill of Rights envisaged by the United Nations, the European countries that are members of the Council of Europe needed less time for a similar exercise. In 1950 they signed in Rome a regional *Convention for the Protection of Human Rights and Fundamental Freedoms*, which covers about the same rights as those set forth in the *International Covenant on Civil and Political Rights*. In drafting this *Convention* they had made use of texts that had been prepared by the UN Commission on Human Rights. Besides this *European Convention* there now exist two other regional human rights treaties: the *American Convention on Human Rights*, signed in 1969 in San José, Costa Rica, under the auspices of the Organization of American States; and the *African Charter on Human and Peoples' Rights*, signed in 1981 in Nairobi under the auspices of the Organization of African Unity.

The *Universal Declaration* and the two *International Covenants*, which together form the *International Bill of Rights*, are by no means the only human rights instruments of the United Nations. Under the auspices of the UN, numerous instruments have been drawn up on special subjects in the field of human rights. As to the legal character of the norms they contain, all such instruments have the status either of recommendations or of binding treaties.

An example of the first category is the *Standard Minimum Rules for the Treatment of Prisoners*, adopted by the first UN Congress on the Prevention of Crime and the Treatment of Offenders in 1955 and approved by the ECOSOC in 1957. Other examples of this category are the following texts adopted by the UN General Assembly: the *Declaration on the Rights of the Child* (1959); the *Declaration on the Elimination of All Forms of Racial Discrimination* (1963); the *Declaration on the Elimination of Discrimination against Women* (1967); the *Declaration on the Protection of All Persons from Being Subjected to Torture and Other Cruel, Inhuman or Degrading Treatment or Punishment* (1975); the *Code of Conduct for Law Enforcement Officials* (1979); the *Declaration on the Elimination of All Forms of Intolerance and of Discrimination based on Religion or Belief* (1981); and the *Principles of Medical Ethics* (1982).

Examples of the second category are the following conventions adopted by the UN General Assembly: the *Convention on the Prevention and Punishment of the Crime of Genocide* (1948); the *Convention Relating to the Status of Refugees* (1951); the *International Convention on the Elimination of All Forms of Racial Discrimination* (1965); the *International Convention on the Suppression and Punishment of the Crime of Apartheid* (1973); the *Convention on the Elimination of All Forms of Discrimination against Women* (1979); and the *Convention against Torture and Other Cruel, Inhuman or Degrading Treatment or Punishment* (1984).

c) *Comparison of declarations and conventions*

Precisely because conventions contain legally binding obligations, the drafting of such instruments often requires a more time-consuming effort than the drafting of declarations. In a declaration rights may be described globally, but a convention has to specify in further detail what these rights involve and what limitations on their exercise are allowed. In order to promote human rights it has therefore frequently proved useful to direct efforts in the first instance to drawing up international declarations. As some of the above-mentioned examples illustrate, such declarations have more than once received a follow-up in the form of a convention.

Even though from a legal point a view declarations and similar instruments are no more than recommendations, their moral and political authority can nonetheless be considerable. Therefore one may in many cases call a government to account by invoking the standards contained in such instruments. In particular the *Universal Declaration of Human Rights*, which was explicitly intended as a common standard of achievement and not as a norm for immediate application, has assumed a far more authoritative and normative character over the years than was foreseen in 1948.

In the final analysis, of course, the protection of human rights benefits most from the conclusion of conventions because these impose obligations of positive law upon States. The value of such conventions is increased if they provide for effective procedures to secure observance of the norms they set forth. In addition, conventions can be useful in that they elaborate norms in greater detail than is commonly done in declarations and in that they outline specific measures for achieving the aims set.

An important difference between the two categories, however, is that declarations address themselves to all members of the organization under whose auspices they have been adopted or even to the entire world, whereas conventions confer obligations exclusively on those States which have become parties to them. In view of a widespread misunderstanding, it has to be pointed out that this is not the same as the States who signed them. In the case of most conventions, signature does not by itself entail a definitive commitment. Binding commitment ensues when the signatory State deposits a specific written pronouncement to that effect, usually named the instrument of ratification. Many conventions also provide for the possibility that non-signatory States enter into a binding commitment by depositing a pronouncement which in this case is named the instrument of accession. The parties to a convention are those States which have deposited instruments of ratification or accession. Even this does not always imply that the obligations set out in the convention are in force for the States concerned, because a multilateral convention normally provides that it will only enter into force after a certain minimum number of States have become Parties to it.

d) *Implementation procedures*

A State for which a convention has entered into force is legally obliged to respect and implement it, but in the present international society this does not mean that such a State can really be forced to do so. In order to promote their actual observance, many human rights conventions include procedures for international supervision of their implementation by the States Parties. Such conventions often also provide for the establishment of international supervisory organs. Current international jargon uses in this connection the terms "implementation procedures" and "implementation organs". From a logical point of view these terms are not wholly correct, for it is up to the States to implement the conventions while the function of those international procedures and organs is to supervise this implementation.

Under the European *Convention for the Protection of Human Rights and Fundamental Freedoms* of 1950, a European Commission of Human Rights as well as a European Court of Human Rights have been created which deal with complaints concerning violations of this convention. Such complaints may be submitted by individuals as well as by States Parties. Eventually, these European procedures can result in decisions which are binding upon the State Party concerned.

The implementation organ created under the *International Covenant on Civil and Political Rights* is the Human Rights Committee, composed of eighteen persons chosen by the States Parties. This Committee, established in 1976, should not be confused with the UN Commission on Human Rights, established in 1946 by the ECOSOC and composed of States. The Human Rights Committee, too, is competent to consider complaints of States and of individuals, but cannot issue binding decisions.

The European State complaint procedure applies to all States which are parties to the *European Convention*. This is called a *mandatory* procedure. On the other hand, the individual complaint procedure under the *European Convention* only applies to those States Parties which have expressly declared that they recognize the competence of the Commission to consider such complaints. This is called an *optional* procedure. The system under the *American Convention on Human Rights* of 1969 is just the reverse: the individual complaint procedure is mandatory whereas the State complaint procedure is optional. In the case of the Human Rights Committee, both the State complaint procedure and the individual complaint procedure are optional. The first procedure is laid down in the *International Covenant on Civil and Political Rights*; the second procedure is embodied in a separate *Optional Protocol*, adopted in 1966 by the UN General Assembly at the same time as the two *Covenants*. The only mandatory implementation procedure under the *Covenant on Civil and Political Rights* relates to reporting by the States Parties on the implementation of the rights concerned.

Meanwhile, the submission of complaints to an international supervisory body under a human rights convention is not the only possibility for international action to counter human rights violations. Year after year, countries who abuse human rights are the targets of sharp criticism in the United Nations. This happens in the General Assembly in New York as well as in the Commission on Human Rights in Geneva. Moreover, these bodies have adopted many resolutions denouncing such abuses and exhorting the governments concerned to restore respect for human rights. In a number of cases special rapporteurs have been appointed with the task of examining the human rights situation in a particular country and of entering into contact with the responsible authorities. Besides, the Commission has sometimes appointed persons with the task of reporting not on a specific country but on a specific category of human rights violations. For instance, there is now a UN working group on enforced or involuntary disappearances, a special rapporteur on summary or arbitrary executions, and a special rapporteur on torture.[1]

---

[1] *Cf. infra* p. 23.

2. Inclusion of the prohibition of torture in international standards

Torture has been practised in many parts of the world in many periods of history, in particular as a method to obtain evidence for judicial proceedings.[2] In Europe this practice assumed large proportions in the later Middle Ages, when confession came to be regarded as the "queen of proofs". One of the most impressive accomplishments of the era of Enlightenment was the abolition of torture as a routine element of criminal procedure. As Edward Peters observes:

> "In revision after revision from 1750 on, the provisions for torture in the criminal codes of Europe were rolled back, until by 1800 they were barely visible. Along with legislative revision, a large literature condemning torture on both legal and moral grounds grew up and was circulated widely. Its best-known example was Cesare Beccaria's immensely influential treatise *On Crimes and Punishments* of 1764... After the end of the eighteenth century torture acquired a universally pejorative association and came to be considered the institutional antithesis of human rights."[3]
>
> "Statutory abolition of torture in criminal law swept virtually all of Europe during the eighteenth and early nineteenth centuries, to the extent that Victor Hugo could announce in 1874 that 'torture has ceased to exist'."[4]

Who would have dared to predict in 1874 that torture would make a terrible come-back in the twentieth century? The totalitarian régimes that established themselves in the period between the First and the Second World Wars deliberately employed torture as one of the mainstays of their power. Extraction of confessions was only a secondary function of their torture practices, the primary function being to spread terror among the population. Besides torture, these régimes also applied many other forms of inhuman treatment to the inmates of their prisons and concentration camps.

It is against this background that the prohibition of all such practices was explicitly included in 1948 in the *Universal Declaration of Human Rights*. Article

---

[2] The history of torture, and of the fight against torture, has been described in many publications. Four major general studies are: *Piero Fiorelli*, La tortura giudiziaria nel diritto comune (two volumes, Milan, 1953-4), *Alec Mellor*, La Torture (Paris, 1949, 2nd edition, Tours, 1961), *Malise Ruthven*, Torture: The Grand Conspiracy (London, 1978), and *Edward Peters*, Torture (New York/Oxford, 1985). The reader is referred to the bibliographical essay included in the work of *Peters* for a detailed introduction into the literature.

An important survey of recent international efforts to combat torture can be found in *Nigel Rodley*, The Treatment of Prisoners under International Law (Oxford, 1987).

[3] *Peters*, *op.cit.*, pp. 74-75.

[4] *Ibidem*, pp. 4-5.

5 of the *Declaration* reads: "No one shall be subjected to torture or to cruel, inhuman or degrading treatment or punishment."

In 1966 the prohibition was included in the *International Covenant on Civil and Political Rights*. Article 7 of the *Covenant* reads: "No one shall be subjected to torture or to cruel, inhuman or degrading treatment or punishment. In particular, no one shall be subjected without his free consent to medical or scientific experimentation." The *Covenant* allows no exceptions to this prohibition. According to article 4, the States Parties may take measures derogating from some of their obligations under the *Covenant* in time of public emergency which threatens the life of the nation; however, the same article mentions article 7 as one of the provisions from which no derogation may be made.

Practically the same rules can be found in the European *Convention for the Protection of Human Rights and Fundamental Freedoms* of 1950. Article 3 of this *Convention* reads: "No one shall be subjected to torture or to inhuman or degrading treatment or punishment." This formulation corresponds to that of the *Universal Declaration* but for the omission of the term "cruel" which was considered to be too subjective. Article 3 is further mentioned in article 15 of the *Convention* as one of the provisions from which no derogation shall be made, even in time of war or other public emergency threatening the life of the nation.

Similar provisions are contained in the two other regional human rights conventions. Article 5, paragraph 2, of the *American Convention on Human Rights* of 1969 reads: "No one shall be subjected to torture or to cruel, inhuman, or degrading punishment or treatment. All persons deprived of their liberty shall be treated with respect for the inherent dignity of the human person." According to article 27, suspension of this provision is not possible, even in time of war, public danger, or other emergency that threatens the independence or security of the State. Article 5 of the *African Charter on Human and Peoples' Rights* of 1981 reads: "Every individual shall have the right to the respect of the dignity inherent in a human being and to the recognition of his legal status. All forms of exploitation and degradation of man, particularly slavery, slave trade, torture, cruel, inhuman or degrading punishment and treatment shall be prohibited." The *African Charter* does not contain any provisions relating to derogation or suspension.

The prohibition of torture has also been included in a *Universal Islamic Declaration of Human Rights* which was issued in 1981. According to article 7 of this *Islamic Declaration*, "No person shall be subjected to torture in mind or body, or degraded, or threatened with injury either to himself or to anyone related to or held dear by him."

Whereas article 3 of the *European Convention* of 1950 was the first treaty provision containing a *general* prohibition of torture, rules against torture had already been included one year earlier in the four *Geneva Conventions* concerning humanitarian law applicable to *armed conflicts* (these conventions are also known as the "Red Cross Conventions"). As to international armed conflicts, the 1949 *Conventions* lay down detailed rules for the treatment of wounded, sick or shipwrecked combatants, prisoners of war, and civilian persons in occupied territory. With regard to those persons, wilful killing, torture or inhuman treatment, including biological experiments, and wilfully causing great suffering or serious injury to body or health are strictly forbidden and qualified as "grave breaches" of the *Conventions* which are punishable as war crimes. As to non-international conflicts such as civil wars, the 1949 *Conventions* only contain some minimum standards for the treatment of persons taking no active part in the hostilities, including combatants who have laid down their arms or who have been rendered *hors de combat* by reason of wounds, sickness or detention. One of these standards is an unconditional prohibition of mutilations, cruel treatment and torture. These minimum standards belong typically to the domain of human rights law, since they have to be observed by States with regard to their own citizens.

Besides the afore-mentioned treaty provisions concerning torture and other inhuman treatment or punishment, relevant norms are also set out in an important non-binding UN document, the *Standard Minimum Rules for the Treatment of Prisoners* of 1955.[5] These rules include detailed directives for the maintenance of discipline, applicable to prisoners under sentence as well as to prisoners awaiting trial and persons arrested or detained without charge. Paragraph 31 of the *Standard Minimum Rules* reads: "Corporal punishment, punishment by placing in a dark cell, and all cruel, inhuman or degrading punishments shall be completely prohibited as punishments for disciplinary offences."

Does the prohibition of torture apply as a norm of international law only to those States which are bound by the above-mentioned regional or world-wide human rights conventions? Nowadays it is the generally accepted view among international lawyers that the prohibition of torture has developed into a rule of *customary* international law applying equally to States which are not parties to any of these conventions. This universally valid rule can be considered a peremptory norm as defined in article 53 of the *Vienna Convention on the Law of Treaties* of 1969, which states that "a peremptory norm of general international law is a norm accepted and recognized by the international community of States as a whole as a norm from which no derogation is permitted and which can be modified only by a subsequent norm of general international law having the same character."

---

[5] Articles 31 to 34 of the *Standard Minimum Rules* are reproduced in Appendix 15.

3. The Declaration on the Protection of All Persons from Being Subjected to Torture and Other Cruel, Inhuman or Degrading Treatment or Punishment

a) *Discussion of the question of torture in the UN General Assembly in 1973 and 1974*

The unambiguous formulation of the prohibition of torture by the United Nations has proved insufficient for eradicating this evil. Moreover, events after the Second World War showed time and again that this evil is not an exclusive characteristic of authoritarian régimes. Full democracy at home may sometimes be accompanied by the application of torture outside the home country. In the context of anti-guerrilla warfare by, for instance, the Dutch in Indonesia, the French in Algeria and the Americans in Vietnam, many captured guerrillas were tortured in order to extract information. Only in France this gave rise to public debate but even here the majority of the population seemed to remain unconcerned. It was not until the 1970s that a reaction in public opinion began to develop when autocratic régimes in Latin America and elsewhere increasingly made use of torture in their repression of domestic opposition.

Against this background the non-governmental human rights organization Amnesty International, which had been founded in 1961, launched a worldwide Campaign for the Abolition of Torture in December 1972. This campaign included the publication of a 200-page report on the current situation concerning this practice[6] and the organization of a Conference for the Abolition of Torture which convened in Paris in December 1973.

Stimulated by this non-governmental campaign some governments decided in the autumn of 1973 to bring the question of torture before the UN General Assembly. Under an item on the agenda concerning the twenty-fifth anniversary of the *Universal Declaration of Human Rights*, the delegation of Sweden together with the delegations of Austria, Costa Rica, the Netherlands and Trinidad and Tobago submitted a draft resolution according to which the General Assembly, "gravely concerned that torture is still practised in various parts of the world", would decide "to examine the question of torture and other cruel, inhuman or degrading treatment or punishment in relation to detention and imprisonment as an item at a future session". Several delegations in the Third Committee of the Assembly considered it improper that the sponsors of the draft resolution utilized a "general" item to concentrate attention on one single provision of the *Universal Declaration*. In reply to this criticism the Netherlands delegate observed that such concentration was "the only way we can ever escape from the abstract vagueness which so often tends to turn our discussions on human rights into academic and frustrating

[6] Report on Torture, Duckworth & Co., London, 1973.

debates". The sponsors accepted two amendments proposed by Denmark, according to which the Assembly would "reject" any form of torture and other cruel, inhuman or degrading treatment or punishment and would urge all governments to become parties to existing international instruments which contain provisions relating to the prohibition of these practices. They also incorporated in their draft an Egyptian proposal according to which the Secretary-General would be requested to inform the Assembly of the consideration which might have been given to this question by the Commission on Human Rights and other bodies concerned.

Eventually, on 2 November 1973 the General Assembly adopted the resolution as amended, without a vote.[7] No doubt this broad support for the Swedish resolution was furthered by the fact that Chile, after the overthrow of the Allende government by a military coup on 11 September 1973, had become the scene of large-scale torture practices which had received worldwide coverage by the mass media.

In 1974 the agenda of the UN General Assembly contained an item "Torture and other cruel, inhuman or degrading treatment or punishment in relation to detention and imprisonment". The delegations of the Netherlands and Sweden, in consultation with the delegations of Austria and Ireland, drew up an elaborate draft resolution which provided for various standard-setting exercises with a view to strengthening the protection against torture. The preamble of this draft stated that "because of the increase in the number of alarming reports on torture, further and sustained efforts are necessary to protect under all circumstances the basic human right to be free from torture and other cruel, inhuman or degrading treatment or punishment". The Netherlands delegation submitted the draft resolution under the new agenda item on behalf of the above-mentioned delegations as well as those of Bangladesh, Costa Rica, Jordan and the Philippines. During consideration of the draft by the Third Committee, the sponsors accepted some textual changes suggested by Iraq. The main thrust of the draft focussed on the Fifth United Nations Congress on the Prevention of Crime and the Treatment of Offenders, which was to be held in September 1975. Replying to the observation that the text seemed to bypass the Commission on Human Rights, the Netherlands delegation explained that the sponsors did not intend to circumvent the Commission, but that the participation of the Commission in dealing with this subject was already adequately ensured.

According to the draft resolution the General Assembly would request the Fifth UN Congress "to give urgent attention to the question of the development of an international code of ethics for police and related law enforcement agencies". It would also request the Congress "to include, in the elaboration of the *Standard Minimum Rules for the Treatment of Prisoners*, rules for the

[7] UNGA resolution 3059(XXVIII).

protection of all persons subjected to any form of detention or imprisonment against torture and other cruel, inhuman or degrading treatment or punishment, and to report thereon to the General Assembly at its thirtieth session". To assist the Congress in implementing this task, the Assembly invited the World Health Organization to draft "an outline of the principles of medical ethics which may be relevant to the protection of persons subjected to any form of detention or imprisonment against torture and other cruel, inhuman or degrading treatment or punishment" and to bring this draft to the attention of the Fifth UN Congress. The General Assembly adopted the resolution on 7 November 1974 with 125 votes in favour, 1 abstention (Zaire) and no votes against.[8]

b) *Preparation of the Declaration by the Fifth UN Congress on the Prevention of Crime and the Treatment of Offenders*

The Congress met in Geneva during the first two weeks of September 1975. At its opening session the Congress set up an open-ended working group to consider all aspects of UNGA resolution 3218 which had been referred to it. In view of the limited time available to the Congress, the working group decided to concentrate on the foundations of the fight against torture and other forms of cruel, inhuman or degrading treatment or punishment. It considered that the cornerstone for any action within the United Nations structure to combat this evil would have to be a further elaboration of article 5 of the *Universal Declaration of Human Rights* in the form of a special declaration which would be issued by the General Assembly. In this way the basic framework would be set out, and the principles contained in the declaration could subsequently be elaborated into rules of conduct for specific categories of people involved in the custody or treatment of persons who are deprived of their liberty. Such further action could then be undertaken by other organs within the UN structure.

The working group therefore decided to commence work on a basic declaration on the basis of a text prepared by Sweden. This text consisted of a substantial set of rules which went clearly beyond the framework of the *Standard Minimum Rules* mentioned in the second request contained in UNGA resolution 3218. As to the first request contained in that resolution, the working group decided to recommend referring the elaboration of a code of conduct for law enforcement officials to the UN Committee on Crime Prevention and Control.

After a more general discussion on the basis of the Swedish text, the matter was delegated to a drafting group which again was open to all members of the working group. This drafting group achieved consensus on a text for the draft

---

[8] UNGA resolution 3218(XXIX).

declaration which in turn was approved by the working group and presented to the fourth section of the Congress. During detailed discussion in this section several amendments were suggested which were again referred to the drafting group. The group took over those amendments that could be incorporated in the text without disturbing its inherent balance and its general thrust. After approval by the working group the amended draft was again presented to the fourth section which approved it unanimously.

In plenary session the Congress took ample time to consider the draft of the declaration which was to be presented to the General Assembly. After some further changes had been made, the Congress unanimously adopted a resolution whose operative paragraph read: "Recommends that the General Assembly adopt the following Declaration on the protection of all persons from being subjected to torture and other cruel, inhuman or degrading treatment or punishment." The text thus submitted to the General Assembly had itself the form of a draft resolution followed by an annex containing the declaration.

c) *Adoption of the Declaration by the UN General Assembly in 1975*

The Third Committee of the General Assembly discussed this draft resolution in mid-November. At the outset of the debate the Netherlands delegate, who had also been a member of the Netherlands delegation to the Congress, explained the drafting history and the main elements of the proposed declaration. He did not conceal that there still remained some questions outstanding. However, while there might be certain imprecisions, he stated that the delegations participating in the Congress had felt that it was not imperative that the declaration should be a tightly drafted all-embracing instrument. It was a political document, expressing the common intent of countries knowing a wide diversity of legal, social and economic structures. It did not purport legal obligations, it imposed a moral obligation on States to ensure that their national legislation would conform to the standards laid down in the declaration. The Netherlands delegate emphasized the unique competence and expertise of the participants in the Congress with regard to the matters dealt with in the draft. He therefore urged the Committee to refrain from commencing a discussion on the specific articles and to take the declaration as it stood and approve it.

Delegations from various regions expressed their support for the draft declaration. Several speakers observed that the declaration should be followed by further action on the international level. The delegate of the Soviet Union pointed to the connection between the attention paid in the UN to the torture question and the current human rights situation in Chile.

As to article 2 of the draft declaration, the Committee agreed to a proposal by the German Democratic Republic's delegation to replace the words "denial of the principles" by "denial of the purposes". With this one change the

Committee approved by acclamation on 24 November the draft resolution submitted by the Congress. The plenary General Assembly adopted the resolution without a vote on 9 December 1975.[9]

The *Declaration on the Protection of All Persons from Being Subjected to Torture and Other Cruel, Inhuman or Degrading Treatment or Punishment* consists of twelve articles. The first article explains what is meant by the term "torture" in this instrument: any act by which severe pain or suffering, whether physical or mental, is intentionally inflicted by or at the instigation of a public official on a person for such purposes as obtaining from him or a third person information or confession, punishing him for an act he has committed or is suspected of having committed, or intimidating him or other persons. The article adds that this does not include pain or suffering arising only from, inherent in or incidental to, lawful sanctions to the extent consistent with the *Standard Minimum Rules for the Treatment of Prisoners.*

The *Declaration* does not contain a comparable explanation of the concept of cruel, inhuman or degrading treatment or punishment. The drafters considered that this concept could not be defined with the same precision because acts are involved which are not all of the same gravity while at the same time the question of intent or purpose is not directly the determining factor. On the other hand, paragraph 2 of article 1 specifies that torture constitutes an aggravated and deliberate form of cruel, inhuman or degrading treatment or punishment.

Besides article 1 only few other articles of the *Declaration* relate specifically to torture. According to article 7 each State shall ensure that all acts of torture are offences under its criminal law. Wherever there is reasonable ground to believe that an act of torture has been committed, the competent authorities of the State shall promptly proceed to an impartial investigation (article 9). If an investigation establishes that such an act appears to have been committed, criminal proceedings shall be instituted against the alleged offender (article 10, first sentence).

All other provisions of the *Declaration* apply equally to torture and to other cruel, inhuman or degrading treatment or punishment. According to article 2, such practices shall be condemned as a denial of the purposes of the *Charter of the United Nations.* Exceptional circumstances such as a public emergency may not be invoked as a justification (article 3). Each State shall take effective measures to prevent such practices (article 5). The prohibition of these practices shall be included in the training of public officials who may be responsible for persons deprived of their liberty, as well as in the general rules or instructions relevant to the custody and treatment of such persons (article 5). With a view to preventing such practices, interrogation methods as well as

[9] UNGA resolution 3452 (XXX). The text of this resolution including the *Declaration* is reproduced in Appendix 2.

arrangements for the custody and treatment of persons deprived of their liberty shall be kept under systematic review (article 6). Any person who alleges that he has been subjected to such practices by or at the instigation of a public official shall have the right to have his case impartially examined by the competent authorities (article 8). Victims of such practices shall be afforded redress and compensation (article 11). Any statement made as a result of these practices may not be invoked as evidence in any proceedings (article 12).

As this summary makes clear, the objective of the *Declaration* is to formulate a coherent set of rules and measures that should contribute to actual compliance with the prohibition of torture and other cruel, inhuman or degrading treatment or punishment of persons deprived of their liberty.

4. Further efforts for strengthening the protection against torture

a) *Further efforts requested by the UN General Assembly*

Immediately after the General Assembly had adopted the *Declaration on the Protection of All Persons from Being Subjected to Torture and Other Cruel, Inhuman or Degrading Treatment or Punishment*, it adopted a second resolution which provided for further international efforts to ensure adequate protection.[10] In paragraph 2 of this resolution the Assembly requested the Commission on Human Rights to study the question of torture and any necessary steps for (a) ensuring the effective observance of the *Declaration*, and (b) the formulation of a body of principles for the protection of all detainees and prisoners. In paragraph 3 it requested the Committee on Crime Prevention and Control to elaborate a code of conduct for law enforcement officials. In paragraph 4 it invited the World Health Organization to give further attention to the elaboration of principles of medical ethics relevant to the protection of detainees and prisoners against torture and other cruel, inhuman or degrading treatment or punishment.

This resolution 3453 had been prepared by the representatives of Greece, the Netherlands and Sweden on the Third Committee in consultation with several of their colleagues. The delegation of Greece introduced the draft resolution to the Committee and later presented a revised version taking into account various suggestions that had been made during the discussion. The revised draft was sponsored by the delegations of Australia, Austria, Belgium, Canada, Colombia, Costa Rica, Cyprus, Denmark, Ecuador, the Federal Republic of Germany, Greece, Ireland, Italy, Japan, Jordan, Mexico, the Nehterlands, New Zealand, Norway, the Philippines, Portugal, Sweden and Venezuela. With some further amendments this revised text was adopted

---

[10] UNGA resolution 3453 (XXX). The text of this resolution is reproduced in Appendix 3.

without a vote by the Third Committee on 28 November and by the plenary General Assembly on 9 December 1975.

b) *Non-governmental initiatives for the formulation of professional codes*

The standard-setting exercises envisaged in resolution 3453 fit into an overall strategy for preventing torture devised in particular by Amnesty International and directed at influencing the behaviour of people who may become involved in situations in which this practice might occur. The *Declaration* adopted on the same occasion is itself an example of that approach. The Conference for the Abolition of Torture convened at Paris in 1973 had explicitly recommended that codes of ethics and conduct be formulated for all those whose professional skills might be perverted in the service of torture: doctors, lawyers, prison officers, military personnel and police. Especially the following non-governmental follow-up actions are worth mentioning.[11]

In June 1975 a seminar on an international code of police ethics was convened by Amnesty International at the Peace Palace in The Hague. Participants were police authorities and members of police forces and of national and international police organizations from eight European countries. This meeting formulated a number of requirements and basic provisions for such a code (the "Declaration of The Hague").

In August 1975 the International Council of Nurses (ICN), meeting in Singapore, adopted a resolution on the "Role of the Nurse in the Care of Detainees and Prisoners". In this resolution it was noted that "in relation to detainees and prisoners of conscience, interrogation procedures are increasingly being employed which result in ill effects, often permanent, on the person's mental and physical health" and it was resolved that "ICN condemns the use of all such procedures harmful to the mental and physical health of prisoners and detainees".

In October 1975 the World Medical Association, meeting in Tokyo, adopted a Declaration of six articles, containing "Guidelines for Medical Doctors concerning Torture and other Cruel, Inhuman or Degrading Treatment or Punishment in relation to Detention or Imprisonment". The first of these articles pronounced that "the doctor shall not countenance, condone or participate in" these practices.

Furthermore, Amnesty International drafted in conjunction with another worldwide human rights organization, the International Commission of Jurists, a "Code of Ethics for Lawyers, relevant to Torture and other Cruel, Inhuman or Degrading Treatment or Punishment".

These non-governmental actions of 1975 had already been preceded by the inter-governmental initiatives embodied in UNGA resolution 3218 of Novem-

[11] *Cf. Alfred Heijder* and *Herman van Geuns*, Professional Codes of Ethics, Amnesty International Publications, London, 1976. This booklet contains, *inter alia*, the text of the ICN resolution of Singapore, the WMA Declaration of Tokyo, and the draft Code of Ethics for Lawyers.

ber 1974, which *inter alia* envisaged the development of an international code of ethics for police and the drafting of principles of medical ethics. UNGA resolution 3453 of December 1975 was a continuation of that line. Most of the objectives of this resolution were actually carried out in the course of subsequent years.

c) *The Code of Conduct for Law Enforcement Officials*

The request contained in paragraph 3 of resolution 3453 had the following background. The recommendations of the seminar on an international code of police ethics, convened by Amnesty International in June 1975, were circulated by the Netherlands government among the delegations attending the Fifth UN Congress on the Prevention of Crime and the Treatment of Offenders in September 1975. However, since the Congress concentrated its efforts on the elaboration of the draft declaration it was to submit to the General Assembly, it did not have sufficient time to work out a code of police ethics; therefore, it recommended that the matter be referred to further expert consideration. In accordance with this recommendation the General Assembly requested the UN Committee on Crime Prevention and Control to elaborate a code of conduct for law enforcement officials.

The Committee on Crime Prevention and Control drew up a complete draft for such a code in July 1976. In 1977 the Economic and Social Council transmitted this draft to the General Assembly, which invited the members of the United Nations to submit their comments. Taking into account the comments received, an open-ended informal working group of the Third Committee discussed the draft in 1978 and 1979. The Swedish representative on the Third Committee acted as chairman-rapporteur of this working group, which achieved full agreement on the contents of the code as well as on a draft resolution for its adoption. The resolution, having as its annex the *Code of Conduct for Law Enforcement Officials*, was adopted without a vote by the Third Committee on 4 December and by the plenary General Assembly on 17 December 1979.[12]

The *Code* consists of eight articles, each followed by an extensive commentary which forms an integral part of the text. Article 5 deals with torture and other cruel, inhuman or degrading treatment or punishment. It is interesting to note that this provision goes beyond the *Declaration* of 1975 in two respects. In the first place, it specifies not only that law enforcement officials may not inflict or instigate but also that they may not *tolerate* any such act. In the second place, it states that they may not invoke *superior orders* as a justification.

[12] UNGA resolution 34/169. Article 5 of the *Code* is reproduced in Appendix 16.

d) *The Principles of Medical Ethics*

Paragraph 4 of UNGA resolution 3453 of 1975, inviting "the World Health Organization to give further attention to the study and elaboration of principles of medical ethics relevant to the protection of persons subjected to any form of detention or imprisonment against torture and other cruel, inhuman or degrading treatment or punishment", was of course a sequel to the invitation that the General Assembly had already addressed to this organization in its resolution 3218 of 1974, to draft an outline of such principles and to bring the draft to the attention of the Fifth UN Congress on the Prevention of Crime and the Treatment of Offenders. At the time of the Congress, however, the WHO had not yet been able to present a draft as envisaged by the General Assembly.

In its resolution 3218 the Assembly had asked the WHO to do such drafting "taking into account the various declarations on medical ethics adopted by the World Medical Association" and "in close co-operation with such other competent organizations... as may be appropriate". In pursuance of UNGA resolutions 3218 and 3453, as well as of UNGA resolution 31/85 of 1976 which contained a similar invitation, the World Health Organization enlisted the co-operation of the World Medical Association and the Council for International Organizations of Medical Sciences. Unlike the World Health Organization, which is an inter-governmental organization and a part of the United Nations system, the WMA and the CIOMS are non-governmental organizations. They differ in that the WMA is a professional association of medical doctors whereas the CIOMS is a global organization concerning medicine as a science.

Taking into account such texts as the above-mentioned resolution of the International Council of Nurses and the Tokyo Declaration of the World Medical Association, the CIOMS prepared a draft body of principles entitled "Principles of medical ethics relevant to the role of health personnel in the protection of persons against torture and other cruel, inhuman or degrading treatment or punishment". In 1979 the WHO endorsed this draft and transmitted it to the UN General Assembly. The Assembly invited the Member States of the UN as well as interested governmental and non-governmental organizations to offer comments on the CIOMS draft. In the light of the comments received it was clear that this draft needed some re-formulation, in particular from a legal point of view, in order to make it more suitable for adoption as a United Nations instrument. At the initiative of the Netherlands representative on the Third Committee, a small number of delegations drafted in 1981 a revised version of the CIOMS text and submitted a draft resolution providing for transmittal of this version to the Member States for their last comments. The General Assembly adopted this resolution without a vote, it being understood that agreement with this procedural resolution did not necessarily imply agreement with the revised text.

In 1982 the Netherlands representative chaired four meetings open to all interested delegations, which resulted in complete agreement with regard to the text of the principles as well as of a resolution for its adoption. On 18 December 1982 the General Assembly adopted without a vote the resolution which set forth in an annex the *Principles of Medical Ethics relevant to the Role of Health Personnel, particularly Physicians, in the Protection of Prisoners and Detainees against Torture and Other Cruel, Inhuman or Degrading Treatment or Punishment.*[13] The text contains six principles. They pronounce *inter alia* that it is a gross contravention of medical ethics for health personnel, particularly physicians, to be actively or passively involved in such practices, and that there may not be derogations from the principles on any ground whatsoever, including public emergency.

e) *The Body of Principles for the Protection of All Persons under Any Form of Detention or Imprisonment*

While the initiatives for bringing about a *Code of Conduct for Law Enforcement Officials* as well as *Principles of Medical Ethics* have led to definitive results within a reasonable time, the same cannot be said of another initiative dealt with in UNGA resolution 3453 of 1975. In sub-paragraph 2 (b) of the resolution, the General Assembly had requested the Commission on Human Rights to study any necessary steps for the formulation of a *Body of Principles for the Protection of All Persons under Any Form of Detention or Imprisonment.* In 1976 the Commission asked its auxiliary organ, the Sub-Commission on Prevention of Discrimination and Protection of Minorities, to draw up such a body of principles. The Sub-Commission appointed one of its members, Erik Nettel (Austria), as rapporteur charged with the task of preparing the first draft for such a document. In 1978 the Sub-Commission presented to the Commission the draft prepared by Mr Nettel, comprising thirty-five principles for the protection of prisoners and detainees. In 1979 the Economic and Social Council invited all governments to submit their comments concerning this draft. In 1980 the General Assembly referred consideration of the draft Body of Principles to its Third Committee, the main committee for social questions and human rights questions. An open-ended working group chaired by the Swedish representative on the Committee started the consideration of the text and adopted eight draft principles in first reading.

After 1980, however, the momentum seemed to get lost. Because the Third Committee was overburdened with other drafting exercises, it had proposed to transfer the examination of the Body of Principles to the Sixth Committee, the main committee for legal affairs. The General Assembly had accepted this

---

[13] UNGA resolution 37/194. The text of this resolution including the *Principles* is reproduced in Appendix 17.

proposal and from 1981 onwards the Body of Principles was studied year after year in an open-ended working group of the Sixth Committee. Each year a number of draft principles was discussed, but by the end of 1987 the work had not yet been completed.

This delay in the finalization of the *Body of Principles for the Protection of All Persons under Any Form of Detention or Imprisonment* is regrettable because the draft contains several rules which, if observed, would provide additional safeguards against torture. The principles would, for instance, severely restrict the practice of *incommunicado* detention; relatives should be promptly informed of the whereabouts of detainees; there should be regular independent visits of inspection to places of detention; and there should be inquests into deaths in custody.

f) *Further actions undertaken by the United Nations*

On the other hand, important results can be registered with regard to the very first request contained in UNGA resolution 3453 of 1975. According to sub-paragraph 2 (a) of the resolution, the General Assembly requested the Commission on Human Rights to study the question of torture and any necessary steps for ensuring the effective observance of the *Declaration on the Protection of All Persons from Being Subjected to Torture and Any Other Cruel, Inhuman or Degrading Treatment or Punishment.* Two major actions undertaken by the Commission on Human Rights may be regarded as just such steps for ensuring the effective observance of the *Declaration.*

In the first place, pursuant to a more specific request which the General Assembly made in 1977, the Commission undertook the elaboration of the *Convention against Torture and Other Cruel, Inhuman or Degrading Treatment or Punishment* which is the subject of this book.

In the second place, three months after this *Convention* had been adopted by the General Assembly, the Commission decided by its resolution 1985/33 of 13 March 1985 to appoint for one year a Special Rapporteur to examine questions relevant to torture. Pursuant to this resolution the Special Rapporteur should seek and receive information concerning torture from governments as well as from intergovernmental and non-governmental organizations, bearing in mind the need to be able to respond effectively to that information. Professor Peter H. Kooijmans (The Netherlands) was appointed to this post. In February 1986 he submitted to the Commission a comprehensive report on his activities as well as on the occurrence and extent of the practice of torture, together with his conclusions and recommendations.[14] He had not limited himself to the collection of information but had also brought a number of cases of alleged torture to the attention of the govern-

[14] Document E/CN.4/1986/15.

ments concerned, sometimes in the form of urgent action. In 1986 and again in 1987, the Commission on Human Rights extended the mandate of the Special Rapporteur. In his second report, of January 1987, professor Kooijmans examined *inter alia* the role of medical personnel in torture.[15]

Besides these steps taken by the Commission on Human Rights for ensuring the effective observance of the 1975 *Declaration*, the General Assembly itself undertook special action with a view to providing assistance to persons who have been subjected to torture. In 1981, the General Assembly decided to set up a Voluntary Fund for Victims of Torture. The task of the Fund is to solicit voluntary contributions from governments, non-governmental organizations and individuals, and then to distribute these funds as humanitarian, legal and financial aid to victims of torture and their families. Since the Fund started operating in 1983, it has given financial support to a large number of aid programmes in different parts of the world.[16]

g) *Further actions undertaken in non-governmental circles*

So far we have mentioned several activities initiated by Amnesty International and various actions undertaken within the United Nations system to combat the evil of torture. This does not imply that Amnesty International and the professional associations mentioned in sub-section (b) were the only non-governmental organizations engaged in this combat, nor that no intergovernmental organizations outside the United Nations undertook efforts for this purpose. As regards the latter aspect it should be pointed out that regional conventions against torture have been concluded in 1985 and 1987 respectively under the auspices of the Organization of American States and of the Council of Europe. These regional conventions will be discussed hereafter in sub-sections (j) and (k). As regards the first aspect, we should like to mention here various activities undertaken in non-governmental circles in the years following the worldwide campaign against torture launched by Amnesty International in 1972.

In June 1974 two French ladies, Hélène Engel and Edith du Tertre, founded Action of Christians for the Abolition of Torture (*Action des Chrétiens pour l'Abolition de la Torture* – ACAT). Their example was followed by the creation of similar groups in several other countries. Since February 1987 all these groups work together in an International Federation (*Fédération Internationale de l'Action des Chrétiens pour l'Abolition de la Torture*).

In January 1977, Jean-Jacques Gautier founded the Swiss Committee Against Torture (*Comité Suisse Contre la Torture* – CSCT).

---

[15] Document E/CN.4/1987/13.

[16] As to the activities of the Fund, see *Hans Danelius*, The United Nations Fund for Torture Victims: The First Years of Activity, Human Rights Quarterly, Volume 8, May 1986, pp. 294–305, and The Review of the International Commission of Jurists, No. 37, December 1986, pp. 35–42.

Especially during the year 1977 the question of torture received considerable attention in non-governmental circles. For instance, the *Revue Internationale de Droit Pénal* (International Review of Criminal Law) devoted a special issue to this question (Volume 1977 No 3/4). The Central Committee of the World Council of Churches, meeting in Geneva from 28 July to 6 August 1977, issued a six-page "Statement on Torture". From 3 to 5 October 1977, a seminar on "Torture and Human Rights" was held in Strasbourg, organized by Amnesty International on behalf of non-governmental organizations interested in human rights and having consultative status with the Council of Europe.

It is of particular interest that 1977 witnessed two non-governmental initiatives for preparing an international convention against torture, even before the UN General Assembly at the end of that year requested the Commission on Human Rights to draw up such a convention. One of these initiatives was taken by the International Association of Penal Law, the other by the Swiss Committee Against Torture. These initiatives will be dealt with hereafter in sub-sections (h) and (i).

In the early 1980s, while the Commission on Human Rights was making progress on the draft convention requested by the UN General Assembly, several non-governmental organizations felt that action for countering the evil of torture should comprise more than the elaboration of conventions and other international standards. At the initiative of the Swiss Committee Against Torture, an International Colloquium on "How to Combat Torture" was held in Geneva on 28–29 April 1983 in order to review all possible forms of action. Some seventy experts from twenty-five countries participated. The report of this colloquium has been published in several languages.[17]

As a follow-up to this colloquium, the Swiss Committee Against Torture was asked by a number of non-governmental organizations to set up a centre for rapid transmission of information concerning torture. This centre, established in Geneva under the name SOS–TORTURE, has started its work in February 1986. It serves a network of more than a hundred non-governmental organizations located all over the world, in particular in countries under authoritarian régimes. SOS–TORTURE disseminates the appeals issued by these organizations and co-ordinates their actions vis-à-vis the United Nations and other intergovernmental organizations. Moreover it sends out missions of inquiry, it assists non-governmental organizations in international procedures, and it provides financial assistance to victims of torture. In April 1986 SOS–TORTURE became an independent organization.

Meanwhile, Amnesty International launched a second worldwide Campaign for the Abolition of Torture in April 1984. This Campaign included

[17] *François de Vargas*, How to Combat Torture, Swiss Committee Against Torture, Geneva, 1984.

the publication of a new report on the current situation in the world with regard to the practice of torture.[18]

h) *The draft convention proposed by the International Association of Penal Law*

The International Association of Penal Law decided in early 1977, in close co-operation with the International Commission of Jurists, a human rights organization based in Geneva, to sponsor the preparation of a draft convention declaring torture a crime under international law. On the basis of a first text drawn up by the ICJ, a tentative draft was worked out in consultation with Amnesty International and the International Committee of the Red Cross and subsequently sent to a great number of experts in international law and comparative penal law. Thereafter the IAPL convened a drafting committee, comprising experts from all parts of the world, at the International Institute of Higher Studies in Criminal Sciences at Siracusa, Sicily, on 16 to 18 December 1977. The meeting, which was chaired by professor M.C. Bassiouni, secretary-general of the IAPL, resulted in agreement on a *Draft Convention for the Prevention and Suppression of Torture*. On 15 January 1978 the IAPL submitted this draft to the United Nations, expressing the hope that it might prove of assistance to the Commission on Human Rights.[19] The general thrust of the IAPL draft was in many respects similar to that of the draft which the government of Sweden presented almost simultaneously for the same purpose. Some elements of the IAPL draft were later incorporated in the revised Swedish draft which became the basis for the deliberations in the Commission.

i) *The preventive system proposed by Jean-Jacques Gautier*

The other non-governmental initiative of 1977 for an international convention against torture represented a basically different approach than the proposals of the IAPL and Sweden. It was developed by Jean-Jacques Gautier (1912–1986), a Swiss lawyer and former banker, who had decided in 1974 to devote himself fully to the struggle against torture. Having studied all the different means of action already in use, Gautier arrived at the conviction that the only effective safeguard against torture would be a system of inspection through regular visits to all places of detention. In view of his special interest in the subject he was invited to take part in a study being conducted by the Henry-Dunant Institute in Geneva on the feasibility of an international convention for the protection of political prisoners. This study, undertaken at the request of the government of Switzerland, was completed in 1976. The Henry-Dunant Institute came to the conclusion that there was no prospect

---

[18] Torture in the Eighties, Amnesty International Publications, London, 1984.

[19] Document E/CN.4/NGO/213. The text of the IAPL draft is reproduced in Appendix 5.

for a special convention on political prisoners, and instead advocated the elaboration of a convention for the protection of *all* prisoners. Such a convention should at first be concluded among only a limited number of States willing to subscribe to strict rules whose observance would be ensured by supra-national control machinery. This convention would then serve as a standard of achievement for other States, and it was hoped that step by step the number of parties to the convention could be increased.

The approach advocated by the Henry-Dunant Institute was inspired to a large extent by the ideas of Gautier. In the following year he founded the Swiss Committee Against Torture (CSCT), which was already mentioned above in sub-section (g). At the request of this Committee a group of experts under the charimanship of prof. Christian Dominicé of the University of Geneva prepared in May 1977 a first draft of a *Convention concerning the Treatment of Persons Deprived of their Liberty*. According to this draft, the States Parties to the convention would establish a supervisory commission which would be empowered to send to the territory of these States on a regular basis delegates authorized to visit, without prior notification, any centre for interrogation, detention or imprisonment. Such a system or routine inspection visits, which by themselves would not imply any accusation or suspicion, would have above all a preventive effect.

Consequently there existed at the beginning of 1978 three draft conventions against torture: the draft of the CSCT, the draft of the IAPL and the draft of the government of Sweden. In this complicated situation Niall MacDermot, secretary-general of the International Commission of Jurists, proposed to Gautier as chairman of the CSCT that the Committee's draft should be transformed into an optional protocol to be added to the convention then under consideration by the Commission on Human Rights. The CSCT welcomed this proposal. MacDermot presented the same idea to a non-governmental meeting of experts on the three draft conventions against torture, which was convened at Sankt Gallen, Switzerland, from 29 June to 1 July 1978.[20]

In the second half of 1978 the CSCT and the ICJ worked together in drafting a suitable text for such an optional protocol. After consultations with a great number of experts they published their proposal in a pamphlet which was widely distributed.[21] The ideas set out in this pamphlet received support in non-governmental circles. For instance, the proposed optional protocol was endorsed by ACAT (*Action des Chrétiens pour l'Abolition de la Torture*) in Paris

[20] The report of this meeting is contained in *Alois Riklin* (ed.), Internationale Konventionen gegen die Folter, Schriftenreihe der Schweizerischen Gesellschaft für Aussenpolitik 6, Bern/Stuttgart 1979.

[21] Torture – How to Make the International Convention Effective: A Draft Optional Protocol, International Commission of Jurists and Swiss Committee Against Torture, Geneva, first edition 1979, revised and enlarged edition 1980.

as well as by seminars on the question of torture organized by the International Institute of Humanitarian Law at San Remo (Italy) and by the Marangopoulos Foundation for Human Rights in Athens.

However, some of the governments who were approached by the ICJ gave a more guarded reaction. They were concerned that submission of the draft protocol to the Commission on Human Rights might complicate and retard the elaboration of the draft convention on the basis of the Swedish proposal that was now under consideration. There would even be the risk that all implementation provisions proposed by Sweden might be removed from the convention and transferred to the optional protocol. On the other hand, some Central American and Caribbean governments expressed their support for the proposed protocol.

On 6 March 1980 the government of Costa Rica, a member of the Commission on Human Rights, formally submitted the Draft Optional Protocol to the Commission.[22] Taking into account the above-mentioned concerns, Costa Rica requested explicitly that consideration of this draft protocol by the Commission be deferred until the convention itself would have been adopted. The governments of Barbados, Nicaragua and Panama declared that they supported the initiative of Costa Rica.

Although the UN convention against torture was adopted in 1984, the Commission has not yet taken up consideration of the optional protocol proposed by Costa Rica. On the other hand, it adopted a resolution on 13 March 1986 (resolution 1986/56) in which it noted a draft European convention based on ideas similar to those contained in the Costa Rican proposal and recommended that other interested regions should consider the possibility of preparing a draft convention containing similar ideas.

Meanwhile, the European convention meant by the Commission was concluded in the framework of the Council of Europe in November 1987. This first convention based on the ideas of Jean-Jacques Gautier will be dealt with hereafter in sub-section (k). As to the possibility of bringing about similar conventions in other regions it is interesting to note that the ICJ and the CSCT organized in April 1987 a colloquium in Montevideo, where some thirty experts discussed a draft for an Inter-American convention along the same lines as the European convention then still under preparation.[23]

Finally it is worth mentioning that professor P.H. Kooijmans, the Special Rapporteur on torture appointed by the UN Commission on Human Rights, expressed explicit support for the proposed system of visits to places of detention or imprisonment in his second report to the Commission (doc.

[22] Document E/CN.4/1409. The text of the Draft Optional Protocol is reproduced in Appendix 8.

[23] In this context it should be pointed out that the *Inter-American Convention to Prevent and Punish Torture* which was concluded in 1985 and which will be dealt with in the next sub-section, does not include a system of inspection visits as advocated by the CSCT.

E/CN.4/1987/13, paragraphs 83–85). He emphasized that the introduction of such a system should be seen as a preventive rather than as a repressive measure.

j) *The Inter-American Convention to Prevent and Punish Torture*

In 1978 the General Assembly of the Organization of American States requested one of the auxiliary organs of the Organization, the Inter-American Juridical Committee, to prepare, in co-operation with the Inter-American Commission on Human Rights, a draft convention defining torture as an international crime. Apparently it was considered useful at that time to initiate work on a separate OAS convention against torture in order to offer an alternative option to Member States of the OAS which might prefer not to become parties to the forthcoming United Nations convention.

In 1980, the Inter-American Juridical Committee presented to the Permanent Council of the OAS a complete draft entitled "Draft Convention Defining Torture as an International Crime". In several respects this draft displayed similarities with the Swedish draft or with the IAPL draft for a worldwide convention. For instance, it stated in its article 1 that torture is "an international crime", which reminds of article 1 of the IAPL draft stating that torture is "a crime under international law". However, the IAJC draft did not couple this statement with specific legal consequences; in particular it did not provide for a system of universal jurisdiction for the purpose of prosecuting alleged torturers.

In subsequent years the IAJC draft underwent a series of modifications. On 9 December 1985 the *Inter-American Convention to Prevent and Punish Torture* was signed at Cartagena de Indias, Colombia.[24] This definitive text differs from the 1980 draft in some important respects. The qualification of torture as an "international crime", for instance, has been removed both from the title and from the text of the convention. On the other hand, the convention does now provide for a system of universal jurisdiction. Needless to say, there is a connection between the latter change in the content of the convention and the changes of government which occurred in several Latin American countries between 1980 and 1985.

k) *The European Convention for the Prevention of Torture and Inhuman or Degrading Treatment or Punishment*

Whereas the Cartagena convention of 1985 does not add much to the UN convention of 1984, since both conventions tackle the question of torture essentially in the same manner, the new European convention on this subject

[24] The text of this *Inter-American Convention* is reproduced in Appendix 18.

really introduces an additional safeguards system based on the ideas developed by Jean-Jacques Gautier.

From the outset, the approach advocated by Gautier and the Swiss Committee Against Torture (CSCT) envisaged the conclusion of an international instrument among a limited number of States who would be ready to accept a system of international inspection through regular visits to all places of detention in their territories. The Draft Optional Protocol submitted to the United Nations in 1980 by Costa Rica was seen as a means for establishing such a nucleus of States accepting the proposed system. Taking into consideration that this Draft Protocol would only be examined in the UN after the adoption of the worldwide convention then still under preparation, the French senator Noël Berrier decided in 1982 to explore the possibility of first establishing such a system among European States, independently of the worldwide convention. At the time Berrier was chairman of the Legal Affairs Committee of the Parliamentary Assembly of the Council of Europe. On his initiative, this Committee requested the CSCT and the ICJ to draft a European convention for this purpose.

On 30 June 1983 the Legal Affairs Committee adopted a report, containing the draft prepared by those two non-governmental organization. On 28 September 1983 the Parliamentary Assembly unanimously adopted its Recommendation 971 (1983) in which it invited the Committee of Ministers of the Council of Europe to adopt the draft European Convention on the Protection of Detainees from Torture and from Cruel, Inhuman or Degrading Treatment or Punishment, the text of which was appended to this Recommendation. The Committee of Ministers charged its Steering Committee for Human Rights with the elaboration of the proposed draft convention. In 1986 the Steering Committee presented a Draft European Convention for the Prevention of Torture and Inhuman or Degrading Treatment or Punishment to the Committee of Ministers, which referred the text to the Parliamentary Assembly for its opinion. After the Assembly had approved the text on 27 March 1987, the Committee of Ministers decided unanimously on 26 June to adopt the Convention as prepared by the Steering Committee and have it opened for signature by Member States of the Council of Europe.

The *European Convention for the Prevention of Torture and Inhuman or Degrading Treatment or Punishment* was signed at Strasbourg on 26 November 1987.[25] Neither Jean-Jacques Gautier nor Noël Berrier witnessed this first concrete result of their endeavours, since they had both died in 1986.

---

[25] The text of this *European Convention* is reproduced in Appendix 19.

Chapter III

The drafting history of the Convention

1. Introduction

The history of the drafting of the *Convention* spans the period 1977 to 1984. The elaboration of the *Convention* has been the work of several bodies under the aegis of the United Nations, namely the General Assembly, which has its regular annual sessions in New York in September-December, the Commission on Human Rights, which meets every year in Geneva during six weeks in February-March, and a number of working groups established by the Commission.

In December 1977, at the initiative of Sweden, the General Assembly requested the Commission on Human Rights to draw up a draft convention against torture and other cruel, inhuman or degrading treatment or punishment. In January 1978 the Swedish government submitted a preliminary draft for such a convention.

During the following session of the Commission, in February-March 1987, a first round of general discussions concerning the Swedish draft took place in a working group created for that purpose. At the end of the session the Commission decided that the subject would be pursued in 1979 by a working group which would meet one week prior to the Commission's next session.

The pre-sessional working group that convened in 1979 was also charged with other tasks and could only devote a few meetings to the proposed convention. After the opening of the session, the Commission transformed the group into a sessional working group, which devoted some further meetings to this subject. In addition, a series of informal meetings was held by delegations interested in the elaboration of the convention. In the course of the session the Swedish delegation submitted a revised draft, taking into account the discussions that had taken place so far. Henceforward this revised draft convention formed the basis of the deliberations. At the end of the 1979 session the Commission decided that the work on the convention would be continued in a working group to be convened exclusively for that purpose during the week preceding the 1980 session.

At the end of each of its four subsequent sessions the Commission again decided to convene a pre-sessional working group in the following year to continue the work on the draft convention. Also, the Commission regularly transformed these pre-sessional groups into sessional working groups after the Commission's session had started. Thus, from 1980 up to 1984 the elaboration of the draft convention took place every year in a special working group which met at the end of January for one full week prior to the Commission's annual session and which furthermore met several times during the session. Since the composition of all these groups showed a considerable degree of continuity over the years, we shall henceforward refer to them simply as "the Working Group".

The Working Group was open-ended, which means that it was open to participation by all members of the Commission.[1] Moreover, States that were not members of the Commission were entitled to participate in the Group as observers. The same applied to non-governmental organizations having consultative status with the Economic and Social Council of the UN. In practice, however, by no means all members of the Commission took part in the Working Group. In particular the smaller delegations often found it difficult to make an expert available for the Group's deliberations.

In point of fact, the Working Group's meetings were mostly attended by only some twenty to thirty delegations of members and observers. Often half of them came from Western countries. Sweden always participated, together with Australia, France, the United Kingdom and the United States. The observer delegation of Switzerland (a non-member of the UN) was also a regular participant. On the non-Western side, Argentina and Brazil as well as the Soviet Union always participated, whereas India, Senegal, Uruguay and Yugoslavia as well as Byelorussia, the German Democratic Republic and the Ukraine played an active role in several sessions. As to non-governmental organizations, the representatives of Amnesty International and the International Commission of Jurists in particular took an active part.

The fact that the Commission had established the Working Group as an "open-ended" group implied that no votes could be taken. Decisions by the Group could only be made by consensus. Where no consensus could be reached, the Working Group could do nothing but report to the Commission the different views that had been expressed.

In 1979 and 1980 the Working Group reached consensus about a great deal of the substantive provisions of the draft convention. However, serious differences of opinion arose with regard to the proposed system of universal jurisdiction. The Group began to consider the implementation provisions of the convention in 1981. In this field too it encountered serious problems. The Group started consideration of the preamble and of the final clauses in 1983. In 1984 the Group finally succeeded in resolving the problem of universal jurisdiction as well as all the other remaining problems except for two provisions of the implementation part. The Working Group now submitted to the Commission a draft convention consisting of a preamble and thirty-two articles. Only article 20 and paragraphs 3 and 4 of article 19 were still placed between square brackets, as no agreement had been achieved in the Group

[1] In 1978 and 1979 thirty-two States were members of the Commission; from 1980 onwards the Commission's membership comprised forty-three States.

with regard to those provisions. All other provisions of the draft had been adopted by consensus.

In March 1984 the Commission on Human Rights decided to transmit to the General Assembly the draft text as submitted by the Working Group. In so doing, it referred to the Assembly the task of finding solutions for the problems that had not been resolved by the Working Group.

During the 1984 session of the General Assembly, informal consultations on the draft convention took place among a great number of delegations, including delegations which had so far not been involved in the work on the convention. In the end acceptable solutions could be achieved by making certain changes in the draft articles 19 and 20 and by inserting a new article 28. On 10 December 1984 the General Assembly adopted in this form the definitive text of the *Convention against Torture and Other Cruel, Inhuman or Degrading Treatment or Punishment*, and opened it for signature, ratification and accession.

A more detailed account of the successive stages of the elaboration of the *Convention* is given on the following pages.

2. Action by the UN General Assembly in 1977

After the *Declaration on the Protection of All Persons from Torture and Other Cruel, Inhuman or Degrading Treatment or Punishment* had been adopted by the United Nations General Assembly on 9 December 1975[2], the question had to be considered as to whether this *Declaration* should be seen as the final international instrument outlawing torture, or whether new efforts should be made in order to obtain more specific and binding international norms.

As has been related in the previous Chapter, several non-governmental organizations, including Amnesty International, the International Commission of Jurists and the Swiss Committee against Torture, advocated the conclusion of an international convention against torture.[3] Among interested governments, opinions were first divided. On the one hand, it was felt that the fact that it had been possible, within a rather short period of time, to have the *Declaration* adopted without a vote by the General Assembly was encouraging and should inspire governments to proceed further in the same direction. On the other hand, it was obvious that it would be more difficult to reach agreement on a binding convention, in particular if the convention should provide for effective measures of international supervision. It was also pointed out that by engaging immediately upon a new endeavour in this field States might weaken the authority and value of the *Declaration*.

---

[2] See *supra* p. 17.
[3] See *supra* p. 25.

However, after extensive consultations among a large number of States at the initiative of Sweden, a group of governments agreed, during the 32nd session of the General Assembly in 1977, to present a draft resolution asking for initiation of work on a convention against torture.

The draft resolution concerned (A/C.3/32/L.13) was submitted on 28 October 1977 and was sponsored by Austria, Cuba, Denmark, Ecuador, Egypt, Ghana, Greece, India, Iran, Jamaica, Kenya, Mexico, Morocco, the Netherlands, New Zealand, Portugal, Spain, Sweden and Yugoslavia. These countries were subsequently joined as co-sponsors by Angola, Australia, Colombia, Costa Rica, Cyprus, the German Democratic Republic, Hungary, Iraq, Ireland, Italy, Lesotho, Mali, Mozambique, Nigeria, Norway, Panama, Poland, the United Republic of Cameroon, the United Republic of Tanzania, the Upper Volta and Zambia. The draft resolution was adopted without a vote on 9 November 1977 by the Third Committee and on 8 December 1977 by the plenary General Assembly (resolution 32/62).[4]

In the resolution's preamble, a reference was made to the *Declaration*, and it was further stated to be the belief of the General Assembly that "further international efforts are needed to ensure adequate protection for all against torture and other cruel, inhuman or degrading treatment or punishment". The General Assembly stated that "a further significant step would be the adoption of an international convention against torture and other cruel, inhuman or degrading treatment or punishment".

In the operative part of the resolution, the General Assembly requested the Commission on Human Rights "to draw up a draft convention against torture and other cruel, inhuman or degrading treatment or punishment, in the light of the principles embodied in the Declaration". A progress report was requested for the 33rd session of the General Assembly, when the same item would again be included in the agenda.

3. Deliberations in the UN Commission on Human Rights in 1978[5]

In view of the resolution of the General Assembly, the item "Torture and Other Cruel, Inhuman or Degrading Treatment or Punishment" was included in the agenda of the Commission on Human Rights at its 34th session in February-March 1978. When the Commission met, it had at its disposal two draft instruments, i.e. a draft International Convention against Torture and Other Cruel, Inhuman or Degrading Treatment or Punishment, submitted on 18 January 1978 by the Swedish government (doc. E/CN.4/1285), and a draft

[4] The text of this resolution is reproduced in Appendix 4.

[5] An account of the item's consideration is given in Chapter VIII of the 1978 report of the Commission on Human Rights which has been published under the symbols E/CN.4/1292 and E/1978/34.

Convention for the Prevention and Suppression of Torture, submitted on 15 January 1978 by the International Association of Penal Law (doc. E/CN.4/NGO/213).

a) *The Swedish proposal*[6]

The Swedish draft was based, in its substantive part, on the 1975 *Declaration*. The definition of "torture" had been taken over from the *Declaration*, and most of the substantive obligations in the Swedish draft corresponded closely to the undertakings laid down in the *Declaration*.

One important obligation which was not included in the *Declaration* had been added in the Swedish draft convention. According to its article 4, no State Party would be allowed to expel or to extradite a person to a State "where there are reasonable grounds to believe that he may be in danger of being subjected to torture or other cruel, inhuman or degrading treatment or punishment". This important additional guarantee had been inspired by the emerging case-law of the European Commission of Human Rights, which had interpreted the prohibition of torture and inhuman or degrading treatment or punishment in article 3 of the *European Convention on Human Rights* so as to imply, in certain circumstances, a prohibition against expulsion or extradition where there is a serious risk that the person concerned would be subjected to treatment contrary to article 3 in the country of destination.

In order to make the undertakings in the convention as effective as possible, the Swedish government further proposed on the one hand that the States Parties should have jurisdiction over the crime of torture wherever it had been committed (the "principle of universality") and that they should exercise that jurisdiction when a suspected torturer is found in their territory. On the other hand, it proposed that the States Parties should subject themselves to a system of international supervision.

With regard to the provisions which set out the principle of universality, the Swedish government had used as a model the corresponding provisions in a number of conventions against various forms of terrorism, in particular the *Convention for the Suppression of Unlawful Seizure of Aircraft*, concluded in The Hague in 1970, the *Convention for the Suppression of Unlawful Acts against the Safety of Civil Aviation*, concluded in Montreal in 1971, and the *Convention on the Prevention and Punishment of Crimes against Internationally Protected Persons, including Diplomatic Agents*, adopted by the UN General Assembly in New York in 1973.

According to the Swedish draft, a State Party would be obliged to have criminal jurisdiction over the offence of torture when the offence was committed in its territory ("principle of territoriality") and also when either the

---

[6] The text of the Swedish draft is reproduced in Appendix 6.

offender or the victim was its national ("principle of nationality"). However, this would not be sufficient. Even if none of these grounds of jurisdiction existed, but the suspected offender was present in the territory of a State Party, that State Party would be obliged to have jurisdiction over the offence, provided it did not extradite the offender to one of the States having jurisdiction on the basis of the territoriality principle or on the basis of the nationality of the offender or of the victim.

Similar to the above-mentioned Hague, Montreal and New York *Conventions*, the Swedish draft also provided that a State Party should not only have jurisdiction over the offence, but it must also exercise that jurisdiction, if it is established that an offence of torture appears to have been committed, and if the State concerned does not choose to extradite the alleged offender to another State which has jurisdiction. The principle is that the torturer shall not find a safe-haven where he is out of reach of the criminal jurisdiction of any State, but the State where he is found shall have a choice between punishing the offender itself or extraditing him to another State which will punish him ("aut dedere aut punire").

With regard to the system of international supervision of the implementation of the convention, the Swedish government had based itself, to a very large extent, on the system laid down in the *International Covenant on Civil and Political Rights* and its *Optional Protocol.* It had even gone so far as to propose that the same body, i.e. the Human Rights Committee set up under the Covenant, should be responsible for supervising the implementation of the convention against torture. There were several advantages in using the same body. It would not be necessary to set up new costly machinery, and there would be no risk of getting conflicts of jurisprudence between article 7 of the *Covenant* and the new convention. But there were also problems connected with the use of the same body, which appeared clearly during the subsequent examination of the Swedish proposal.

As in the system embodied in the *Covenant* and its *Optional Protocol*, the international supervision would be exercised in three different ways, i.e. through (a) examination of reports submitted by the States Parties; (b) examination of communications in which one State Party alleges that another State Party is not fulfilling its obligations under the convention; and (c) examination of communications by individuals claiming to have been subjected to treatment contrary to the convention and in contravention of the obligations of a State Party under the convention. While a State Party would be obliged to submit reports for examination under (a), the Swedish proposal did not make it compulsory for a State Party to subject itself to examination under (b) and (c). Such examination would be dependent on whether the State Party concerned had made a specific declaration accepting the competence of the Human Rights Committee to receive and consider such communications directed against the State concerned.

While these parts of the implementation system were based on the corresponding rules in the *Covenant* and its *Optional Protocol*, the Swedish draft contained one provision – in article 17 – which extended the international supervision beyond what had been accepted in the *Covenant* and in other human rights conventions. Article 17 provided that if the Human Rights Committee received information that torture was being *systematically* practised in a certain State Party, the Committee could designate one or more of its members to carry out an inquiry and to report to the Committee urgently. The inquiry could include a visit to the State concerned, but only if that State consented to such a visit. However, the inquiry as such would not require the consent of the State Party concerned.

Through this provision, an element of mandatory international control would be introduced into the convention, although this would only apply when systematic use of torture was said to occur. The idea behind the provision was that it would be unsatisfactory if a convention concluded with the specific purpose of preventing torture in the States Parties, left the Committee unable to act in a situation of serious suspicion of systematic torture in a State Party. For that reason, the Swedish government considered that there should be a general competence for the Committee to act at least in such situations, and that specific consent beyond that implied in becoming a party to the convention should therefore not be required. To some extent, the proposal on this point was inspired by the procedure adopted under ECOSOC resolution 1503(XLVIII) of 1970, under which the Commission on Human Rights and its Sub-Commission on Prevention of Discrimination and Protection of Minorities have competence, irrespective of consent, to examine communications which appear to reveal a consistent pattern of gross and reliably attested violations of human rights in a particular country.

Nevertheless, despite its very restricted scope, it soon became clear that this part of the Swedish proposal would cause special difficulties. The development of the discussions on this point is reflected in Sections 6. to 11. of this Chapter.

b) *The proposal of the International Association of Penal Law*[7]

The draft convention proposed by the International Association of Penal Law (IAPL) was the result of the work of experts who met at Siracusa in December 1977. It differed from the Swedish draft on a number of points.

Unlike the Swedish proposal, the draft of the IAPL dealt only with torture and not with other cruel, inhuman or degrading treatment or punishment. Torture was declared to be a crime under international law. There was to be no time bar for prosecution and punishment less than that applicable to the

[7] *Cf. supra.* p. 26 regarding the preparation of this proposal. The text of the IAPL draft is reproduced in Appendix 5.

most serious offence in the laws of the Contracting Parties. A ranking order for the claims to jurisdiction on different grounds was established, and there was to be an obligation, in principle, to extradite a suspect to a Contracting Party having prior jurisdiction. Torture should not be considered a political offence.

Like the Swedish proposal, the draft of the IAPL also gave the Human Rights Committee responsibility for supervising the implementation of the new convention. The Human Rights Committee was to be assisted by a Special Committee on the Prevention of Torture, appointed by the chairman of the Human Rights Committee from among the members of the Committee who were also nationals of States Parties to the convention. According to the proposal, the competence of the two committees would be limited to the examination of reports submitted by the States Parties, and no complaint machinery was provided for. On the other hand, there was a provision for referral to the International Court of Justice of disputes between the States Parties regarding the interpretation or application of the convention.

c) *Consideration by the Commission*

The Commission on Human Rights first decided to set up an informal open-ended Working Group to draw up a first draft of a convention on torture and other cruel, inhuman or degrading treatment or punishment. The Working Group held four meetings under the chairmanship of Mrs. V. Pandit (India).[8]

The draft conventions of Sweden and of the IAPL were introduced to the Working Group, which decided to take the Swedish draft as the basis of its work. Since, however, a number of participants in the Working Group considered that they had not had sufficient time to examine the Swedish draft in detail, the discussion which took place was not far-reaching. It was agreed that no articles should be adopted at that session of the Commission and that States should be given the opportunity of submitting suggestions and amendments at a later date. Some attention was given to the question as to whether or not the convention ought to contain a provision recognizing torture as a crime under international law, as proposed by the IAPL but not by Sweden.

The Working Group started a discussion on article 1 of the Swedish draft which contained a definition of torture identical to the definition in the 1975 *Declaration* and which also dealt with the relationship between "torture" and "cruel, inhuman or degrading treatment or punishment" by stating, in conformity with the *Declaration*, that torture is "an aggravated and deliberate form" of such treatment or punishment. While some delegates found the definition in the Swedish draft an acceptable basis for further consideration, others

---

[8] The report of the working group is contained in document E/CN.4/L.1400 and is also reproduced on pages 30-33 of the 1978 report of the Commission on Human Rights which has been published under the symbols E/CN.4/1292 and E/1978/34.

pointed out that it needed more clarification and precision, since what was acceptable in a *Declaration* was not necessarily acceptable in a binding legal instrument such as a convention.

Different views were expressed on the question as to whether or not the convention should deal with "other cruel, inhuman or degrading treatment or punishment", since this concept was difficult to define. Without reaching any conclusions, the Working Group also discussed whether torture under the convention should be restricted to acts committed by, or at the instigation of, public officials only, and whether the concept of torture presupposed that the act was committed for a specific purpose.

On the basis of the discussions within the Working Group, the Commission on Human Rights, by its resolution 18 (XXXIV), decided to request the Secretary-General of the United Nations to transmit all relevant documents to the Member States of the UN and other States wishing to express themselves on this subject, for their comments, and subsequently to prepare a summary of these comments. The Commission also recommended to ECOSOC to authorize the holding of a meeting of a Working Group for one week immediately before the 35th session of the Commission in February 1979 with the task of preparing concrete drafting proposals. The ECOSOC subsequently authorized the holding of such a meeting (decision 1978/24).

4. Deliberations in the Commission's Working Group in 1979[9]

The pre-sessional Working Group met in the beginning of February 1979. Its work was continued in a sessional Working Group which met in the course of the Commission's session in February and March 1979. Co-chairman-rapporteurs of the pre-sessional Working Group were Nina Sibal from India and Allioune Sene from Senegal. Mrs Sibal continued as chairman-rapporteur of the sessional Working Group. The Group could only devote part of its time to the draft convention against torture, because its mandate also covered another item of the agenda which related to "further promotion and encouragement of human rights and fundamental freedoms, including the question of the programme and methods of work of the Commission". After the pre-sessional week a number of delegations particularly interested in the elaboration of the draft convention held a series of informal consultations which were chaired by the Swedish representative, Hans Danelius.

As stated above, the Commission, in order to facilitate further work on this subject, had requested the Secretary-General to invite governments to present their comments on the draft convention and to prepare a summary of these

[9] The 1979 report of the Working Group is contained in document E/CN.4/L.1470 and is also reproduced on pages 35-44 of the 1979 report of the Commission on Human Rights which has been published under the symbols E/CN.4/1347 and E/1979/36.

comments. Such comments were received before and during the Commission's session in 1979 from seventeen governments, and a summary of these comments was prepared by the Secretary-General and duly presented to the Commission (doc. E/CN.4/1314 with Addenda 1, 2 and 3).

Many governments expressed their support for the idea of drawing up a convention against torture and other cruel, inhuman or degrading treatment or punishment. On the whole, the draft convention by Sweden was well received by the governments concerned. With some nuances, it was supported, in particular, by Austria, Denmark, the Federal Republic of Germany, Norway, Portugal, Somalia, Switzerland and the United States of America.

However, some of the commenting States had reservations on specific points. Austria thought that essential provisions of the Swedish draft could be usefully combined with certain elements of the draft of the IAPL. Portugal noted that the provisions on universal jurisdiction could be regarded as contrary to Portuguese public order, while the United Kingdom stated that it would find it difficult to accept even a limited degree of extraterritorial jurisdiction. On the other hand, the United States attached special importance to this aspect of the Swedish draft. At the same time, however, the United States considered that the convention should be focussed on torture rather than on other acts of cruel, inhuman or degrading treatment or punishment. The German Democratic Republic and Spain also found that it might be advisable to limit the convention to torture. Switzerland considered it essential to ensure that the new convention should not weaken the protection afforded by other international instruments, in particular the *International Covenant on Civil and Political Rights* and the four *Geneva Conventions* for the protection of war victims of 1949 and their two *Additional Protocols* of 1977. For that reason, Switzerland took the view that the convention should not be limited to torture but should also provide protection against other cruel, inhuman or degrading treatment or punishment.

The German Democratic Republic further considered that the tasks, the subject and the objectives of the proposed convention should be defined more precisely. The Soviet Union was of the opinion that any draft convention should be based on the 1975 *Declaration* and also found it necessary to study more closely the jurisdiction problems, since the legislation of many States did not recognize jurisdiction based on the nationality of the offender or the victim.

A number of comments relating to specific provisions in the Swedish draft will be referred to below.

On the basis of the written comments submitted by governments as well as of the discussions which took place in the pre-sessional Working Group and in the subsequent informal consultations, the delegate of Sweden presented on 19 February 1979 a revised draft which, however, only included the substantive provisions of the convention (doc. E/CN.4/WG.1/WP.1).[10] This revised draft was taken as the basis for further discussions in the Working Group.

a) *Definition of torture*

A great deal of attention was given to the definition of torture in article 1 of the Swedish draft. Various suggestions and proposals were made in regard to this article, but the Working Group finally managed to adopt by consensus the text of article 1, paragraphs 1 and 3, while consideration of paragraph 2 was postponed.

In order to give a full picture of the discussions which finally resulted in the adopted text, the proposals which were made will first be quoted, and on the basis of these proposals a summary of the discussion will be given.

The wording proposed in the original Swedish draft[11] was as follows:

> "1. For the purpose of the present Convention, torture means any act by which severe pain or suffering, whether physical or mental, is intentionally inflicted by or at the instigation of a public official on a person for such purposes as obtaining from him or a third person information or confession, punishing him for an act he has committed or is suspected of having committed, or intimidating him or other persons. It does not include pain or suffering arising only from, inherent in or incidental to, lawful sanctions to the extent consistent with the Standard Minimum Rules for the Treatment of Prisoners.
> 2. Torture constitutes an aggravated and deliberate form of cruel, inhuman or degrading treatment or punishment."

In their written comments, some governments submitted alternative text proposals.

The United States suggested that article 1 should read as follows:

> "1. For the purpose of the present Convention, the offence of torture includes any act by which extremely severe pain or suffering, whether physical or mental, is deliberately and maliciously inflicted on a person by or with the consent or acquiescence of a public official.
> 2. Torture does not include pain or suffering arising only from, inherent in or incidental to sanctions lawfully imposed; but does include sanctions imposed under colour of law but in flagrant disregard of accepted international standards."

[10] The text of the revised Swedish draft is reproduced in Appendix 7.
[11] *Cf.* Appendix 6.

Moreover, the United States proposed that the term "public official" be defined in article 2 of the convention as follows:

> "1. A public official is any person vested with exercise of some official power of the state, either civil of military.
> 2. Any public official who (a) consents to an act of torture, (b) assists, incites, solicits, commands, or conspires with others to commit torture, or (c) fails to take appropriate measures to prevent or suppress torture when such person has knowledge or should have knowledge that torture has or is being committed and has the authority or is in a position to take such measures, also commits the offence of torture within the meaning of this Convention."

Portugal suggested that a new paragraph 3, couched in the following or in similar terms, should be inserted in article 1:

> "3. For the purposes of the present Convention, the use of psychiatry for one of the objects referred to in paragraph 1 or the abuse of psychiatry with a view to prolonging the confinement of any person subjected to a measure or penalty involving deprivation of freedom shall be regarded as torture."

Switzerland considered that article 1, paragraph 2, might read as follows:

> "2. The term "torture" includes cruel, inhuman or degrading treatment or punishment."

Moreover, Switzerland considered that the following should be inserted after the first sentence of paragraph 1:

> "It (the term "torture") also means medical or scientific experiments that are not justified by a person's state of health and serve no therapeutic purpose."

Denmark suggested that in the second sentence of article 1 the reference to the *Standard Minimum Rules for the Treatment of Prisoners* might be changed to read:

> "... to the extent consistent with international rules for the treatment of persons deprived of their liberty".

During the pre-sessional Working Group's discussions, the following new texts were submitted and discussed: (a) the chairman's summary of the Group's discussion, including one main text proposal and two alternatives submitted by the United States and Denmark (doc. CHR/XXXV/Items 10 and 11/WP.1), (b) a proposal of Sweden (doc. CHR/XXXV/Items 10 and 11/WP.2), and (c) a proposal of the International Commission of Jurists (CHR/XXXV/Items 10 and 11/WP.3 and WP.4).

The main text submitted by the chairman was as follows:

"1. For the purpose of the present Convention, torture means any act or omission by which severe pain or suffering, whether physical of mental, is intentionally inflicted by or at the instigation of or with the acquiescence of a person acting in an official capacity, on a person [for such purposes as obtaining from him or a third person information or a confession, punishing him for an act he has committed or is suspected of having committed, or intimidating him or other persons]. It does not include pain or suffering arising only from, inherent in or incidental to, lawful sanctions.
[2. Torture constitutes an aggravated and deliberate form of cruel, inhuman or degrading treatment or punishment.]"

The alternative proposal of the United States was to replace the second sentence of paragraph 1 by the following sentence:

"Torture does not include pain or suffering arising only from, inherent in or incidental to sanctions lawfully imposed; but does include sanctions imposed under colour of law but in flagrant disregard of accepted international standards."

The alternative proposal of Denmark was to replace the second sentence of paragraph 1 by the following sentence:

"It does not include pain or suffering arising only from, inherent in or incidental to, lawful sanctions to the extent consistent with international rules for the treatment of persons deprived of their liberty."

The text proposed by Sweden was as follows:

"1. For the purpose of the present Convention, torture means any act by which severe pain or suffering, whether physical or mental, is intentionally inflicted on a person by or at the instigation or with the consent or the acquiescence of a public official or other person acting in an official capacity for such purposes as obtaining from him or a third person information or a confession, punishing him for an act he has committed or is suspected of having committed, intimidating or coercing him or other persons, or for any reason based on discrimination of any kind. It does not include pain or suffering arising only from, inherent in or incidental to, lawful sanctions.
2. This Article is without prejudice to any international instrument or national legislation which does or may establish wider prohibitions."

The version proposed by the International Commission of Jurists, orally amended, was as follows:

"1. The present Convention applies only to torture inflicted by or at the instigation of or with the consent or acquiescence of a public official or other person acting in an official capacity.

2. For the purposes of this Convention, torture means any act by which a person intentionally inflicts severe pain or suffering, whether physical or mental, on another person for such purposes as obtaining from the person tortured or a third person information or a confession; punishing the person tortured for an act he has committed or is suspected of having committed; or intimidating or coercing the person tortured or a third person; or for any reason based on discrimination of any kind. It does not include pain or suffering arising only from, inherent in or incidental to lawful sanctions.
3. This Article is without prejudice to any international instrument or national legislation which does or may establish prohibitions of wider application or definition."

The revised Swedish draft which was subsequently submitted was worded as follows (doc. E/CN.4/WG.1/WP.1):[12]

"1. For the purposes of this Convention, torture means any act by which severe pain or suffering, whether physical or mental, is intentionally inflicted on a person for such purposes as obtaining from him or a third person information or a confession, punishing him for an act he or a third person has committed or is suspected of having committed, or intimidating or coercing him or a third person, or for any reason based on discrimination of any kind, when such pain or suffering is inflicted by or at the instigation of or with the consent or acquiescence of a public official or other person acting in an official capacity. It does not include pain or suffering arising only from, inherent in or incidental to lawful sanctions.
[2. Torture is an aggravated and deliberate form of cruel, inhuman or degrading treatment or punishment.]
3. This Article is without prejudice to any international instrument or national legislation which does or may contain provisions of wider application relating to the subject matter of this Convention."

The Working Group adopted paragraphs 1 and 3 of this draft by consensus but agreed to postpone consideration of paragraph 2.

The discussions which preceded the adoption of two paragraphs and the postponement of the consideration of the remaining paragraph, including the remarks made in the written comments, may be summarized as follows.

With regard to *the character of the act constituting torture*, the United States considered that it might be useful to develop the negotiating history which indicates that although conduct resulting in permanent impairment of physical or mental faculties is indicative of torture, it is not an essential element of the offence. On the other hand, the negotiating history should also reflect the

[12] *Cf.* Appendix 7.

requisite intensity and severity inherent in torture. The United Kingdom considered that the definition of torture should be more restrictive: *systematic and intentional* infliction of *extreme* pain or suffering rather than *intentional* infliction of *severe* pain or suffering.

Some States wished to make it clear that certain specific acts were included in the concept of torture. Barbados suggested, in this respect, that it should be considered to expand the definition of torture to include the use of means such as "truth drugs" where no physical or mental suffering is apparent. Portugal suggested a new provision (see above) in order to clarify that abuse of psychiatry would, in certain circumstances, be regarded as torture. Switzerland submitted a proposal (see above) which would make the concept of torture applicable to medical and scientific experiments not justified by a person's state of health and not serving any therapeutic purpose.

There were different opinions on the question as to whether or not the definition of torture in the convention should be limited to *acts of public officials*. It was pointed out by many States that the purpose of the convention was to provide protection against acts committed on behalf of, or at least tolerated by, the public authorities, whereas the State could normally be expected to take action according to its criminal law against private persons having committed acts of torture against other persons. However, France considered that the definition of the act of torture should be a definition of the intrinsic nature of the act of torture itself, irrespective of the status of the perpetrator.

Although there was little support for the French view on this matter, most States agreed that the convention should not only be applicable to acts committed by public officials, but also to acts for which the public authorities could otherwise be considered to have some responsibility. While in the original Swedish draft reference was made to acts "inflicted by or at the instigation of a public official", the United States preferred the concept of "acquiescence of" rather than "instigation by" a public official. Austria believed that the concept of "public official" could be expanded, for example by using the words "persons, acting in an official capacity". The United Kingdom suggested that the convention should refer to a "public official or any other agent of the State", whereas the Federal Republic of Germany felt that it should be made clear that the term "public official" referred not only to persons who, regardless of their legal status, have been assigned public authority by State organs on a permanent basis or in an individual case, but also to persons who, in certain regions or under particular conditions, actually hold and exercice authority over others and whose authority is comparable to government authority or – be it only temporarily – has replaced government authority or whose authority has been derived from such persons. The United States proposed a more elaborate definition of the concept of "public official", the text of which is quoted above. In the end, it was generally agreed that the definition of acts committed by public officials should be expanded to cover acts committed by, or at the instigation of, or with the consent or acquiescence of a public official or any other person acting in an official capacity.

There was some discussion as to whether *the purpose for which an act was committed* was a relevant element in characterizing the act as "torture". France considered the motives of the perpetrators to be irrelevant. The United States suggested that the definition of torture should state that the act must be deliberate and malicious and that the inclusion of these terms could replace the purposes mentioned in the original Swedish draft. In the end, it was agreed that the enumeration of purposes in the original Swedish draft should be extended so as to include discriminatory and coercive purposes, and moreover that the enumeration of purposes should not be exhaustive but merely indicate the most characteristic examples.

With regard to the words "or for any reason based on discrimination of any kind", which were included in the revised Swedish draft, the following statement by the United Kingdom was included in the Working Group's report (doc. E/CN.4/L.1470, para. 27):

> "The United Kingdom shares the concern to eliminate all forms of torture, including any motivated by discrimination. The United Kingdom is doubtful of the need to isolate this particular motivation and in practical terms the United Kingdom thinks that there will in any case be difficulties in doing so with the necessary degree of precision for a criminal offence."

The original Swedish draft contained an exception relating to "pain or suffering arising only from, inherent in or incidental to, lawful sanctions to the extent consistent with the Standard Minimum Rules for the Treatment of Prisoners". Several delegations pointed out that, as a matter of principle, it was difficult in a binding convention to base a definition on a non-binding instrument such as the *Standard Minimum Rules*. However, the views differed as to how the exception concerned should be worded.

On the one hand, it was held that a general exception should be made for lawful sanctions, since the purpose of the convention was not to make criminal sanctions provided for in different legal systems more humane but to prohibit torture not allowed under the law of any country. On the other hand, it was pointed out that it would be unsatisfactory if a State was permitted to continue applying punishments of such cruelty that they would, by normal standards, be considered to fall under the definition of torture. France advocated a clear distinction to be made between, on the one hand, penalties affecting the person and honour of the criminal (*peines afflictives et infamantes*), which could legitimately be imposed as punishment and, on the other, treatment which, by causing violent physical pain or extreme mental suffering, altering the physical capacity of the victim or making the victim an object of derision or hatred, tortures the person to whom it is applied. The United States accepted, in principle, an exception for lawful sanctions but added that the exception should not apply to "sanctions imposed under colour of law but in flagrant disregard of accepted international standards".

However, it was not possible to reach agreement on any reference to accepted international standards, since it was widely considered that no such standards exist. The text which was adopted therefore contains a general exception for pain and suffering resulting from lawful sanctions, and it is left open whether this exception refers only to the contents of national law or whether a sanction, in order to be lawful, must also comply with certain international humanitarian standards.

The paragraph on which no agreement could be reached during the session of the Working Group in 1979 was the paragraph dealing with *cruel, inhuman or degrading treatment or punishment*. There were different views in regard to the desirability of dealing with such treatment and punishment in the convention. It was held that the concept of "cruel, inhuman or degrading treatment or punishment" was too vague to be included in a convention which was to form the basis for criminal legislation in the Contracting States. On the other hand, it was pointed out that other international instruments, such as the *International Covenant on Civil and Political Rights*, dealt not only with torture but also with other cruel, inhuman or degrading treatment or punishment and that is was not desirable to give the convention against torture a more limited scope. France considered that cruel, inhuman or degrading treatment or punishment involved acts of physical or mental torture, that no distinction should be drawn between the two concepts, and that torture should be defined in such a way as to encompass both. Switzerland even proposed a specific provision in the convention, according to which the term "torture" would include cruel, inhuman or degrading treatment or punishment.

Since no solution to this problem could be reached during the 1979 session of the Working Group, consideration of the matter was postponed.

b) *Basic obligations of States*

The Working Group further considered articles 2 and 3 of the original Swedish draft in which the basic obligations of States in respect of torture were formulated. These articles read as follows:

> *Article 2*
> "1. Each State Party undertakes to ensure that torture or other cruel, inhuman or degrading treatment or punishment does not take place within its jurisdiction. Under no circumstances shall any State Party permit or tolerate torture or other cruel, inhuman or degrading treatment or punishment.
> 2. No exceptional circumstances whatsoever, whether a state of war or a threat of war, internal political instability or any other public emergen-

cy, may be invoked as a justification of torture or other cruel, inhuman or degrading treatment or punishment.
3. An order from a superior officer or a public authority may not be invoked as a justification of torture or other cruel, inhuman or degrading treatment or punishment."

Article 3
"Each State Party shall, in accordance with the provisions of the present Convention, take legislative, administrative, judicial and other measures to prevent torture and other cruel, inhuman or degrading treatment or punishment from being practised within its jurisdiction."

It was agreed that article 2, paragraph 1, and article 3 of the Swedish draft could well be merged. As to the character of the undertaking in the new merged paragraph, it was pointed out that while a State could undertake to adopt measures to prevent torture, it could not undertake to ensure that torture would never occur. The United Kingdom suggested a rewording of the paragraph along the following lines: "Each State Party undertakes to ensure that its public officials or any other of its agents do not commit torture or other cruel, inhuman or degrading treatment or punishment."

It was further suggested by France that the words "within its jurisdiction" should be replaced by "in its territory" throughout the draft. It was pointed out, in this regard, that the phrase "within its jurisdiction" might be interpreted too widely so as to cover citizens of one State who are resident within the territory of another State. In support of a proposal to use the wording "any territory under its jurisdiction", it was emphasized that such wording would cover torture inflicted aboard ships or aircraft registered in the State concerned as well as occupied territories.

There were different views on whether article 2 should refer only to torture or also to other cruel, inhuman or degrading treatment or punishment.

The United States considered that although orders from a superior officer could not justify torture, it was a factor which should be considered in mitigation of punishment. It was discussed whether a provision to this effect should be added to article 2, paragraph 2, but no agreement was reached.

Switzerland proposed the introduction of a safeguard clause, according to which the provision stating that no exceptional circumstances could justify torture or other cruel, inhuman or degrading treatment or punishment would be without prejudice to the provisions of the four *Geneva Conventions* of 12 August 1949 for the protection of victims of armed conflicts as well as the two *Additional Protocols* thereto of 10 June 1977.

On the basis of the discussion in the Working Group, the delegate of Sweden presented a proposal for a revision of article 2 which was intended to replace both article 2 and article 3 in the previous draft (doc. E/CN.4/WG.1/WP.1). According to this proposal, which was adopted by the Working Group, article 2 read as follows:

"1. Each State Party shall take effective legislative, administrative, judicial or other measures to prevent acts of torture in any territory under its jurisdiction.
2. No exceptional circumstances whatsoever, whether a state of war or a threat of war, internal political instability or any other public emergency may be invoked as a justification of torture.
3. An order from a superior officer or a public authority may not be invoked as a justification of torture. [However, this may be considered in mitigation of punishment if justice so requires.]"

In the Working Group, one delegation indicated that it had some reservations regarding paragraph 3 of this text.

c) *Expulsion and extradition*

The Working Group further discussed, but without reaching any final conclusion, article 4 of the original Swedish draft, which read as follows:

"No State Party may expel or extradite a person to a State where there are reasonable grounds to believe that he may be in danger of being subjected to torture or other cruel, inhuman or degrading treatment or punishment."

Subsequently, the Swedish delegate presented a revised draft of this provision, which then became article 3 and which was worded as follows (doc. E/CN.4/WG.1/WP.1):

"No State Party shall expel, return ("refouler") or extradite a person where there are substantial grounds for believing that he would be in danger of being subjected to torture."

In its written comments, France proposed an alternative draft in which the following wording was suggested:

"No State may in any way expel, turn back or extradite a person to a State where there are serious grounds for believing that he may be in danger of being subjected to torture."

This article gave rise to considerable discussion. The idea of having a provision prohibiting expulsion and extradition in certain circumstances received wide, although not general, support. Switzerland considered that extradition was inconceivable unless the State believes that the person extradited from its territory will be given a proper trial by a court guaranteeing a fair judgement and that the person will be detained in humane conditions. Since the aim of the convention was not to create new categories of victims but to ensure the equitable punishment of the perpetrators of acts of torture, Switzerland considered that steps must be taken to prevent the alleged offenders from being subjected to the rigours of summary justice as a result of extradition. Consequently, Switzerland supported the retention of this article.

Further discussion took place as to whether or not a provision of this kind would create problems in relation to already existing extradition agreements. Austria thought it would be useful to include a further article, according to which States Parties should re-examine extradition treaties already in force to determine whether or not they conform with this article. Spain saw a problem in the existence of extradition treaties with States suspected of practising torture but who were not party to the convention on torture, since the latter convention would necessarily prevent mandatory extradition under such extradition treaties.

However, the Working Group did not find it advisable to include an exception for cases of extradition from States Parties to the convention under extradition treaties to States who were not Parties to the convention. It was considered that such an exception might be interpreted as encouraging extradition to countries where the persons concerned would be subjected to torture. Instead, it was proposed that the following remark be included in the report of the Commission on Human Rights:

> "Some representatives indicated that their States might wish, at the time of signature or ratification of the Convention or accession thereto, to declare that they did not consider themselves bound by Article 3 of the Convention, in so far as that Article might not be compatible with obligations towards States not party to the Convention under extradition treaties concluded before the date of signature of the Convention."

The advisability of including the word "return" ("refouler") gave rise to considerable discussion. On the one hand, it was said that there were strong humanitarian reasons to include that word, which broadened the protection of the persons concerned. Moreover, the concept was already found in article 33, paragraph 1, of the 1951 *Convention relating to the Status of Refugees*. On the other hand, the view was expressed that the 1951 *Convention* concerned a different subject and was not broadly accepted. It was further suggested that the inclusion of the concept of "return" might require a State to accept a mass influx of persons when it was not in a position to do so.

As indicated above, the original Swedish draft prohibited expulsion and extradition where there were "reasonable grounds to believe" that the person concerned might be in danger of being subjected to torture. The United Kingdom considered that the criteria should be more precise and suggested that the wording in the Swedish draft should be replaced by "substantial grounds for believing that he would be" in danger of being subjected to torture. This wording was adopted in the revised Swedish draft.

However, other words were also proposed, such as "substantial evidence indicating" and "substantial indications". It was pointed out in this connection that the evidentiary requirement should not be too rigorous and that the burden of proof should not fall solely upon the person concerned.

Certain minor amendments to this revised draft were also proposed. It was agreed that the words "to a State" should be added after the word "person". It was proposed that the word "where" should be replaced by "as long as" or "when" so as to allow for extradition or expulsion in cases where new developments had removed the danger of torture. It was also stated that the word "where" was adequate to cover such situations.

Of a more fundamental nature was a proposal submitted by the Soviet Union (doc. E/CN.4/WG.1/WP.2), according to which article 3 should be worded as follows:

> "1. No State Party shall expel or extradite a person to another State where substantial evidence indicates that he may be in danger of being subjected to torture.
> 2. The evidence referred to in the preceding paragraph of this article includes above all situations characterized by flagrant and massive violations of human rights brought about when *apartheid*, racial discrimination or genocide, the suppression of national liberation movements, aggression or the occupation of foreign territory are made State policy.
> 3. The provisions of this article shall not be invoked as grounds for refusing to institute proceedings against persons who have committed crimes against peace or mankind, or war crimes as defined in the relevant international instruments."

The Soviet delegate pointed out that in this proposal an attempt had been made to develop and illustrate the concept of "substantial evidence" by citing certain types of situations which arose as a result of State policy and which were highly conducive to torture practices. It was not possible to make an exhaustive list of such situations. The term "colonialism" was not included because it was encompassed in the broader reference to "the suppression of national liberation movements". Other delegations could not accept the Soviet proposal. They considered that the listing of specific types of situations might be misinterpreted to imply that there were other situations in which torture could be tolerated. Moreover, the main purpose of the article was to ensure an evaluation of each individual case, and a reference to general situations was not helpful for that purpose. The Soviet delegate also pointed out that paragraph 3 of the Soviet proposal was aimed at ensuring that the article could not be invoked as a pretext for refusing to institute proceedings against persons who have committed the crimes specified. The paragraph would secure punishment for such criminals, but did not oblige States to extradite them if there was a danger of torture.

While one delegation favoured the deletion of article 3 altogether, most delegations were in favour of retaining an article on this subject. However, since no agreement could be reached on the wording of the article, the discussion was suspended in order to allow further consideration and consultation.

d) *Education of personnel and control of interrogation methods*

The Working Group considered two further articles, namely articles 5 and 6 of the original Swedish draft, which were worded as follows:

> *Article 5*
> "1. Each State Party shall ensure that education and information regarding the prohibition against torture and other cruel, inhuman or degrading treatment or punishment are fully included in the curricula of the training of law enforcement personnel who may be responsible for persons deprived of their liberty.
> 2. Each State Party shall include this prohibition in the general rules or instructions issued in regard to the duties and functions of anyone who may be involved in the custody or treatment of persons deprived of their liberty."
>
> *Article 6*
> "Each State Party shall keep under systematic review interrogation methods and practices as well as arrangements for the custody and treatment of persons deprived of their liberty in its territory, with a view to preventing any cases of torture or other cruel, inhuman or degrading treatment or punishment."

With regard to article 5, Spain proposed a minor amendment to the Spanish text, a consequence of which was that in the English text the word "vocational" would be inserted before the words "training of law enforcement personnel". The United Kingdom proposed that in article 5, paragraph 2, the word "include" should be replaced by "give effect to". The United States proposed a rewording of the whole article as follows:

> "Each State Party shall ensure that education and information regarding the prohibition against torture and other cruel, inhuman or degrading treatment or punishment:
> 1. is fully included in the curricula of the training of medical personnel, law enforcement personnel, and other public officials who may be involved in the custody or treatment of persons deprived of their liberty, and
> 2. is included in the instructions issued in regard to the duties of anyone who may be involved in the custody or treatment of persons deprived of their liberty."

As regards article 6, the United States again proposed a redrafting as follows:

> "Each State Party shall keep under systematic, periodic review interrogation practices, and arrangements for the custody and treatment of

persons deprived of their liberty within its jurisdiction with a view towards preventing cases of torture or other cruel, inhuman or degrading treatment or punishment."

In the revised Swedish draft, the two articles, renumbered articles 10 and 11, were worded as follows:

Article 10

"1. Each State Party shall ensure that education and information regarding the prohibition against torture are fully included in the training of law enforcement personnel, civil or military, medical personnel, public officials and other persons who may be involved in the custody, interrogation or treatment of any individual subjected to any form of arrest, detention or imprisonment.

2. Each State Party shall include this prohibition in the rules or instructions issued in regard to the duties and functions of any such persons."

Article 11

"Each State Party shall keep under systematic review interrogation methods and practices as well as arrangements for the custody and treatment of persons subjected to any form of arrest, detention or imprisonment in any territory under its jurisdiction, with a view to preventing any cases of torture."

Article 10 as redrafted was adopted by consensus by the Working Group.

As regards article 11, it was agreed that the phrase "territory under its jurisdiction" had the same meaning as in article 1, paragraph 1, or in other words it covered ships and aircraft registered in the State as well as territories occupied by that State (doc. E/CN.4/L.1470, para. 55).

It was further agreed to harmonize articles 10 and 11 by adding in article 11 a reference to "interrogation rules and instructions".

In the form in which article 11 was finally adopted by the Working Group, it was worded as follows:

"Each State Party shall keep under systematic review interrogation rules, instructions, methods and practices as well as arrangements for the custody and treatment of persons subjected to any form of arrest, detention or imprisonment in any territory under its jurisdiction, with a view to preventing any cases of torture."

5. Deliberations in the Commission's Working Group in 1980[13]

The Working Group met at the end of January 1980 for a full week immediately before the 36th session of the Commission on Human Rights. Anestis Papastefanou, the Greek representative on the Commission, was elected chairman-rapporteur. During the Commission's session the Group held a number of further meetings in February.

After the session of the Commission on Human Rights in 1979, written observations on the draft convention had been received from three more governments, and these observations were summarized in a document which was at the disposal of the Working Group in 1980 (doc. E/CN.4/1314/Add. 4). However, the basic working document of the Group in 1980 was the revised Swedish draft convention which had been submitted during the 1979 session of the Commission.[14]

a) *Expulsion and extradition*

While the discussion on article 3 of the draft convention had started in 1979, it had not been possible to reach an agreement on any particular text. The discussion was therefore resumed in 1980, the basis still being the revised Swedish draft. In 1979, the Soviet Union had introduced an alternative proposal, which was re-introduced in the Working Group in 1980.

As the Soviet proposal caused problems of principle for a great many delegations, attempts were made to find a suitable compromise. In particular, the International Commission of Jurists made such an effort by proposing the following wording of paragraph 2 of the article (doc. HR/XXXVI/WG.10/WP.7):

> "For the purpose of determining whether there is such evidence all relevant considerations shall be taken into account, including, where applicable, the existence in the State concerned of a consistent pattern of gross violations of human rights, such as those resulting from a state policy of *apartheid*, racial discrimination or genocide, the suppression of national liberation movements or the occupation of foreign territory. "

As regards the first paragraph of article 3, the Working Group adopted the text in the revised Swedish draft which read as follows:

> "No State Party shall expel, return ("refouler") or extradite a person to

[13] The 1980 report of the Working Group is contained in document E/CN.4/1367 and is also reproduced on pages 52-73 of the 1980 report of the Commission on Human Rights which has been published under the symbols E/CN.4/1408 and E/1980/13.

[14] See Appendix 7.

another State where there are substantial grounds for believing that he would be in danger of being subjected to torture."

However, there was disagreement as to whether a second sentence should be added to that rule. Argentina stated that its acceptance of the first sentence was conditional on a second sentence being added, and proposed that the second sentence should be worded as follows (doc. HR(XXXVI)/WG.10/WP.8/Add. 1):

"If a State which otherwise would be obliged to extradite did not do so for the reasons mentioned, it shall take the necessary measures to bring the person, whose extradition it refuses to grant, to trial."

It was obvious that a proposal of this kind would create problems for many States which would not necessarily have criminal jurisdiction over the offences concerned. A person whose extradition to another country was refused because of risk of torture could be suspected of having committed any kind of offence, and the offence would normally have been committed outside the territory of the requested State. In these circumstances, the requested State would often lack criminal jurisdiction, and many States would be unwilling to introduce criminal jurisdiction simply on the grounds that extradition had been refused. The Argentinian proposal was considered to be based on a Latin American practice which was unknown in other parts of the world.

In this situation, attempts were made to find a compromise. Sweden proposed the following wording (doc. HR(XXXVI)/WG.10/WP.8/Add. 2):

"A State Party which refuses extradition in the circumstances described in paragraph 1 shall consider, on the basis of its national law, whether to institute criminal proceedings in that State against the person whose extradition was refused."

Along the same lines, the International Commission of Jurists proposed the following text (doc. HR(XXXVI)/WG.10/WP.11):

"If a State Party, which is under a treaty obligation to extradite a person to another State, refuses to do so in the circumstances described in paragraph 1, it shall, if its national legislation so permits, institute criminal proceedings against the person whose extradition it refuses."

However, no agreement on this matter was reached in the Working Group in 1980. While some delegations considered that in the last-mentioned proposal the words "if its national legislation so permits" were not acceptable, others took the view that the whole sentence was undesirable. Similarly, there was no agreement on whether there should be a specific remark in the Commission's report to the effect that some States might wish to make a reservation so as not to be obliged to refuse extradition to States not Party to the convention where such extradition was required under already existing treaties.

With regard to the Soviet proposal to add a paragraph 2 which would give a number of examples of situations in which there would be a risk of torture, opinions were divided. A number of delegations favoured the deletion either of the whole paragraph or of the specific examples given as they were considered to have political overtones and to restrict the scope of the article. On the other hand, some delegations considered that the examples given should be extended so as to include references to "colonialism" and "neo-colonialism". The delegation of the United States suggested that if there were to be a list of situations creating a specific risk of torture, this list would have to include religious persecution, denial of free speech, suppression of political dissent and of the free flow of information, and armed intervention in the affairs of a sovereign State.

No agreement could be reached on this matter and its discussion was deferred for further consideration.

With regard to the additional paragraph 3 proposed by the Soviet Union – the paragraph dealing with persons who have committed crimes against peace or mankind, or war crimes – the Working Group agreed not to include it in the convention.

b) *Punishment for torture*

The Working Group further discussed article 4 of the revised Swedish draft which corresponded to article 7 of the original Swedish draft. The two articles read as follows:

> *Article 7 of the original Swedish draft*
> "1. Each State Party shall ensure that all acts of torture as defined in Article 1 are offences under its criminal law. The same shall apply in regard to acts which constitute participation in, complicity in, incitement to or an attempt to commit torture.
> 2. Each State Party undertakes to make the offences referred to in paragraph 1 of this Article punishable by severe penalties."
>
> *Article 4 of the revised Swedish draft*
> "1. Each State Party shall ensure that all acts of torture are offences under its criminal law. The same shall apply to an attempt to commit torture and to an act by any person which constitutes complicity or participation in torture.
> 2. Each State Party shall make these offences punishable by appropriate penalties which take into account their grave nature."

The rewording of paragraph 2 was based on article 2, paragraph 2, of the *Convention on the Prevention and Punishment of Crimes against Internationally*

Protected Persons, including Diplomatic Agents and had been suggested by the United Kingdom.

The discussion which took place mostly concerned the concept of "complicity or participation". The question was raised as to whether this concept covered the concept of "encubrimiento" (approximately: "concealment") in Spanish law. Although other delegates found this to be the case, it was agreed, for the sake of clarity, to add the word "encubrimiento" in the Spanish text of the convention. Article 4 of the revised Swedish draft was then adopted, although one delegate reserved his position because of his concern that the word "complicity" was not broad enough to cover the notion of "accessory after the fact" under his country's domestic law.

c) *Jurisdiction over the offence of torture*

A thorough discussion took place with regard to article 5 of the revised Swedish draft, which corresponded to article 8 of the original Swedish draft. The two articles read as follows:

> *Article 8 of the original Swedish draft*
> "1. Each State Party shall take such measures as may be necessary to establish its jurisdiction over the offences referred to in Article 7 in the following cases:
> (a) when the offences are committed in the territory of that State or on board a ship or aircraft registered in that State;
> (b) when the alleged offender is a national of that State;
> (c) when the victim is a national of that State.
> 2. Each State Party shall likewise take such measures as may be necessary to establish its jurisdiction over these offences in cases where the alleged offender is present in its territory and it does not extradite him pursuant to Article 14 to any of the States mentioned in paragraph 1 of this Article.
> 3. This Convention does not exclude any criminal jurisdiction exercised in accordance with internal law."
>
> *Article 5 of the revised Swedish draft*
> "1. Each State Party shall take such measures as may be necessary to establish its jurisdiction over the offences referred to in Article 4 in the following cases:
> (a) when the offences are committed in any territory under its jurisdiction;
> (b) when the alleged offender is a national of that State;
> [(c) when the victim is a national of that State.]
> 2. Each State Party shall likewise take such measures as may be necessary to establish its jurisdiction over such offences in cases where the alleged offender is present in any territory under its jurisdiction and it

> does not extradite him pursuant to Article 8 to any of the States mentioned in paragraph 1 of this Article.
> 3. This Convention does not exclude any criminal jurisdiction exercised in accordance with internal law."

In the opinion of Sweden this article was a cornerstone in the convention. By providing for wide domestic jurisdiction – often, with some simplification, called "universal jurisdiction" – over offences of torture, the article was aimed at making it as difficult as possible for torturers to find a safe-haven in a foreign country. In the frequent situations where a regime under which torture was practised is overthrown, and the new regime in the country is anxious to bring the torturers to justice, it would be more difficult for the perpetrators to escape the consequences of their acts by fleeing to another country. The proposed provisions on universal jurisdiction had been inspired by similar provisions in a number of treaties on various forms of terrorism, in particular article 4 of the 1970 *Hague Convention for the Suppression of Unlawful Seizure of Aircraft*, article 5 of the 1971 Montreal *Convention for the Suppression of Unlawful Acts against the Safety of Civil Aviation*, article 3 of the 1973 New York *Convention on the Prevention and Punishment of Crimes against Internationally Protected Persons, including Diplomatic Agents* and article 5 of the 1979 *International Convention against the Taking of Hostages*.

The Swedish view on this matter was supported, in principle, by a considerable number of delegations. For instance, the United States considered that universal jurisdiction was appropriate, since torture, like piracy, might well be considered an "offence against the law of nations". Some delegations, however, in particular those of Australia, France, the Netherlands and the United Kingdom, had reservations on this point. These countries considered that universal jurisdiction over an offence such as torture would create problems under their domestic legal systems. The United Kingdom pointed out, for instance, that in contrast to offences of a more obviously international character, such as hijacking and attacks on internationally protected persons, the exceptionally wide extra-territorial jurisdiction conferred by article 8 in the original Swedish proposal went beyond the practicable. In fact, the United Kingdom would find it difficult to breach the territorial principle normally applied in its criminal law and accept even a limited degree of extra-territorial jurisdiction with regard to offences of torture.

Italy considered that it would be desirable to establish an order of precedence between the different grounds of jurisdiction and suggested the following wording:

> "Each Member State shall take such measures as may be necessary to establish its jurisdiction over the offences referred to in article 4 above in the following cases and according to the order of priority indicated below:
> (a), (b), (c) – as in the Swedish proposal

(d) when the accused is on its territory."

With regard to the proposed paragraph 1 (a) of the article, there was general agreement that territoriality should be a ground for jurisdiction. The only question was to what extent offences committed on board ships or aircraft or on the continental shelf should be assimilated to offences committed in the territory of a State, and how this should be reflected in the text of the article. France considered that it would be preferable to keep to the single concept of "territory", which could then be clarified as necessary by the legislation of each particular State. Another suggestion was to use the following form of words: "on board an aircraft registered in that State or a ship flying the flag of that State".

The following text of article 5, paragraph 1 (a), was finally adopted:

> "Each State shall take such measures as may be necessary to establish its jurisdiction over the offences referred to in Article 4 in the following cases:
> (a) When the offences are committed in any territory under its jurisdiction or on board an aircraft or ship registered in that State".

With regard to the proposed paragraph 1 (b) of the article, there was widespread support for using the nationality of the offender as one criterion for establishing jurisdiction over the offence. However, some alternative suggestions were made, for instance to use as the decisive criterion not the nationality of the offender but his function as a public official or employee of a certain State, or the fact of having committed torture with the consent or acquiescence of such public officials or other persons acting in an official capacity on behalf of a certain State.

Greece even proposed a much wider formula by amending paragraph 1 (b) in the following way (HR(XXXVI)/WG.10/WP.10):

> "(b) When the alleged offender belongs to one of the categories of individuals named under Article 1, para. 1 and is present in any territory under the jurisdiction of that State".

No final conclusion was reached as to the wording of article 5, paragraph 1 (b).

With regard to paragraph 1 (c), opinions were divided. The nationality of the victim was a criterion which caused difficulties for many delegations in view of their domestic legal systems. On the other hand, it was pointed out that a similar criterion had been used in previous conventions, in particular in the *Convention on the Prevention and Punishment of Crimes against Internationally Protected Persons, including Diplomatic Agents*, and the *Convention against the Taking of Hostages*. It was also proposed to make the provision optional, as had in fact been done in the *International Convention against the Taking of Hostages*, whose article 5, paragraph 1 (d), requires a State to establish jurisdiction on the basis of the nationality of the victim, "if that State considers it appropriate".

No agreement was reached on whether paragraph 1 (c) should be retained and, if so, how it should be worded.

It should be added that a more fundamental change was proposed by the Soviet Union, which suggested that the whole of paragraph 1 of article 5 should be replaced by the following text (doc. HR(XXXVI)/WG.10/WP.9):

> "1. Each State Party shall take such measures as may be necessary to prosecute persons who have committed the crime mentioned in Article 4 of this Convention and who are in its territory and under its jurisdiction."

Paragraph 2, as proposed by Sweden, caused particular difficulties for those delegations which were opposed to the idea of universal jurisdiction with regard to torture. The French delegation proposed that the words "after receiving a request for extradition" should be added after the words "and it does not extradite him". This proposal was supported by the Netherlands delegation which was in favour of making the exercise of universal jurisdiction dependent upon the rejection of an extradition request. Several other delegations favoured retention of the paragraph as proposed by Sweden. They pointed out that either the omission of paragraph 2 or the proposed amendment could create a loophole in the convention, thereby creating potential safe-havens for torturers. Despite the discussions no agreement was reached regarding this paragraph.

Paragraph 3 in the Swedish proposal did not give rise to any substantial discussion in the Working Group.

Eventually, while agreement had been reached on the text of paragraph 1 (a), it was decided to suspend the consideration of paragraph 1 (b) and (c) and of paragraphs 2 and 3.

(d) *Custody and other preliminary measures*

Article 6 of the revised Swedish draft read as follows:

> "1. Upon being satisfied that the circumstances so warrant, any State Party in territory under whose jurisdiction a person alleged to have committed any offence referred to in Article 4 is present, shall take him into custody or take other measures to ensure his presence. The custody and other measures shall be as provided in the law of that State but may be continued only for such time as is necessary to enable any criminal or extradition proceedings to be instituted.
> 2. Such State shall immediately make a preliminary enquiry into the facts.
> 3. Any person in custody pursuant to paragraph 1 of this Article shall

be assisted in communicating immediately with the nearest appropriate representative of the State of which he is a national.
4. When a State, pursuant to this Article, has taken a person into custody, it shall immediately notify the States referred to in Article 5, paragraph 1, of the fact that such person is in custody and of the circumstances which warrant his detention. The State which makes the preliminary enquiry contemplated in paragraph 2 of this Article shall promptly report its findings to the said States and shall indicate whether it intends to exercise jurisdiction.
5. Any person regarding whom proceedings are being carried out in connection with any of the offences referred to in Article 4 shall be guaranteed fair treatment at all stages of the proceedings."

This article had no equivalent in the original Swedish draft. It was inserted on the basis of a proposal by the United States and of informal consultations, using as a model similar provisions which appear in article 6 of the *Convention for the Suppression of Unlawful Seizure of Aircraft*, article 6 of the *Convention for the Suppression of Unlawful Acts against the Safety of Civil Aviation*, article 6 of the *Convention on the Prevention and Punishment of Crimes against Internationally Protected Persons, including Diplomatic Agents* and article 6 of the *International Convention against the Taking of Hostages.*

There was some concern that paragraph 1 of this article might be interpreted too widely, that persons might be taken into custody on weak grounds and that other measures of an undesirable nature might be taken to ensure a person's presence. It was therefore agreed to indicate in paragraph 1 that the decision to take a person into custody must be based on an examination of available information and that any other measures taken to ensure a person's presence must be of a legal nature.

With regard to the right of a person in custody to contact his nearest diplomatic or consular representative as provided for in paragraph 3, it was agreed to add a provision about stateless persons who would have a similar right to contact the representative of their country of residence.

Since there was a clear connection between, on the one hand, paragraph 4 of this article dealing with notification to States having jurisdiction under article 5, paragraph 1, and on the other hand articles 5 and 7, it was agreed to defer consideration of paragraph 4 until after further consideration of these two articles.

Consequently, the Swedish proposal, with some modifications, was adopted insofar as paragraphs 1, 2, 3 and 5 were concerned, whereas the wording of paragraph 4 was left open. The adopted paragraphs read as follows:

"1. Upon being satisfied, after an examination of information available to it, that the circumstances so warrant, any State Party in whose territory a person alleged to have committed any offence referred to in

Article 4 is present, shall take him into custody or take other legal measures to ensure his presence. The custody and other legal measures shall be as provided in the law of that State but may be continued only for such time as is necessary to enable any criminal or extradition proceedings to be instituted.
2. Such State shall immediately make a preliminary enquiry into the facts.
3. Any person in custody pursuant to paragraph 1 of this Article shall be assisted in communicating immediately with the nearest appropriate representative of the State of which he is a national, or, if he is a stateless person, with the representative of the State where he usually resides.
4. ...
5. Any person regarding whom proceedings are being carried out in connexion with any of the offences referred to in Article 4 shall be guaranteed fair treatment at all stages of the proceedings."

e) *Extradition or prosecution*

An important element in the Swedish draft was the obligation of a State in whose territory a suspected torturer is present, either to extradite him to another State which has jurisdiction over the offence, or to submit his case to its own authorities for the purpose of prosecution. This principle – *aut dedere aut judicare* – also appears in the above-mentioned anti-terrorism conventions (article 7 of the *Convention for the Suppression of Unlawful Seizure of Aircraft*, article 7 of the *Convention for the Suppression of Unlawful Acts against the Safety of Civil Aviation*, article 7 of the *Convention on the Prevention and Punishment of Crimes against Internationally Protected Persons, including Diplomatic Agents* and article 8 of the *International Convention against the Taking of Hostages).* In the original Swedish draft, the obligation appeared in article 11 which read as follows:

"1. Each State Party shall, except in the cases referred to in Article 14, ensure that criminal proceedings are instituted in accordance with its national law against an alleged offender who is present in its territory, if its competent authorities establish that an act of torture as defined in Article 1 appears to have been committed and if that State Party has jurisdiction over the offence in accordance with Article 8.
2. Each State Party shall ensure that an alleged offender is subject to criminal, disciplinary or other appropriate proceedings, when an allegation of other forms of cruel, inhuman or degrading treatment or punishment within its jurisdiction is considered to be well founded."

The United States agreed with the principle behind this provision – a choice between extradition and prosecution and no indication of preference for either of these measures – but proposed an alternative wording as follows:

> "The State Party in whose territory there is present a person who is alleged to have committed an offence under article 1 or article 2 shall, if it does not extradite him, submit the case to its competent authorities without exception whatsoever and without undue delay, for the purpose of prosecution through criminal proceedings in accordance with the laws of that State."

> "Each State Party shall take such measures as may be necessary to assure that criminal, disciplinary or other appropriate proceedings are instituted in accordance with its national law if its competent authorities have a reasonable basis for belief that an act of cruel, inhuman or degrading treatment or punishment has been committed."

Switzerland also considered that paragraph 1 of the article could be strengthened by requiring that proceedings be instituted without exception or undue delay. It proposed the following rewording:

> "Other than in the case of extradition under article..., each State Party undertakes to ensure that criminal proceedings are instituted without exception and without undue delay, in accordance with its national law, against an alleged offender who is present in its territory, if the competent authorities establish that an act of torture as defined in article 1 appears to have been committed and if that State Party has jurisdiction over the offence in accordance with article...".

France considered that the words "ensure that criminal proceedings are instituted" should be replaced by the phrase "submit the case to its competent authorities for the institution of criminal proceedings".

After informal consultations, Sweden submitted its revised draft, in which the corresponding provision appeared in article 7 and read as follows:

> "The State Party in territory under whose jurisdiction a person alleged to have committed any offence referred to in Article 4 is found shall, if it does not extradite him, be obliged, without exception whatsoever and whether or not the offence was committed in any territory under its jurisdiction, to submit the case to its competent authorities for the purpose of prosecution. Those authorities shall take their decision in the same manner as in the case of any offence of a serious nature under the law of that State."

The Working Group considered that it should examine this article together with article 5 because of the complementary nature of the two articles and decided to defer this consideration until a later stage.

f) *The convention as basis for extradition*

Since some States can only extradite a person on the basis of a treaty obligation to this effect, Sweden considered it desirable to make the convention against torture itself the basis for the extradition of suspected torturers. Provisions to this effect also appear in article 8 of the *Convention for the Suppression of Unlawful Seizure of Aircraft*, article 8 of the *Convention for the Suppression of Unlawful Acts against the Safety of Civil Aviation*, article 8 of the *Convention on the Prevention and Punishment of Crimes against Internationally Protected Persons, including Diplomatic Agents* and article 10 of the *International Convention against the Taking of Hostages.*

In the original Swedish draft, the corresponding article 14 read as follows:

> "Instead of instituting criminal proceedings in accordance with paragraph 1 of Article 11, a State Party may, if requested, extradite the alleged offender to another State Party which has jurisdiction over the offence in accordance with Article 8."

Austria suggested that the wording "may... extradite" should be reconsidered and possibly be replaced by the mandatory phrase "shall... extradite".

The question was raised as to whether it should be possible, in some cases, to refuse extradition on the ground that the offence was a political one. On this point different views were expressed. While France considered that the principle of non-extradition for political offences should be maintained in this connection, Switzerland favoured the inclusion of a provision to the effect that acts of torture shall not be considered political offences.

After informal consultations and taking into account a text proposal made by the United States, Sweden submitted its revised draft in which article 8 read as follows:

> "1. The offences referred to in Article 4 shall be deemed to be included as extraditable offences in any extradition treaty existing between States Parties. States Parties undertake to include such offences as extraditable offences in every extradition treaty to be concluded between them.
> 2. If a State Party which makes extradition conditional on the existence of a treaty receives a request for extradition from another State Party with which it has no extradition treaty, it [may] [shall] consider this Convention as the legal basis for extradition in respect of such offences. Extradition shall be subject to the other conditions provided by the law of the requested State.
> 3. States Parties which do not make extradition conditional on the existence of a treaty shall recognize such offences as extraditable offences between themselves subject to the conditions provided by the law of the requested State.
> 4. Such offences shall be treated, for the purpose of extradition between

States Parties, as if they had been committed not only in the place in which they occurred but also in the territories of the States required to establish their jurisdiction in accordance with Article 5, paragraph 1."

The alternative in paragraph 2 – "may" of "shall" – reflected a difference of opinion between different delegations. This problem could not be resolved at this stage, and the Working Group therefore adopted the text proposed by Sweden, including the two alternatives in paragraph 2 which were left for further consideration at a later stage.

g) *Legal assistance*

In the original Swedish draft, article 15 read as follows:

"1. States Parties shall afford one another the greatest measure of assistance in connection with proceedings referred to in Article 11, including the supply of all evidence at their disposal necessary for the proceedings.
2. The provisions of paragraph 1 of this Article shall not affect obligations concerning mutual judicial assistance embodied in any other treaty."

The United States proposed a rewording as follows:

"1. Each State Party shall, consistent with its own laws, afford the greatest measure of assistance in connexion with proceedings brought under this Convention in any other State Party, including the supply of all evidence at its disposal necessary for the proceeding. The law of the State requested shall apply in all cases.
2. The provisions of paragraph 1 of this article shall not affect obligations under any other treaty, bilateral or multilateral, which governs or will govern, in whole or in part, mutual assistance in criminal matters."

France considered that the phrase "the greatest measure of assistance in connection with proceedings" should be replaced by the phrase "the greatest measure of assistance in all criminal proceedings" and that paragraph 2 should follow the lines of the corresponding provisions of the *Convention for the Suppression of Unlawful Seizure of Aircraft* and the *Convention for the Suppression of Unlawful Acts against the Safety of Civil Aviation.*

In the revised Swedish draft, article 9 was reworded as follows:

"1. States Parties shall afford one another the greatest measure of assistance in connection with criminal proceedings brought in respect of any of the offences referred to in Article 4, including the supply of all evidence at their disposal necessary for the proceedings.
2. The provisions of paragraph 1 of this Article shall not affect obligations under any other treaty, bilateral or multilateral, which governs or will govern, in whole or in part, mutual assistance in criminal matters."

As a result of the discussion in the Working Group, paragraph 2 of this article was redrafted, and the whole article, in its modified form, was adopted by the Working Group. It reads as follows:

> "1. States Parties shall afford one another the greatest measure of assistance in connection with criminal proceedings brought in respect of any of the offences referred to in article 4, including the supply of all evidence at their disposal necessary for the proceedings.
> 2. States Parties shall carry out their obligations under paragraph 1 of this article in conformity with any treaties on mutual judicial assistance that may exist between them."

h) *Complaints and investigations*

Articles 9 and 10 of the original Swedish draft read as follows:

> *Article 9*
> "Each State Party shall guarantee to any individual who alleges to have been subjected within its jurisdiction to torture or other cruel, inhuman or degrading treatment or punishment by or at the instigation of its public officials, the right to complain to and to have his case impartially examined by its competent authorities without threat of further torture or other cruel, inhuman or degrading treatment or punishment."

> *Article 10*
> "Each State Party shall ensure that, even if there has been no formal complaint, its competent authorities proceed to an impartial, speedy and effective investigation, wherever there is reasonable ground to believe that an act of torture or other cruel, inhuman or degrading treatment or punishment has been committed within its jurisdiction."

With regard to article 9, Austria considered that the phrase "the right to complain to its competent authorities" should be replaced by "the right to an effective remedy before a national authority". Denmark considered that the words "without threat of further torture or other cruel, inhuman or degrading treatment or punishment" should be deleted, since they might give the false impression that other forms of threat could be used. A similar proposal was made by the United Kingdom which also considered that in article 9 as well as in article 10 the word "jurisdiction" should be replaced by "territory".

Regarding article 10, France considered that "reasonable ground" should be replaced by "serious ground". The United States proposed a new article which would replace both articles 9 and 10 and would read as follows:

> "If there is reasonable basis for belief that an act of torture or other cruel, inhuman or degrading treatment or punishment has been or is being committed within a State Party's jurisdiction, its competent authorities

> shall initiate and carry out an impartial, speedy and effective investigation."

The revised Swedish draft contained articles 12 and 13 which read as follows:

> *Article 12*
> "Each State Party shall ensure that any individual who alleges he has been subjected to torture in any territory under its jurisdiction has the right to complain to and to have his case promptly and impartially examined by its competent authorities. Steps shall be taken to ensure that the complainant is protected against ill-treatment in consequence of his complaint."
>
> *Article 13*
> "Each State Party shall ensure that, even if there has been no formal complaint, its competent authorities proceed to a prompt and impartial investigation, wherever there is reasonable ground to believe that an act of torture has been committed in any territory under its jurisdiction."

During the discussion of this revised proposal in the Working Group, it was agreed to reverse the order of the two articles in order to demonstrate that the primary responsibility for taking measures against torture is on the authorities and not on the victim. Moreover, it was agreed to indicate explicitly that not only the complainant but also any witnesses would be protected against reprisals which would include not only ill-treatment but also other forms of intimidation.

Articles 12 and 13 were finally adopted by the Working Group in the following form:

> *Article 12*
> "Each State Party shall ensure that its competent authorities proceed to a prompt and impartial investigation, wherever there is reasonable ground to believe that an act of torture has been committed in any territory under its jurisdiction."
>
> *Article 13*
> "Each State Party shall ensure that any individual who alleges that he has been subjected to torture in any territory under its jurisdiction has the right to complain to and to have his case promptly and impartially examined by its competent authorities. Steps shall be taken to ensure that the complainant and witnesses are protected against all ill-treatment or intimidation as a consequence of his complaint or any evidence given."

i) *Right to compensation*

The right to compensation granted to a victim of torture was dealt with in article 12 of the original Swedish draft in the following manner:

> "Each State Party shall guarantee an enforceable right to compensation to the victim of an act of torture or other cruel, inhuman or degrading treatment or punishment committed by or at the instigation of its public officials. In the event of the death of the victim, his relatives or other successors shall be entitled to enforce this right of compensation."

Several governments had made observations on this question in their written comments.

Austria considered that this right to compensation should be as comprehensive as possible. In the event of the death of the victim, the right of relatives to compensation regarding alimony should however be limited to cases where the victim was legally obliged to pay such alimony. All other forms of claims for compensation – with the exception of those of a purely personal nature – should be open to the victim's heirs as successors.

Barbados considered that it should be specified whether the State, the public official or the individual is liable to pay compensation.

The United Kingdom suggested that the word "relatives" should be replaced by "dependants".

The United States was of the opinion that the right to compensation as such should be limited to victims of torture. However, it should be possible for "heirs, dependants or successors" to enforce that right in the event of the victim's death. The United States proposed that the article should be redrafted as follows:

> "Each State Party shall take such measures as may be necessary to assure an enforceable right to compensation to the victim of an act of torture committed by or with the consent or acquiescence of its public officials. In the event of the death of the victim, his heirs, dependants or successors shall be entitled to enforce this right."

Article 14 of the revised Swedish draft read as follows:

> "1. Each State Party shall ensure that the victim of an act of torture has an enforceable right to compensation. In the event of the death of the victim as a result of an act of torture, his dependants shall be entitled to compensation.
> 2. Nothing in this Article shall affect any other right to compensation which may exist under national law."

A number of questions relating to this article were discussed by the Working Group. A suggestion was made that the entitlement should be not only to "compensation" but to "fair and adequate compensation". Some delegates considered it important that the term "compensation" should include "means for the rehabilitation of the victim", but other delegates pointed out that the term "rehabilitation" was vague and ambivalent. There was also a discussion on which persons should be entitled to compensation in the case of the death of the victim. Reference was made to the case of a friend or a neighbour who had helped the victim and supported him financially before he died.

While leaving it open as to whether or not the term "rehabilitation" should be used in the text, the Working Group adopted the article worded as follows:

> "1. Each State Party shall ensure in its legal system that the victim of an act of torture be redressed and have an enforceable right to fair and adequate compensation including the means for his [rehabilitation]. In the event of the death of the victim as a result of an act of torture, his dependants shall be entitled to compensation.
> 2. Nothing in this article shall affect any right of the victim or other persons to compensation which may exist under national law."

j) *The use of statements made under torture*

Article 13 of the original Swedish draft read as follows:

> "Each State Party shall ensure that any statement which is established to have been made as a result of torture or other cruel, inhuman or degrading treatment or punishment shall not be invoked as evidence against the person concerned or against any other persons in any proceedings."

It was pointed out, however, that an exception to this rule should be made because it should be possible to invoke the statement made under torture as evidence against the torturer. The United Kingdom therefore suggested that at the end of the article the words "except against a person accused of obtaining such statement by torture" should be added. Similar proposals were made by Austria and the United States.

Consequently, in its revised draft Sweden proposed the following wording of article 15:

> "Each State Party shall ensure that any statement which is established to have been made as a result of torture shall not be invoked as evidence in any proceedings, except against a person accused of obtaining that statement by torture."

After some redrafting the Working Group adopted the article, which in this final version reads as follows:

> "Each State Party shall ensure that any statement which is established to have been made as a result of torture shall not be invoked as evidence

in any proceedings, except against a person accused of torture as evidence that the statement was made."

k) *Cruel, inhuman or degrading treatment or punishment*

The request which had been addressed by the General Assembly to the Commission on Human Rights had been to draft a convention against torture and other cruel, inhuman or degrading treatment or punishment. However, it soon appeared that is was not possible to define in precise terms the concept of "cruel, inhuman or degrading treatment or punishment" and it therefore proved difficult to take this concept as the basis for specific legal obligations in the convention. On the other hand, a number of delegations considered that it would be unfortunate if "cruel, inhuman or degrading treatment or punishment" were left outside the convention, not only because this would be contrary to the request of the General Assembly, but also because in several other international instruments torture and other cruel, inhuman or degrading treatment or punishment are dealt with side by side and without any distinctions being made in the applicable rules.

In the original Swedish draft, most of the articles dealt with torture and cruel, inhuman or degrading treatment or punishment along the same lines. Exceptions were made, however, in certain articles imposing specific obligations to legislate, for instance article 7 which would oblige State to make torture a punishable offence and article 8 which would oblige States to establish their universal jurisdiction over offences of torture.

However, in the course of discussions in the Working Group and in informal consultations it appeared that most delegates wished the convention to deal primarily with torture, while leaving it open whether some of its provisions could in the end be made applicable also to other cruel, inhuman or degrading treatment or punishment.

In the revised Swedish draft, no final solution to this problem was proposed. This draft merely contained an article 16 reading as follows:

> "This Convention shall be without prejudice to any provisions in other international instruments or in national law which prohibit cruel, inhuman or degrading treatment and punishment."

In the Working Group the suggestion was made that the convention should contain one article dealing with the problem of cruel, inhuman and degrading treatment and punishment and indicating specifically that some of the other articles in the convention should also apply to such treatment and punishment. Along these lines, the International Commission of Jurists proposed an additional paragraph in article 16 which would read as follows (doc. HR(XXXVI)/WG.10/WP.5):

> "2. Each State Party shall take effective measures to prevent in any

> territory under its jurisdiction other acts of cruel, inhuman or degrading treatment or punishment which do not amount to torture as defined in Article 1. In particular, the obligations contained in Articles 3, 10, 11, 12, 13, 14 and 15 shall apply with the substitution for references to torture of references to other forms of cruel, inhuman or degrading treatment or punishment."

Subsequently the International Commission of Jurists submitted a revised text intended to be inserted as paragraph 1 of article 16 and reading as follows (doc. HR(XXXVI/WG.10/WP.5/Rev.1):

> "1. Each State Party shall undertake to prevent in any territory under its jurisdiction other acts of cruel, inhuman or degrading treatment or punishment which do not constitute torture as defined in Article 1, when such acts are committed by or at the instigation of or with the consent or acquiescence of a public official or other person acting in an official capacity. In particular, the obligations contained in Articles [3], 10, 11, 12, 13, [14] and [15] shall apply with the substitution for references to torture of references to other forms of cruel, inhuman or degrading treatment or punishment."

No agreement could be reached on whether or not articles 3 (prohibition in some cases of expulsion and extradition), 14 (right to compensation) and 15 (prohibition of the use of statements in evidence) should also apply to cruel, inhuman or degrading treatment or punishment. While leaving this question open, the Working Group adopted article 16 which read as follows:

"1. Each State Party shall undertake to prohibit in any territory under its jurisdiction other acts of cruel, inhuman or degrading treatment or punishment which do not constitute torture as defined in Article 1, when such acts are committed by or at the instigation of or with the consent or acquiescence of a public official or other person acting in an official capacity. In particular, the obligations contained in Articles [3], 10, 11, 12, 13, [14] and [15] shall apply with the substitution for references to torture, of references to other forms of cruel, inhuman or degrading treatment or punishment.
2. The provisions of this Convention are without prejudice to the provisions of any other international instrument or national law which prohibit cruel, inhuman or degrading treatment or punishment."

6. Deliberations in the Commission's Working Group in 1981[15]

In 1981 the Working Group met again for a full week before the session of the Commission and continued its work during the session both in public meetings and in informal consultations. Under the guidance of Mr Papastefanou the Group made assiduous efforts to solve major problems; nevertheless it made less progress than in the preceding years. It spent much time on discussing the question of universal jurisdiction without coming to conclusions. It only achieved agreement with regard to some other provisions of the substantive part of the convention. Furthermore, it started its consideration of the problems concerning the implementation provisions, again without reaching any definite conclusions.

a) *The question of universal jurisdiction*

In respect of this question, the position of most delegations had not substantially changed since the previous year. Several delegations argued that a system of universal jurisdiction was desirable in order not to provide torturers with any place of refuge. Other delegations considered such a system not appropriate for the prosecution of torture, either for reasons of principle or for practical reasons. Some delegations indicated that they had difficulties in accepting a clause of universal jurisdiction which was not subject to certain conditions.

The Netherlands delegation now accepted universal jurisdiction in principle and no longer advocated making the exercise of such jurisdiction dependent on the rejection of a request for extradition. Instead, it tabled a formal proposal to make the exercise of universal jurisdiction dependent "upon complaint by any interested party" (doc. E/CN.4/1981/WG.2/WP.2). Only the Australian delegation gave support to this proposal. Other Western delegations felt that this formula could give rise to loose interpretations and open up loopholes. The Brazilian delegation preferred to make universal jurisdiction conditional on the refusal of a request for extradition.

During the session of the Commission the Working Group held a series of informal consultations to try to find a generally acceptable solution for the question of universal jurisdiction. The discussions were highly complicated, in particular because this question could be dealt with either in the article on jurisdiction (article 5) or in the article on prosecution (article 7) while moreover both these articles gave rise to several other problems. Numerous formulas were suggested during these consultations, but in the end the Working

[15] The 1981 report of the Working Group is contained in document E/CN.4/L.1567 and is also reproduced on pages 51-69 of the 1981 report of the Commission on Human Rights which has been published under the symbols E/CN.4/1475 and E/1981/25.

Group had to decide to postpone the discussion of this question to the following year.

b) *Other provisions of the substantive part*

The Working Group discussed a number of questions relating to articles 1, 2, 3, 5, 6, 7, 8, 14 and 16.

The Group reached no agreement about the question of maintaining or deleting the proposed second paragraph of article 1, which stated that torture is an aggravated and deliberate form of cruel, inhuman or degrading treatment or punishment. In particular the delegations of the United Kingdom and the United States advocated maintaining this provision.

In the proposed third paragraph of article 1, the final words "relating to the subject matter of this Convention" were deleted.

The Working Group decided that article 2, paragraph 3, would simply read "An order from a superior officer or a public authority may not be invoked as a justification of torture", *without* the addition of the phrase "however, this may be considered a ground for mitigation of punishment, if justice so requires".

No agreement could be reached about maintaining, changing or deleting the proposed second paragraph of article 3, containing an illustrative list of situations which may result in gross violations of human rights. On the other hand, the Group agreed to replace the words "whether there is such evidence" in the first line of the proposed paragraph by the words "whether there are such grounds". The Argentine delegation maintained its position that a State Party which refuses extradition in the circumstances described in article 3, paragraph 1, shall, if its national legislation so permits, institute criminal proceedings against the person whose extradition it refuses.

With regard to article 5, paragraph 1, the Working Group decided that subparagraphs (b) and (c) would read as follows:

"(b) When the alleged offender is a national of that State;
(c) When the victim is a national of that State if that State considers it appropriate."

Paragraph 2 of article 5 was retained between square brackets since no agreement could be achieved about the question of universal jurisdiction.

The Group adopted by consensus paragraph 3 of article 5, which reads "This Convention does not exclude any criminal jurisdiction exercised in accordance with internal law."

The Group considered paragraph 4 of article 6, but made no decision because this paragraph was connected with the question of universal jurisdiction.

The Group decided to transfer paragraph 5 of article 6, relating to fair treatment of alleged offenders, to the end of article 7. No results were achieved concerning the further contents of article 7 because of the disagreement about the question of universal jurisdiction.

In respect of article 8, paragraph 2, concerning the possible use of the convention as a legal base for extradition, most speakers felt that the verb should read "shall". Other delegations, in particular those of the United Kingdom and the United States, maintained their position that the verb should read "may".

As to article 14, paragraph 1, concerning compensation to be given to torture victims, the Group adopted a Netherlands proposal to insert the words "committed in any territory under its jurisdiction" after the word "torture". It further decided to qualify the term "rehabilitation" by adopting the expression "as full a rehabilitation as possible".

With regard to article 16, paragraph 1, concerning other acts of cruel, inhuman or degrading treatment or punishment, the Group agreed not to include references to articles 3 and 15. However, no agreement was reached on the question of including a reference to article 14. Nor was any conclusion reached on the suggestion to insert in article 16 a provision which would exclude suffering due to lawful sanctions from the scope of this article. With regard to paragraph 2 of article 16 the Group decided to replace the words "of this Convention" by the words "of this article" and to add at the end of the paragraph the words "or which relate to extradition or expulsion".

c) *Implementation provisions*

An important step forward in 1981 was that now, for the first time, the Working Group addressed the question of the implementation provisions. The Swedish proposals thereon were contained in articles 16 to 21 of the original Swedish draft.[16] Provisions on implementation were also contained in the draft of the International Association of Penal Law.[17] Moreover, there was the draft optional protocol submitted by Costa Rica, providing for a special verification system.[18] In addition, the Netherlands submitted elaborate amendments to the Swedish implementation proposals.

In the Swedish proposals, the task of monitoring compliance with the convention was entrusted to the Human Rights Committee established under the *International Covenant on Civil and Political Rights*. The States Parties would have to submit reports on measures taken to suppress and punish torture and other cruel, inhuman or degrading treatment or punishment (article 16). Such reports would be considered by the Committee in accordance with the procedures set up under the *Covenant*. The Committee would also be authorized to initiate an inquiry if it received information that torture

[16] See Appendix 6.
[17] See Appendix 5.
[18] See Appendix 8.

was being systematically practised in a certain State Party (article 17). Moreover, the Swedish proposals provided for two optional procedures concerning the consideration of complaints, one relating to complaints by States Parties (articles 18 and 19) and the other relating to complaints by individuals (article 20). These procedures would only apply to those States Parties which had at any time expressly declared that they recognized the competence of the Committee to deal with such complaints. The Committee would deal with complaints of States Parties in accordance with articles 41 and 42 of the *Covenant*; it would deal with complaints of individuals in accordance with the *Optional Protocol* to the *Covenant*.

On the first day of the pre-sessional meetings in 1981 the Netherlands delegation submitted to the Working Group a comprehensive implementation proposal in the form of amendments to the Swedish draft (doc. E/CN.4/1981/WG.2/WP.3). According to this alternative proposal the text of articles 16, 17, 18 and 20 would be modified, article 19 would be deleted and four new articles would be added. The main differences between the Dutch proposal and the Swedish proposal were as follows.

The task of international supervision would not be given to the Human Rights Committee as such but to a new Committee; however, this would be a new body in a formal sense only, for according to the Dutch formula it would be composed of the members of the existing Human Rights Committee. The competence of the Committee to initiate inquiries would not only relate to systematic torture practices but to any occurrence of repeated violations of the convention. The optional procedure for the consideration of State complaints would be replaced by a mandatory system, *i.e.* this procedure would apply to all States Parties. On the other hand, the Dutch proposal maintained the optional character of the procedure for considering complaints of individuals. One of the additional articles proposed by the Netherlands stated that between States Parties to the convention, which were also Parties to the *International Covenant on Civil and Political Rights* and which had accepted the competence of the Human Rights Committee under article 41 of the *Covenant* and/or under the *Optional Protocol*, the procedures provided for in the *Covenant* and/or in the *Protocol* would apply instead of the procedures provided for in the convention.

The principal innovative element of the Dutch proposals was embodied in the other additional articles, which provided for an entirely new function for the Committee. According to these articles the Committee might designate a fact-finding commission to carry out visits to places of detention. This fact-finding commission would be authorized to visit places under the jurisdiction of a State Party where persons were detained for any reason whatever. It would have the right to discuss with such a State Party appropriate solutions to particular questions, and would submit a report on its findings to the Committee. On the basis of this report the Committee might itself take up the matter with the State Party concerned. All these proceedings would be confidential, but if the Committee thought that a serious violation of the convention had taken place and if the State Party concerned would not take satisfactory steps to restore respect for the convention, the Committee would have the right to make public its own report. It is evident that the Netherlands, in designing this additional verification scheme based on visits to places of detention, had been inspired by the draft optional protocol submitted by Costa Rica. Unlike the Costa Rican proposal, however, this scheme would form a mandatory part of the implementation system.

The Netherlands delegation gave an oral introduction of its alternative implementation proposals to the Working Group, but these proposals were never thoroughly discussed. The Group's deliberations on the implementation issue focussed almost exclusively on the question of who was to be charged with monitoring compliance with the convention.

On the third day of the pre-sessional meetings Mr Papastefanou informed the Working Group of a telegram received from the Legal Counsel of the UN, Erik Suy. This telegram, dated 26 January 1981, read as follows:

> "A. Have carefully examined the proposals contained in document E/CN.4/1285 by which the Human Rights Committee established under article 28 of the Covenant on Civil and Political Rights would function as the implementation organ of the proposed torture convention.
> B. In my view this proposal presents serious legal obstacles and if adopted its legal validity could be challenged on the ground that it constitutes a modification of the terms of the Covenant which has established the Human Rights Committee and defined its terms of reference. Such modification can only be effected by the procedure specified in article 51 of the Covenant.
> C. As a treaty organ the Human Rights Committee must function in accordance with the provision of its constituent treaty. It is not sufficient in my view that there is a general concordance in purpose between the proposed convention and article 7 of the Covenant on Civil and Political Rights." (doc. E/CN.4/1981/WG.2/WP.6)

Several delegations shared the objections voiced by the Legal Counsel, pointing out that the States Parties to the convention against torture would not necessarily be the same as the States Parties to the *Covenant*. Other delegations considered that the difficulties referred to by the Legal Counsel were not insurmountable, and that the idea of using the services of the Human Rights Committee merited examination. Several delegations recommended that a separate international body be charged with the task of supervising implementation. Some delegations suggested that the monitoring functions be entrusted to the UN Commission on Human Rights or to a sub-organ of that body. The Soviet delegation advised against the creation of new machinery and preferred to stick to the implementation system established under the *Covenant*.

The delegations of Argentina and Brazil questioned the necessity for setting up a system of international supervision; in their view the implementation of the convention should basically be assured by each State Party itself within the context of its own legal system. The Argentine delegation suggested therefore that all provisions concerning international supervision should be made optional. This position was countered by the remark that self-enforcement had been shown to be a failure because, despite internal laws and international instruments prohibiting torture, torture was still widely practised. The debate made it clear that a majority of the delegations in principle favoured some form of international supervision.

The Swedish delegation submitted an alternative suggestion for the establishment of a supervisory body (doc. E/CN.4/1981/WG.2/WP.7). According to this formula the members of that body would be nationals of States Parties to the convention, serving in their personal capacity. They would be elected by the States Parties and they should as far as possible be chosen among members of the Human Rights Committee. There was divided reaction to this alternative suggestion which, at any rate, would need further elaboration before being incorporated in the convention.

Owing to lack of time, the Working Group decided to continue its discussion of the implementation issues in the following year.

7. Deliberations in the Commission's Working Group in 1982[19]

When the Working Group reconvened in 1982, it had to elect a new chairman-rapporteur because Mr Papastefanou had resigned as the Greek representative to the Commission on Human Rights. The Group chose as his successor J. Herman Burgers, deputy head of the Netherlands delegation to the Commission. The Group met during a full week before the Commission's session and held seven additional meetings during the course of the session.

The new chairman felt that the time had come for a slightly different approach to the Working Group's task. Since the Group could only decide on the basis of consensus and fundamentally different positions continued to exist, there seemed to be no prospect that the Group would be able to solve all these issues. In some such cases, instead of seeking endlessly for consensus formulas, the Group would do better to identify the issues as clearly as possible and to explore what measure of support might be expected for specific solutions. With regard to such issues the Group would then leave it to the Commission or to the General Assembly to make definitive decisions, either by consensus or by majority vote.

---

[19] The 1982 report of the Working Group is contained in document E/CN.4/1982/L.40 and is also reproduced in an addendum to the 1982 report of the Commission on Human Rights which has been published under the symbol E/1982/12/Add.1.

Generally speaking, the deliberations of the Working Group in 1982 had an animated character. Although final agreement was only achieved with regard to some of the unsolved questions, this round of debate could be considered valuable, first of all because remarkable progress was made concerning the jurisdiction issue, and secondly because for the first time the implementation questions were thoroughly discussed.

a) *The question of universal jurisdiction*

A certain evolution in the position of several delegations could be observed as to the question of universal jurisdiction. France and the Netherlands now explicitly supported the system proposed by Sweden. Consequently, Australia remained the only Western country participating in the Working Group which did not support the inclusion of universal jurisdiction in the convention. This led the Australian delegation to consult with its government on the new situation. The Netherlands delegation announced the withdrawal of its proposal submitted in 1981, which would make the exercise of universal jurisdiction dependent upon complaint by any interested party. The Brazilian delegation expressed its concern that universal jurisdiction could be exploited for political reasons and that it could result in trials on the basis of spurious accusations and fabricated evidence. This delegation repeated its plea for making the exercise of universal jurisdiction dependent on the refusal of a request for extradition.

The Brazilian proposal was not supported by Argentina. Together with the Uruguayan delegation, the Argentine delegation declared itself firmly opposed to any system of universal jurisdiction with regard to the prosecution of torture because this crime is not international in its nature. The Argentine delegation argued that the primary objective of the convention should be to ensure compliance with its norms by any State which does not punish acts of torture carried out by its public officials. Universal jurisdiction would not contribute to this end, since such a system would only apply to the improbable case in which a torturer would leave his own State where he enjoyed impunity for his crime. The system proposed to face this highly hypothetical case could be a source of controversy between States. The intention of a State to prosecute a case of torture on the basis of universal jurisdiction could be interpreted by the State where the crime had been committed as a demonstration of lack of trust in its judicial system, a violation of its sovereignty and even as an interference in its internal affairs.

The United States delegate showed himself a highly articulate advocate of the inclusion of universal jurisdiction in the convention. Replying to the Argentine delegation he stated that such jurisdiction was intended primarily to deal with situations where torture is a State policy and, therefore, the State in question does not, by definition, prosecute its officials who conduct torture. For the international community to leave enforcement of the convention to such a State would be essentially a formula for doing nothing. Therefore in such cases universal jurisdiction would be the most effective weapon against torture which could be brought to bear. It could be utilized against official torturers who travel to other States, a situation which was not at all hypothetical. It could also be used against torturers fleeing from a change of government in their States if, for legal or other reasons, extradition was not possible.

In the light of suggestions which had been made during the discussion, the chairman-rapporteur consulted several delegations regarding the possibility of adapting the text of article 7. Before the end of the pre-sessional meetings he submitted a modified version of this article to the Working Group (doc. E/CN.4/1982/WG.2/WP.5). The principal new element in this text made it clear that in the case of the exercise of universal jurisdiction the standards of evidence required for prosecution and conviction should in no way be less stringent than those which apply in the case of jurisdiction on a nationality or territorial basis. Mr Burgers explained that his proposal was intended to meet the concern of those who feared that the exercise of universal jurisdiction might lead to trials on the basis of spurious accusations inspired by political motives. He further explained that his proposal implied that article 5, paragraph 2, and article 6, paragraph 4, of the Swedish draft would be maintained.

The discussion of this proposal in meetings of the Working Group during the session of the Committee showed a growing support for the inclusion of universal jurisdiction in the convention. The Australian delegation announced that its government, although retaining its reservations, had now decided to accept such inclusion with a view to facilitating progress towards agreement on a final text. The Brazilian delegation stated that it could accept the proposal of the chairman-rapporteur while maintaining its position on article 5, paragraph 2, namely that the establishment of universal jurisdiction should be made conditional on the refusal of a request for extradition. If such a clause could not be included in the text of the convention itself, Brazil would consider making a declaration or reservation to that effect when becoming a Party to the convention.

Several speakers who supported the proposal of the chairman in general terms suggested drafting changes. Mr Burgers therefore tabled a revised version, which subsequently underwent further amendments during the discussion. The Soviet delegation, which had already welcomed the proposal as a step in the right direction, now made it clear that it could support the text. Explicit support was also voiced by the delegation of Senegal. The delegations of Argentina and Uruguay maintained their opposition. Since no other delegations which participated in the Working Group spoke out against including universal jurisdiction in the convention, these two delegations found themselves isolated.

The report of the Working Group to the Commission stated explicitly that most speakers had indicated that their governments were prepared to support the inclusion of a system of universal jurisdiction in the draft convention. The revised text of article 7, as it emerged finally from the discussion, was reproduced in the first annex of the report. The report noted that all delegations who could accept the inclusion of universal jurisdiction in the draft convention could support this text of article 7, as well as the text of article 5, paragraph 2, and of article 6, paragraph 4.

b) *Other provisions of the substantive part*

The Working Group further discussed some questions relating to articles 1, 3, 8 and 16.

The Group decided to delete the proposed second paragraph of article 1, which characterized torture as an aggravated and deliberate form of cruel, inhuman or degrading treatment or punishment. This decision was made after new language had been incorporated in article 16, implying that torture is the gravest form of such treatment of punishment.

As to article 3, once again the Group could not reach agreement on maintaining, changing or deleting the proposed second paragraph, which contained an illustrative list of situations which may result in gross violations of human rights.

With regard to article 8, paragraph 2, the Group decided that the verb should read "may", not "shall". Accordingly, States Parties *may* consider the convention as the legal basis for extradition in respect of acts of torture, attempts at torture and complicity and participation in torture.

With regard to article 16, the Group decided to replace the words in paragraph 1 "which do not constitute torture" by "which do not amount to torture". This had been proposed by the United States delegation to make it clear that torture is the gravest form of cruel, inhuman or degrading treatment or punishment. On the other hand, a consensus was not achieved on including in this paragraph a reference to article 14.

c) *Implementation provisions*

The Working Group discussed at great length the implementation provisions to be included in the convention. Taking into account the objections raised by the UN's Legal Counsel in January 1981, Sweden had submitted towards the end of that year a complete set of alternative implementation provisions (doc. E/CN.4/1493).[20] In these new Swedish proposals the task of monitoring compliance with the convention was no longer assigned to the Human Rights Committee but to a separate "Committee against Torture", consisting of nine nationals of the States Parties to the convention. As far as possible they were to be members of the Human Rights Committee, and they would be elected

[20] See Appendix 10.

by the States Parties. The composition and the functioning of this new Committee was set out in eighteen articles, largely along the lines of the corresponding provisions of the *International Covenant on Civil and Political Rights*.

In the pre-sessional meetings of the Working Group a preliminary discussion took place on whether first to consider the nature and composition of the implementation organ or the functions of this organ. The Group decided to begin with a debate on the functional aspects, as a decision on the type of organ to be chosen would depend to a great extent upon the kind of functions assigned to it. During the last two days of the pre-sessional meetings the Group considered mainly the organizational aspects. After the completion of these meetings, the chairman-rapporteur submitted a new set of implementation provisions as a possible alternative to the Swedish draft articles (doc. E/CN.4/1982/WG.2/WP.6).[21] This new proposal was discussed at several meetings in the middle of the Commission's session.

Starting with a discussion regarding the provisions on the functions of the implementation organ, the Working Group first took up article 29 of the new Swedish draft, which provided for the submission of reports and other information by the States Parties and the consideration thereof by the supervisory body. Some delegations objected to the inclusion of "other information" in this procedure. The Brazilian delegation tabled amendments to both paragraphs of the proposed article, in which *inter alia* the element of "other information" was removed (doc. E/CN.4/1982/WG.2/WP.3). During the discussion some changes were suggested and these were accepted by the Brazilian delegation. The revised version of article 29 was also acceptable to the Swedish delegation.

The Working Group discussed at some length the proposed inquiry procedure as contained in article 30 of the new Swedish draft. Initially this proposal was discussed together with the Netherlands proposal for a mandatory verification system based on visits to places of detention. The latter proposal was embodied in amendments which the Netherlands delegation had submitted in 1981.[22] Only the Australian delegation gave support to the Dutch proposal. Some other delegations remarked that, while their governments might be prepared to accept for themselves a system as proposed by the Netherlands, they felt that such a system was too stringent for the purpose of a convention which was intended to obtain worldwide support.

With regard to the Swedish proposal, several points of criticism were raised. In particular, the Brazilian delegation argued that the text of article 30 should make it clear that a step-by-step approach would be required. It was also recommended for inclusion in the text that all the proceedings under this article should be confidential. On the other hand, the Australian delegation

[21] See Appendix 11.
[22] See *supra* p. 75.

observed that torture is an evil of such a grave nature that publicity would be justified if a government would clearly fail to take the necessary measures to suppress this evil. In the light of the debate the Swedish delegation presented a revised text of article 30 (doc. E/CN.4/1982/WG.2/WP.4). During the discussion of this new version several delegates suggested further changes. All these suggestions were accepted by the Swedish delegation.

The Working Group also discussed the complaint procedures contained in the Swedish draft articles 31 and 32. Several delegations expressed their support for these procedures. On the other hand, it was pointed out that there might be a risk of duplication, even conflict, between these procedures and the corresponding procedures under the *Covenant* and the *Protocol* of 1966. Taking into account as well that the proposed procedures would be optional, some delegations wondered whether it would not be preferable to omit these procedures from the convention.

The Netherlands delegation invited comments regarding the proposal for a mandatory State complaint procedure as contained in the amendments it had tabled in 1981.[23] Only the Australian delegation expressed its support for such a mandatory procedure. On the other hand, the delegation of the United Kingdom stated that it could only accept an optional procedure. Several other delegations also manifested their preference for an optional procedure.

The Brazilian delegation recommended replacing the proposed complaint procedures by a mandatory conciliation procedure. According to this delegation, States would be more likely to accept such a procedure as it would fall into the generally accepted treatment of inter-state disputes concerning the interpretation or the application of a treaty.

As to which body was to be charged with supervising the convention's implementation, several delegations considered the new Swedish formula a constructive proposal. Other delegations expressed reservations about the multiplication of international organs. The delegation of the Soviet Union reiterated its preference for seeking a solution in the framework of existing structures. The delegation of the Byelorussian Soviet Socialist Republic observed that the system established under the *International Convention on the Suppression and Punishment of the Crime of Apartheid*, where the monitoring task is performed by a Group of Three Members of the Commission on Human Rights, might constitute a useful precedent.

At the end of the pre-sessional meetings, the chairman-rapporteur outlined to the Working Group some ideas he had in mind for a different set-up of the implementation provisions as a possible alternative basis of discussion. The Group authorized him to work these ideas out in a text. On the first day of the Commission's session he submitted his alternative implementation proposals, consisting of four draft articles and an annex (doc. E/CN.4/1982/

[23] See *supra* p. 75.

WG.2/WP.6).[24]

The first of these draft articles dealt with the nature and composition of the supervisory body. It provided for the creation of a group of five persons whom the Chairman of the Commission on Human Rights would appoint from among representatives to the Commission who were nationals of States Parties to the convention. Mr Burgers explained that this solution would avoid the creation of an entirely new body as well as the need for spelling out election procedures etc. in considerable detail. He had taken as his starting point the supervisory machinery provided for in the *Anti-Apartheid Convention*. The second and the third of the proposed articles contained no really new elements but simply reflected the outcome of the discussions that had taken place concerning articles 29 and 30 of the Swedish draft. However, the fourth draft article and the accompanying annex were new and provided for a mandatory conciliation procedure as suggested by the Brazilian delegation. This article and the annex were copies, with some necessary adaptations, of the corresponding provisions of the *Vienna Convention on the Law of Treaties*. In this context Mr Burgers also mentioned the new *Convention on the Law of the Sea*. He further explained that in his alternative set-up the convention would contain no complaint procedures.

The text presented by the chairman-rapporteur was discussed by the Working Group in the third week of the Commission's session, after delegations had had an opportunity to consult their governments. Generally, the reactions to these alternative suggestions were not enthusiastic.

Only the delegations of Argentina and Uruguay supported the proposal for a Group of Five as the supervisory body. Most speakers did not favour the idea of a body organically linked to the Commission on Human Rights. The view was expressed that this would introduce strong political factors which were especially undesirable as regards implementation of a convention designed to eliminate torture by public officials. A number of delegations stated their preference for the following basic elements: election of the implementation organ by the States Parties to the convention, requirement that all or part of the members should also belong to the Human Rights Committee, and functions to be carried out in a personal capacity.

The proposed mandatory conciliation procedure was only supported by the Brazilian delegation. Other delegations expressed their hesitations with regard to this proposal. The Argentine delegation pointed out that the precedents mentioned by the chairman-rapporteur related to treaties regarding matters entirely different from those dealt with in the envisaged convention against torture. The Indian delegation observed that there was a difference between disputes concerning the application of such provisions of the convention as those in the field of jurisdiction and extradition, which would often

[24] See Appendix 11.

lend themselves to judicial or quasi-judicial settlement, and disputes regarding the occurrence of torture practices. In the last case it was preferable that the matter would not be dealt with exclusively between the parties to the dispute but that the supervisory body would have a certain role to play.

The Working Group did not arrive at final conclusions about any of the proposed implementation provisions in 1982. However, the comprehensive exchange of views that had taken place prepared the ground for future solutions which could obtain broader support.

8. Deliberations in the Commission's Working Group in 1983[25]

The Working Group conducted its business in a very constructive atmosphere in 1983. The principal outcome of its deliberations was the formulation of a comprehensive implementation system supported by a sizable majority within the Group. Another important step forward was that for the first time the Working Group also dealt with the preamble and the final clauses to be included in the convention. Consequently, the Group could now annex to its report to the Commission a complete text for the draft convention, although many of the provisions contained therein were still placed between square brackets.[26]

a) *Preamble*

The Working Group discussed the preamble on the basis of a draft submitted by Sweden in 1980.[27] A suggestion to delete the words "of the inherent dignity and" in the first paragraph, so as to avoid duplication with the second paragraph, appeared to be generally acceptable. With regard to the third paragraph, suggestions were made for including a reference to the principle of non-discrimination. A proposal to do so by referring to article 55 of the *Charter of the United Nations* obtained general support. Several speakers criticized the last paragraph of the draft preamble. The observer for Amnesty International argued that it risked undermining the authority of the 1975 *Declaration*. There was general support for the proposal of the Argentine delegation to replace this formula by the following text: "Desiring to make more effective the struggle against torture and other cruel, inhuman or degrading treatment or punishment".

In the light of the discussion the chairman-rapporteur submitted a revised set of draft preambular clauses (doc. E/CN.4/1983/WG.2/WP.14). These were adopted on a second reading by the Working Group. On the same occasion

[25] The 1983 report of the Working Group is contained in document E/CN.4/1983/63.
[26] See Appendix 13.
[27] Document E/CN.4/1427. The text of this draft preamble is reproduced in Appendix 9.

the Peruvian observer delegation proposed the following paragraph for inclusion in the preamble: "Recognizing that the essential rights of man are not derived from one's being a national of a certain State, but are based upon attributes of the human personality and that they therefore justify international protection in the form of a convention". The Group felt that this proposal deserved careful consideration at a later stage.

b) *Provisions of the substantive part*

The Working Group devoted several discussions to those provisions of the substantive part of the convention upon which decisions had not been reached at previous sessions, but it did not arrive at final conclusions.

Several delegations favoured deletion of the proposed second paragraph of article 3, other delegations opposed this. Some speakers considered that, if this provision were retained, references to other types of gross violations of human rights should be added, such as all forms of religious intolerance, denial of freedom of expression and denial of the right to form and join trade unions.

The system of universal jurisdiction included in draft articles 5, 6 and 7 was again supported by many delegations, but rejected by the delegations of Argentina and Uruguay. The Brazilian delegate proposed a modified system under which the principle of universal jurisdiction would apply under certain conditions and on a subsidiary basis, only if the States of territorial or national jurisdiction did not request extradition within a set period or if such a request were denied (doc. E/CN.4/1983/WG.2/WP.12). He observed that this modified system would not satisfy those governments which held objections of principle to the inclusion of universal jurisdiction in the convention against torture; nevertheless he hoped that it might make the convention more acceptable to some other governments. As a preliminary comment, some delegations stated that such a system might constitute a sound basis for compromise. On the other hand, the French delegation declared that its government preferred to adhere as closely as possible to the formulations concerning universal jurisdiction used in a number of recent international conventions. The Working Group decided that the Brazilian proposal should be further studied at a later stage. A similar decision was made with regard to a proposal submitted by Senegal for inserting an additional paragraph in article 5 (doc. E/CN.4/1983/WG.2/WP.13).

As in previous years, the Working Group could not agree on the question of including or excluding a reference to article 14 in article 16.

c) *Implementation provisions*

The Working Group made remarkable progress with regard to the implementation provisions of the convention. After the 1982 session the chairman-rapporteur had reconsidered the draft articles which he had suggested during that session as an alternative basis for discussion.[28] He had come to the conclusion that these suggestions offered no prospect for finding a generally acceptable solution. A majority within the Working Group clearly preferred an implementation organ to be elected by the States Parties to the convention as had been proposed by Sweden. The main disadvantage of the Swedish draft[29] appeared to be that it regulated the organizational aspects of the implementation organ in considerable detail, in twelve articles modelled on the corresponding articles of the *International Covenant on Civil and Political Rights.* Therefore, the chairman-rapporteur had drafted a revised set of provisions, taking into account the simpler provisions on implementation organs contained in the 1965 *International Convention on the Elimination of All Forms of Racial Discrimination* and the 1979 *Convention on the Elimination of All Forms of Discrimination against Women.* After ascertaining that the Swedish delegation would have no objection to this, he submitted to the UN Secretariat at the end of 1982 four draft articles together with an explanatory note for consideration by the Working Group.[30] The first and second of these draft articles (articles 17 and 18) contained his revised set of provisions on the organizational aspects of the implementation organ. The third and the fourth draft article (articles 19 and 20) reflected the outcome of the discussions that had taken place in 1982 on articles 29 and 30 of the Swedish draft. In his explanatory note, Mr Burgers pointed out that these draft articles did not cover the implementation issue in its entirety and that the Working Group would also continue to discuss complaint and/or settlement of dispute provisions as well as a provision on annual reporting by the implementation organ itself.

At the first pre-sessional meeting in 1983 the Working Group agreed to take the draft articles submitted by the chairman-rapporteur as its basis for discussion instead of the Swedish proposals of 1981, although most members of the Group had not yet seen these draft articles before that meeting.

Draft article 17 provided for the creation of a new body, the Committee against Torture, consisting of nine experts serving in their personal capacity, to be elected by the States Parties. Essentially, this corresponded to the Swedish proposal of 1981, but in a simplified form. In principle, this idea was now also accepted by the Soviet delegation. With regard to paragraph 1 there were divergent opinions on the question of whether the proposed number of nine Committee members was appropriate. Some delegates criticized paragraph 6 concerning the filling of vacancies, which had been taken verbatim from the corresponding provisions in the above-mentioned anti-discrimination conventions of 1965 and 1979. Paragraph 7 concerning the expenses of

[28] See Appendix 11.
[29] See Appendix 10.
[30] Document E/CN.4/1983/WG.2/2. These draft articles and explanatory note are reproduced in Appendix 12.

the Committee members elicited comments from several delegations. In the light of this discussion the chairman-rapporteur submitted a revised text for paragraphs 6 and 7 of article 17 (doc. E/CN.4/1983/WG.2/WP.9). Some speakers observed that the new version of paragraph 7, although a step in the right direction, was still too complicated.

With reference to draft article 18, Mr Burgers informed the Working Group that the second paragraph contained an error: instead of "five members shall constitute a quorum" the text sould read "six members shall constitute a quorum". The discussion of article 18 concentrated on financial aspects. The delegation of the United States proposed to add to this article a new final paragraph determining that the States Parties would be responsible for expenses incurred in connection with the meetings of the States Parties and of the Committee, including reimbursement of such costs to the United Nations (doc. E/CN.4/1983/WG.2/WP.2). Some delegations, including the Soviet delegation, supported this amendment. Other delegations stated they could not accept the amendment which, in their view, might make it difficult for the less affluent States to decide to become parties to the convention.

Draft article 19 dealt with the submission of reports by the States Parties and the consideration of these reports by the Committee. With regard to paragraph 1 the Australian delegation felt that the requirement to submit reports "whenever new measures have been taken" would place too great a burden on the States Parties and could best be replaced by a requirement to submit supplementary reports periodically. As to paragraphs 2 and 3, the Australian delegation observed that the text did not make it clear whether or not the report could lead to a dialogue between the Committee and the State Party concerned. This delegation submitted several informal suggestions for a reformulation of paragraphs 1, 2 and 3 (doc. E/CN.4/1983/WG.2/WP.1 and WP.3). Other delegations also made suggestions concerning the drafting of these provisions. In the light of the discussion the chairman-rapporteur submitted consolidated proposals for the text of article 19, comprising four paragraphs (doc. E/CN.4/1983/WG.2/WP.7). The discussion of these proposals resulted after some further amendments in a final version which seemed to meet with no objections from the Working Group.

Draft article 20 dealt with action that might be taken if the Committee received information which appeared to indicate the occurrence of systematic torture practices in the territory of a State Party. With regard to paragraph 1, a number of suggestions were made for including a requirement of reliability with respect to the information upon which action would be based. In relation to paragraph 2 it was pointed out that the Committee should give special attention to the observations submitted by the State Party concerned. As to paragraph 3, several speakers felt that the last part, that began with the words "unless the government", was not satisfactory. Moreover it was stressed that the Committee should always seek the co-operation of the State Party concerned when it had decided to initiate an enquiry. With reference to paragraph

4 it was observed that the Committee, if it had any comments or suggestions, should always transmit them to the State Party concerned. Furthermore the Working Group agreed that the State Party concerned was entitled to be informed of the enquiry's findings. With regard to paragraph 5, all delegations agreed that the proceedings referred to in paragraphs 1 to 4 should remain confidential as long as they were in progress. On the other hand, the Australian delegation proposed that, after such proceedings had been finalized in respect of a particular case, the Committee should be able to include a summary account of the enquiry in its annual report. This proposal, which was made on the first day of the pre-sessional meetings, elicited various comments, in particular from the delegations of Argentina, Brazil, Senegal and Uruguay.

In the light of the discussion the chairman-rapporteur submitted a revised text for article 20 (doc. E/CN.4/1983/WG.2/WP.4). On this basis the article was discussed again on the third day of the pre-sessional meetings. The discussion resulted in minor changes to paragraphs 1 and 5. The delegation of Uruguay now explicitly supported the proposed paragraph 5 as its earlier observations had been taken into account in the text. No delegation explicitly rejected this paragraph, which entailed the possibility that the Committee would publish, albeit in summary form, the findings of an enquiry into systematic torture practices.

A new development which took place on the same day was that the delegation of the Soviet Union expressed the view that the implementation system of the convention should have an optional character. In this context it proposed to include all implementation provisions in an optional protocol. The USSR delegation argued that the inclusion of such provisions in the convention itself was not necessary for those States which were already bound by the implementation provisions of the *International Covenant on Civil and Political Rights*; therefore the proposed Committee against Torture would not have much work to do. Moreover, since it was the intention to draw up a convention that could obtain worldwide support, it should be borne in mind that it might be easier for some States to consider becoming a party if the convention did not contain mandatory implementation provisions.

The delegation of the Ukrainian Soviet Socialist Republic stated that it wished to suggest a compromise. It proposed to retain the implementation provisions in the convention itself but to amend these articles in such a way that they would only bind those States which would have made statements recognizing the competence of the implementation body. To this end the Ukrainian delegation submitted alternative versions for article 17, paragraphs 1, 2, 3, 4 and 7, article 19, paragraphs 1 and 2, and article 20, paragraph 1 (doc. E/CN.4/1983/WG.2/WP.5).

The proposal to make all implementation provisions optional received full support from the Argentine delegation. The Indian delegation considered that at any rate the provisions relating to enquiries should be optional. Some other delegations stated that they were not yet able to take a definitive position on this matter. On the other hand, all Western delegations expressed the view that a mandatory character should be given to the provisions on the nature and composition of the implementation organ, on reporting by States Parties and on enquiries initiated by the Committee.

In contrast with the intensive discussion devoted to the draft articles concerning these questions, the Working Group spent little time on discussing the complaint procedures contained in articles 31, 32 and 33 of the Swedish draft.[31] It was recalled that in the previous year some delegations had expressed misgivings as to the advisability of including such procedures in the convention against torture. The Swedish delegation indicated that it wished to maintain its proposals. The Swiss observer delegation pleaded forcefully for including at any rate a procedure for individual complaints in the convention. The Group agreed to come back to these proposals at a later stage.

The Working Group discussed the question of annual reporting by the implementation organ on the basis of article 34 of the Swedish draft. In the light of the comments that had been made the chairman-rapporteur submitted a revised text which met with no objection from the Group (doc. E/CN.4/1983/WG.2/WP.8).

The Working Group did not formally adopt any provision of the implementation part of the draft convention. However, with the agreement of the Swedish delegation, it decided that in the annex of its report to the Commission the implementation articles proposed by Sweden, as far as they did not relate to the complaint procedures, would be replaced by the draft articles submitted by the chairman-rapporteur and adapted in the light of the discussions thereon.[32] This was decided without prejudice to the question as to whether these implementation provisions, and in particular draft article 20, should have a mandatory or an optional character.

d) *Final clauses*

The Working Group discussed the final clauses to be included in the convention on the basis of a draft submitted by Sweden in 1980.[33] This draft consisted of six articles, listed as A, B, C, D, E and F. Moreover, the delegations of Australia and the Netherlands submitted additional proposals. During the general debate on the final clauses it was recalled that at the previous session Brazil had proposed the inclusion of a mandatory conciliation system. Furthermore the view was expressed that the convention should contain an article on denunciation.

---

[31] See Appendix 10.

[32] The text of these articles as adapted was contained in a consolidated revised draft of implementation provisions, submitted by the chairman-rapporteur (doc. E/CN.4/1983/WG.2/WP.11).

[33] Document E/CN.4/1427. The text of these draft final clauses is reproduced in Appendix 9.

During the consideration of the separate articles a contradiction was observed between article A and article C as to the possibility of accession to the convention before its entry into force. With regard to article C there was a divergence of opinions on the number of ratifications or accessions required for the entry into force of the convention. In relation to article D several delegations stated that they preferred provisions concerning a procedure for amendments instead of the proposed provisions for revision of the convention. As regard article E some suggestions were made for complementing the text. Article F did not give rise to any comments.

The Australian delegation submitted a draft article concerning the obligations of federal or non-unitary States, reading as follows:

> "The obligations of a Federal or non-unitary State Party which has a system of government under which executive, judicial and legislative powers are distributed or shared between the federal authority and the constituent states, provinces or cantons, shall be the same as for non-federal States but the provisions of the convention may be implemented by the State Party through its federal, constituent state, provincial or canton authorities, having regard to their respective constitutional powers and arrangements concerning their exercise." (doc. E/CN.4/1983/WG.2/WP.6)

An initial exchange of views took place on this proposal in which several members of the Working Group participated who were themselves representatives of federal States. The Canadian delegation supported the proposal on the basis that it could provide practical assistance to at least some federal States in becoming parties to the convention. The delegations of Brazil and the Federal Republic of Germany observed that, although such a clause was not needed for their own State, they appreciated the underlying reasons for the proposals. The delegates of India and Senegal considered the proposed clause unnecessary as it related only to an internal matter of the State Party concerned. In this context they referred to article 50 of the *International Covenant on Civil and Political Rights*, which stipulates that the Covenant's provisions shall extend to all parts of federal States without any limitations or exceptions. The Argentine delegation stated that it preferred the formula as found in article 50 of the Covenant, but that it was prepared to give the Australian proposal further consideration. The Working Group agreed that the matter should be further examined at a later stage.

The Netherlands delegation submitted a draft article concerning the settlement of disputes, reading as follows:

> "Any dispute between two or more States Parties with respect to the interpretation or application of this Convention, which is not settled by negotiation, shall, at the request of any of the parties to the dispute, be

referred to the International Court of Justice for decision, unless the disputants agree to another mode of settlement." (doc. E/CN.4/ 1983/WG.2/WP.10).

The Netherlands delegation explained that this text followed the example of article 22 of the *International Convention on the Elimination of All Forms of Racial Discrimination.* Some delegations expressed support for the idea underlying the Netherlands proposal. However, the French delegation stated that a second paragraph should be added, enabling States Parties to declare, at the time of signature or at the time of ratification or accession, that they would not be bound by the obligation to refer disputes to the International Court of Justice.

In the light of the discussions the chairman-rapporteur submitted a revised set of clauses concerning signature, ratification, accession, entry into force, amendments and denunciation (doc. E/CN.4/1983/WG.2/WP.15). Mr Burgers pointed out that these proposals did not cover the whole field of possible final clauses. Due to lack of time the Working Group was not able to formally adopt any of the proposed final clauses. However, with the agreement of the Swedish delegation the Group decided that in the annex of its report to the Commission the part on final clauses should consist of the draft articles submitted by the chairman-rapporteur and a draft article identical with article F of the Swedish proposals.

9. Deliberations in the Commision's Working Group in 1984[34]

In 1984 the Working Group achieved a consensus on almost all provisions of the draft convention. Whereas its deliberations during the period 1979-1983 had resulted in formal adoption of only eleven articles, now fifteen articles were adopted in the pre-sessional meetings. At the end of the pre-sessional week the chairman-rapporteur declared that in his view the work of the Group had reached a stage which made it desirable that the Commission itself should devote a substantial debate to the draft convention well before the close of the session, instead of holding the brief and largely procedural debate which usually took place towards the end of each session. This implied that the Group would have to submit its report to the Commission at a much earlier date than in the past. The Working Group authorized the chairman-rapporteur to take the necessary steps thereto. In the second week of the Commission's session the Group held one additional meeting in which it adopted its report. In the meantime Mr Burgers had pursued informal consultations with a number of delegations concerning the remaining unsolved questions. As a result of these consultations, four articles and the half of a fifth article

[34] The 1984 report of the Working Group is contained in document E/CN.4/1984/72.

could be adopted by consensus at the Working Group's last meeting. Consequently, the Group submitted to the Commission a complete draft convention consisting of a preamble and thirty-two articles, in which only article 20 and the second half of article 19 were still undecided and thus were placed between square brackets.

Some of the factors which had contributed to this gratifying result were the radical change in the Argentine position after the end of military rule, the very active support of the Senegalese delegation, the constructive role of the Indian delegation and the flexible and co-operative attitude of the Soviet delegation. However, the flexibility of the Soviet Union had its limits where two elements of the proposed implementation system were concerned as in the Soviet view these entailed risking unlawful interference in internal affairs.

The Working Group took as its basis for discussions the compilation of draft provisions which it had annexed to its 1983 report.[35]

a) *Preamble*

In the convention's preamble the only unsettled question related to the amendment proposed in 1983 by the Peruvian delegation.[36] Some delegations felt that this amendment, although highly commendable in spirit, was based on controversial concepts and couched in terms too general for inclusion in the convention. Taking into account the views expressed during the discussion, the Peruvian delegation withdrew its proposal. The Working Group thereupon decided that the preamble would consist of the revised set of preambular clauses adopted in 1983.

b) *Provisions of the substantive part*

The Working Group eventually achieved consensus in respect of all provisions of the substantive part of the convention that had not been decided upon in previous years, namely article 3, paragraph 2, article 5, paragraph 2, article 6, paragraph 4, article 7, and article 16, paragraph 1.

With regard to article 3, paragraph 1, which had already been adopted in 1979, several delegations made statements. Some delegations indicated that their government might wish to declare, at the time of signature or ratification of the convention or of accession thereto, that they did not consider themselves bound by article 3 insofar as that article might not be compatible with obligations under extradition treaties concluded earlier.

With regard to article 3, paragraph 2, the delegation of the Federal Republic of Germany proposed adding the following sentence:

[35] See Appendix 13.
[36] See *supra* p. 85.

"It shall be decisive, however, that there are in the individual case substantial grounds to believe that the person to be expelled, returned or extradited would be in danger of being subjected to torture."

Several delegations felt that such an addition was not needed, because the draft paragraph already specified that "all relevant considerations" should be taken into account. At a later stage the delegation of the Federal Republic announced that it would not insist on its proposal.

The main problem concerning article 3, paragraph 2, related to the illustrative list of situations which many Western delegations took exception to. In order to gain a consensus on article 3, the delegations of India and Senegal proposed the deletion of the illustrative list beginning wich "such as". The Soviet delegate, while accepting this proposal in principle, drew attention to a difference between the Russian and the English version of the draft paragraph. He proposed to make the English text, which spoke of "a consistent pattern of gross violations of human rights", consistent with the Russian text which spoke of "persistent gross and mass violations of human rights". After informal consultations the Working Group accepted a compromise suggested by the Indian delegation, namely to replace the current formulas in all languages by the following: "a consistent pattern of gross, flagrant or mass violations of human rights".

Another problem with regard to article 3, paragraph 2, was its passive formulation which, in the view of several speakers, did not make it sufficiently clear by whom the relevant considerations should be taken into account. In the light of this discussion the United Kingdom delegation proposed a formulation according to which "the competent authorities" should take these considerations into account. The Working Group adopted the text of the paragraph as contained in a revised version of the working paper submitted by the United Kingdom delegation (doc. E/CN.4/1984/WG.2/WP.4/Rev.1). After the adoption of this paragraph the delegations of China, the German Democratic Republic, the Soviet Union and the United States of America made explanatory statements for the record.

The representative of the Soviet Union said that, although he had supported the compromise solution, he would have preferred the original version of the paragraph. He attributed great importance to the concept of "mass violations of human rights". In his understanding the concept of a consistent pattern of human rights violations already implied that such violations occurred on a massive scale. Therefore, the word "or" in the text was not to be interpreted as indicating opposition between the concept of "gross" and that of "mass" violations of human rights. The two concepts were complementary and should be read together.

The representative of the United States said that, according to his delegation's interpretation, the paragraph included situations covered by ECOSOC resolution 1503.

The Working Group discussed at considerable length the system of universal jurisdiction included in draft articles 5, 6 and 7. The discussions indicated that there had been important changes of position as compared to the 1983 session of the Group. The inclusion of universal jurisdiction in the convention was no longer opposed by any delegation.

At the outset of the debate on this question, the delegation of Argentina announced that it would make every effort to help finalize the draft convention against torture and declared that the new Argentine government supported universal jurisdiction as provided for in draft articles 5, 6 and 7, as well as the implementation system provided for in draft articles 17 to 24.

The delegation of Uruguay stated that it retained its doubts as to the wisdom of including universal jurisdiction in the convention, but that it did not wish to stand in the way of consensus on this question. At the same time it announced that the inclusion of universal jurisdiction in the convention might eventually make it difficult for Uruguay to become a party to the convention.

The Chinese delegation stated that it favoured the inclusion of universal jurisdiction, but that it considered the current formulation of the draft articles concerned not entirely satisfactory.

The delegation of Senegal, with a view to expediting the work on the convention, withdrew its proposal as submitted in 1983 for the insertion of an additional paragraph in article 5.[37]

The Brazilian delegation explained its compromise text on universal jurisdiction which it had submitted in 1983.[38] At the same time it stated that it would not insist on these proposals if they were not generally acceptable. In reply to a question, the Brazilian delegation further explained that, while its alternative proposal was aimed at giving priority to the establishment of jurisdiction by States on a territorial or nationality basis, it had not been intended to create an automatic obligation for the requested State to extradite the alleged offender to those States, since extradition was a sovereign act to be decided in each case by the competent court of the requested State. Some speakers observed that it was both legally and politically proper to leave the State in which the offender was found such freedom to refuse extradition, because if extradition was requested by the State in which the acts of torture had taken place, it was doubtful whether the requesting State would really punish the offender.

Most speakers expressed their preference for the current text of draft articles 5, 6 and 7. It was pointed out that the formulation concerning universal jurisdiction should be as close as possible to that used in earlier treaties, such as the *Convention for the Suppression of Unlawful Seizure of Aircraft*, the

[37] See *supra* p. 85.
[38] See *supra* p. 85.

Convention for Suppression of Unlawful Acts against the Safety of Civil Aviation and the *International Convention against the Taking of Hostages*. On the other hand, several speakers expressed an interest in exploring the possibility of achieving consensus by introducing in the current text the essence of, or certain elements borrowed from, Brazil's alternative proposals.

The chairman-rapporteur strongly advised against deviating substantially from the formulations on universal jurisdiction used in those and similar recent treaties, although he considered these formulations far from ideal. On the contrary, from a theoretical point of view they contained various flaws. However, devising a text that could be considered perfect would require a time-consuming effort that would stand in the way of a rapid conclusion of the work on the convention. Moreover, any substantial deviation from the formulations that had already been accepted by the international community might cause problems of interpretation.

At the end of the pre-sessional meetings all delegations except the Chinese delegation were prepared to accept the current text of articles 5, 6 and 7. This delegation considered that the exercise of jurisdiction in accordance with article 5, paragraph 1 (a), (b) and (c), should have priority over the exercise of jurisdiction based exclusively on the presence of an alleged offender in the territory of a State Party. Only if the States having primary jurisdiction did not wish to exercise it, should jurisdiction be exercised by the State where the offender was found.

After the close of the pre-sessional meetings informal consultations continued with the Chinese delegation, taking into account that most delegations were not prepared to accept an automatic obligation for the requested State to grant extradition requests by States having primary jurisdiction. At the final meeting of the Working Group in the second week of the Commission's session, the Chinese delegation announced that it could now in principle accept universal jurisdiction as set out in the draft convention. The Group thereupon agreed to adopt the current text of articles 5, 6 and 7, without prejudice to the reservations of certain delegations which would be reflected in the report.

As regards article 16, it was not possible during the pre-sessional meetings to reach agreement on the question of including in the first paragraph of this article a reference to article 14. Such inclusion was firmly opposed by the delegations of the United Kingdom and the United States, while it was favoured by most other Western delegations. The Spanish delegation went a step further and proposed also to include references to articles 3 and 15. Following this discussion, however, the Spanish delegation later withdrew its proposal.

Most non-Western delegations participating in the Working Group had no strong preference for including or excluding a reference to article 14 in article 16. The Indian delegation recalled the general reservation concerning article 14 which India had entered at previous sessions. The delegate of the Soviet

Union, in an effort to overcome the difficulties that divided the Western delegations, submitted a proposal according to which the obligation of article 14 would apply to cruel, inhuman or degrading treatment or punishment only in the event that such treatment or punishment caused its victim material loss or loss of health (doc. E/CN.4/1984/WG.2/WP.5). In other words, this obligation would not apply to "moral damages".

After the close of the pre-sessional meetings informal consultations took place on this question. The delegations of the United Kingdom and the United States maintained their opposition and were not prepared to accept the Soviet proposal. At the final meeting of the Working Group the chairman-rapporteur announced that several delegations which had favoured a reference to article 14 in article 16 had now indicated that they would not insist on such a reference if this created an obstacle to reaching agreement. The Group thereupon decided to adopt article 16, limiting the reference in the first paragraph to articles 10, 11, 12 and 13.

After the adoption of article 16, the delegations of Canada and Ireland stated that they wished to have recorded in the report of the Working Group that their governments retained a strong preference for including a reference to article 14 in this article.

c) *Implementation provisions*

The Working Group reached consensus with regard to most articles of the implementation part of the convention, but did not achieve agreement on draft articles 19 and 20.

At the opening of the debate on the implementation issues, the delegation of the Soviet Union informed the Group that it would no longer insist on giving all elements of the implementation system an optional character. This delegation was now prepared to accept mandatory provisions concerning the creation of an implementation organ and concerning reporting by States Parties. However, it maintained its fundamental objections against the mandatory character of the proposed article 20 concerning inquiries. The delegation of the Ukrainian Soviet Socialist Republic took a similar stand and withdrew its alternative suggestions in respect of draft articles 17 and 19.

As to draft article 17, the Working Group decided that the Committee against Torture would not consist of nine experts but of ten experts; in this connection it also replaced the word "four" in both parts of the second sentence of paragraph 5 by "five". With these amendments article 17 was formally adopted by the Group.

In respect of article 18 the Working Group discussed the proposal for the addition of a paragraph on the financial responsibilities of States Parties, submitted in 1983 by the delegation of the United States.[39] There was some opposition to this proposal, but since no delegation insisted on its objections, the new paragraph was added to the draft article. With this amendment article 18 was adopted by the Group.

With regard to article 19 on reporting by States Parties and consideration of the reports by the Committee against Torture, the delegation of the Soviet Union objected to the formulation of paragraphs 3 and 4, which authorized the Committee to make "comments or suggestions" on the report of a State Party and to include such "comments or suggestions" in its own annual report. The Soviet delegation proposed replacing the words "comments" in both paragraphs by "general comments", in conformity with article 40 of the *International Covenant on Civil and Political Rights.* The Soviet delegate explained that the current formulation entailed the possibility that the Committee would express a value judgment on measures taken by a State Party and would even recommend changing or abolishing such measures. The delegation of the Ukrainian SSR, supporting the proposal of the Soviet Union, further proposed to delete the words "or suggestions" in both paragraphs. The delegation of the German Democratic Republic supported the proposals of the Soviet and Ukrainian delegations. Most speakers, however, wished to retain the formulation "comments or suggestions", which had met with no opposition during the discussions in 1982 and 1983. One delegation indicated that it could not accept insertion of the word "general" but that it might agree to delete the words "or suggestions" if that would make consensus on the article possible.

Another matter discussed in connection with article 19 was whether the reports of States Parties could be transmitted to the UN General Assembly. The Working Group agreed to add to paragraph 4 a sentence proposed by the delegation of India, reading: "If so requested by the State Party concerned, the Committee may also transmit a copy of the report submitted by the State under paragraph 1."

Since no agreement was reached on replacing the formula "comments or suggestions" by "general comments" the Working Group decided at its final meeting to adopt paragraphs 1 and 2 of article 19 but to retain paragraphs 3 and 4 between square brackets.

The Working Group discussed repeatedly and at considerable length draft article 20, which authorized the Committee to initiate an inquiry in connection with reliable indications that torture was being systematically practised in the territory of a State Party. The delegation of the Soviet Union explained that it had objections of a fundamental and principled nature against the mandatory character of the proposed provision. In the view of this delegation, systematic torture had always indicated that there was a situation characterized by mass and gross violations of human rights. Such situations immediately

[39] See *supra* p. 87.

became widely known, and therefore there was no need to create a special body for their recognition as such. However, if there was no certainty about the existence of such a situation, the proposed system might be misused for the purpose of unlawful interference in the internal affairs of sovereign States. The Soviet delegation could only accept draft article 20 if it was given an optional character. This delegation also pointed out that, since primarily States or individuals or non-governmental organizations could be the sources of information mentioned in article 20, all such information should be dealt with in accordance with articles 21 and 22. The delegation of the German Democratic Republic supported the position of the Soviet Union. The delegation of the Ukrainian SSR proposed to insert the words "which has made a declaration in accordance with article 21, paragraph 1" after the words "in the territory of a State Party" in paragraph 1 of article 20.

Most delegations expressed themselves strongly in favour of maintaining the mandatory character of draft article 20, which they considered essential to effective implementation of the convention. Among those who expressed this position were the delegations of Argentina and Uruguay. The Argentine delegation remarked that the inquiry procedure proposed in draft article 20 was not new in the United Nations system, since it had been used in the International Labour Organization for a long time and with considerable success.

As no agreement was reached on the question of giving the proposed inquiry system a mandatory or an optional character, draft article 20 could not be adopted by the Working Group.

The subsequent draft articles of the implementation part did not meet with objections from the Working Group. Accordingly, the Group formally adopted articles 21, 22, 23 and 24.

d) *Final clauses*

The deliberations of the Working Group resulted in complete agreement concerning the final clauses to be included in the convention. Already at the first pre-sessional meeting the Group adopted articles 25, 26, 27 and 31 as contained in the annex to the 1983 report. Because of the insertion of a new article among the final clauses, article 31 was later renumbered as article 32.

At the same meeting the Australian delegation withdrew its proposal as submitted in 1983 regarding the obligations of federal or non-unitary States.[40]

The proposal which the Netherlands delegation had submitted in 1983 concerning the settlement of disputes[41] was supported by some delegations as an important mechanism that was well tested in international law. Some

---

[40] See *supra* p. 90.

[41] See *supra* pp. 90–91.

other delegations restated their objections against inserting in the convention any clause of compulsory jurisdiction of the International Court of Justice. The French delegation proposed an alternative draft article which followed the example of several international conventions concluded under the auspices of the UN in recent years (doc. E/CN.4/1984/WG.2/WP.1). The Working Group adopted the French proposal and decided to place the new article after the current draft article 28.

With regard to draft article 28 concerning the procedure for amending the convention, the Working Group adopted a suggestion by the United States delegation to insert the words "within four months from the date of such communication" in the third sentence of the first paragraph after the words "In the event that". With this amendment article 28 was adopted by the Group.

The Working Group gave thorough consideration to former draft article 29, now renumbered as article 30, which dealt with denunciation of the convention. The delegation of the United States proposed to add a new paragraph stipulating that denunciation would not release the denouncing State Party from its obligations with regard to any act or omission which had occurred before the date at which the denunciation became effective, nor prejudice the continued consideration of any matter which was already being dealt with by the Committee before that date (doc. E/CN.4/1984/WG.2/WP.2). In the light of the discussion regarding this proposal and after informal consultations, the United States delegation proposed to add another paragraph to the draft article, specifying that after that date the Committee would not commence consideration of any new matter regarding the State which had denounced the convention. The Working Group agreed to include in the article the two additional paragraphs proposed by the United States, with some drafting changes. In this form article 30 was adopted by the Group.

The Working Group also adopted former draft article 30, which was now renumbered as article 31, after having replaced the reference to "article 29" by a reference to "article 30". The Working Group thus completed its consideration of the final clauses.

10. Consideration by the plenary Commission in 1984[42]

After the Working Group had established its report, it was open to question what action the Commission would take. One option for the Commission was to settle by voting the still unresolved issues regarding articles 19 and 20 of the draft convention. Another option was to renew the mandate of the Work-

[42] The 1984 report of the Commission has been published under the symbols E/CN.4/1984/77 and E/1984/14.

ing Group and to request it to seek consensus on the remaining issues in 1985. Informal contacts between members of the Commission indicated a preference for a third option, namely to transmit the draft as it stood (with two passages still between square brackets) to the General Assembly and to leave it to the Assembly to determine the definitive text of the convention.

An important reason for not pressing now for a vote on the controversial issues was the fact that only a limited part of the members of the Commission had actively participated in the Working Group and that many of the other members were not familiar with the issues relating to articles 19 and 20. This problem was aggravated by a delay in the publication of the Group's report. The Working Group had made an effort to draw up its report rapidly and had adopted it in the second week of the Commission's session, on 16 February. At that time it was hoped that the document would come out at the beginning of the third week of the session in order to give Commission delegations ample opportunity to prepare themselves for the debate. However, the document did not become available to delegations until 28 February, the very day on which the debate on this item was opened.

On the other hand, most delegations felt that the draft convention had now been prepared to such a degree as to make its examination by the General Assembly possible. Bearing in mind that the original request of the General Assembly dated back to 1977, many delegations hoped that the Assembly would see its way to finally adopt the convention against torture before the end of 1984.

With these considerations in mind, the delegations of Finland and the Netherlands held consultations with delegations from other geographical regions in order to draw up a draft resolution for the Commission. The resulting draft resolution was submitted, also on 28 February, by the delegations of Argentina, Finland, India, the Netherlands, Senegal and Yugoslavia (doc. E/CN.4/1984/L.36). According to this text, the Commission on Human Rights would:

- decide to transmit to the General Assembly, through the Economic and Social Council, the report of the Working Group as well as the summary records of the Commission's debate on this item during its present session;
- request the Secretary-General to bring these documents to the attention of the governments of all States and to invite these governments to communicate to him, preferably before 1 September 1984, their comments on the draft convention contained in the annex to the Working Group's report;
- request the Secretary-General to submit the comments received from governments to the General Assembly; and
- recommend to the General Assembly to consider the draft convention as a matter of priority with a view to the early adoption of a convention against torture and other cruel, inhuman or degrading treatment or punishment.

The Commission discussed the report of the Working Group on 28 and 29

February. The following members of the Commission took part in this debate: Argentina, Australia, Bangladesh, Bulgaria, Canada, Colombia, Costa Rica, the Federal Republic of Germany, France, the German Democratic Republic, India, Italy, Senegal, Spain, the United Kingdom, the United States, Uruguay and the USSR. The observer delegations of Denmark, Norway, Peru and Switzerland as well as the representative of the Centre for Social Development and Humanitarian Affairs of the UN Secretariat also participated. Further statements were made on behalf of the non-governmental organizations Amnesty International, the International Association of Penal Law, the International Commission of Jurists, the International Movement for Fraternal Union among Races and Peoples, and Pax Romana. The statement for Amnesty International was delivered by its secretary-general, Thomas Hammarberg, who had especially come over from London for this occasion.

Most speakers expressed their appreciation for the draft convention drawn up by the Working Group. Many Western delegations as well as the delegations of Argentina, Senegal and Uruguay gave explicit support to the current formulation of articles 19 and 20. Several delegations expressed reservations regarding the exception contained in the last sentence of article 1, paragraph 1, with regard to lawful sanctions. The United Kingdom delegation criticized article 1 in some other respects as well. The delegations of the Soviet Union, Bulgaria and the German Democratic Republic explained their objections concerning articles 19 and 20 and discussed some other problems relating to the text adopted by the Working Group. The Soviet representative argued that the text could be improved in several respects, *inter alia* with regard to the preamble, article 3, article 16 and the articles on jurisdiction. His delegation therefore preferred that the Commission would request the Working Group to continue its work. However, his delegation would not oppose transmission of the present text to the General Assembly if this were the prevailing feeling in the Commission. The debate was concluded with a statement by the chairman-rapporteur of the Working Group.[43]

On 6 March the delegation of Finland introduced the above-mentioned draft resolution, which was now also co-sponsored by the delegations of Colombia, Costa Rica, Denmark, Jordan, Norway, Peru and Sweden. The Commission thereupon adopted the resolution without a vote (resolution 1984/21 of the Commission on Human Rights).

[43] The main part of this statement has been reproduced in the June 1984 issue of *The Review of the International Commission of Jurists.*

11. Final consideration and action by the UN General Assembly in 1984[44]

On 26 March 1984 the Secretary-General of the UN forwarded the Working Group's report and the summary records of the Commission's debate to the governments of all States, in accordance with the request contained in the Commission's resolution 1984/21. In this way all governments which had not followed the proceedings in the Working Group and in the Commission concerning this question were informed accurately about the state of affairs with regard to the preparation of a convention against torture and other cruel, inhuman or degrading treatment or punishment.

More than thirty governments responded to the invitation to communicate to the Secretary-General their comments concerning the draft convention annexed to the Working Group's report. These comments have been reproduced in documents A/39/499, A/39/499/Add.1 and A/39/499/Add.2 which were issued on 2 October, 24 October and 6 November respectively. About half of these comments were submitted by governments that had not actively participated in the work of the Working Group.

After the opening of its 39th session in September 1984, the General Assembly established its agenda of which item 99 read: "Torture and other cruel, inhuman or degrading treatment or punishment". The Assembly assigned this agenda item to its Third Committee. The main subject under this item was of course the draft convention. In the first meeting of the Third Committee the Netherlands representative Alphons Hamer announced his intention to establish contact with interested delegations in order to explore the possibility of reaching agreement on the outstanding problems regarding the draft convention before the Committee formally dealt with agenda item 99. Under the chairmanship of Mr Hamer informal meetings were held on 31 October, 6 November, 13 November and 20 November, in which a considerable number of delegations, representing all geographical regions, exchanged views on the draft convention. Besides, many informal discussions on a bilateral basis took place throughout the session.

These bilateral and multilateral consultations were useful for clarifying the principal elements of the draft convention and for identifying the problems which delegations had with certain of its provisions. At the same time they made it clear that the support for rapid finalization of the convention was less strong among the total membership of the United Nations than it had been among the members of the Commission on Human Rights. All Western and

---

[44] The summary records of the Third Committee of the General Assembly on the debate in which *inter alia* the draft convention against torture was discussed are contained in documents A/C.3/39/SR.44-46 and 48-52. The summary records of the meetings in which the Third Committee dealt with the draft resolution concerning this convention are contained in documents A/C.3/39/SR.60 and 61. The report of the Third Committee on the agenda item concerned is contained in document A/39/708. The verbatim record of the meeting in which the plenary General Assembly finally adopted the convention is contained in document A/39/PV.93.

most Latin American States favoured adoption of the convention, including the provisions of articles 19 and 20 which still stood between square brackets, at the current session of the General Assembly. This position was shared by a limited number of African and Asian States. The Soviet Union and other East European States were prepared to support adoption of the convention if the questions regarding articles 19 and 20 were settled in accordance with their views. However, many African and Asian States were not eager to take a definitive stand on the draft convention already at this stage. Several had misgivings about the inquiry system contained in article 20 and some even preferred the complete deletion of this article. Moreover, a number of problems were raised in respect of other provisions of the draft convention, in particular with regard to articles 1, 3 and 16. Several Islamic States expressed concerns about the interpretation of the concepts of "torture" and of "cruel, inhuman or degrading treatment or punishment" and sought assurances that the death penalty and certain forms of punishment prescribed by Islamic law were compatible with the convention.

The Third Committee dealt with agenda item 99 together with four other agenda items. The debate on this cluster of items lasted from 19 to 28 November. The views on the draft convention expressed during this debate corresponded to those which had come to the fore in the informal discussions.

Some time before the opening of this debate it became known that certain delegations were considering submitting a procedural draft resolution which would postpone action on the draft convention to the next session of the General Assembly. Against this background the delegations of Argentina, the Netherlands and Sweden decided that they should wait no longer in putting before the Third Committee a concrete proposal to adopt the convention as prepared at Geneva. On 23 November these delegations, together with the delegations of Bolivia, Colombia, Costa Rica, Denmark, the Dominican Republic, Finland, Gambia, Greece, Norway, Samoa and Spain, submitted a draft resolution to that effect (doc. A/C.3/39/L.40). Subsequently, Australia, Austria, Belgium, France, Iceland, Panama, Portugal, Singapore and the United Kingdom joined the sponsors. According to this draft the General Assembly would adopt and open for signature, ratification and accession the convention contained in the resolution's annex. The annex contained the text as drawn up by the Working Group but without square brackets with respect to articles 19 and 20.

Three days later the delegation of the Soviet Union, together with the delegations of Afghanistan, Bulgaria, Czechoslovakia, the German Democratic Republic, Hungary, Mongolia, Poland, the Ukrainian Soviet Socialist Republic and Vietnam, submitted amendments with regard to articles 19 and 20 (doc. A/C.3/39/L.49 and L.50). In document A/C.3/39/L.49 these delegations proposed to replace the words "comments or suggestions on the report" in the third paragraph of article 19 by "general comments" and to delete the words "or suggestions" in the fourth paragraph. In document

A/C.3/39/L.50 they proposed to insert, after the words "in the territory of a State Party" in the first paragraph of article 20, the words "which has made a declaration in accordance with article 21, paragraph 1, and article 22, paragraph 1". The last part of this amendment implied a further emphasis on the optional character these delegations wished to give to article 20. Whereas in February 1984 the Ukrainian SSR had proposed to the Working Group that article 20 should apply to those States Parties which accepted the procedure for State complaints, the new amendment meant that article 20 could only apply to States Parties which accepted *both* the procedure for State complaints *and* the procedure for individual complaints.

Again three days later, on 29 November, further amendments to the annex of the draft resolution were submitted by the Soviet Union and by the Byelorussian Soviet Socialist Republic. With regard to article 1, paragraph 1, the Soviet Union proposed in document A/C.3/39/L.63 to delete the word "severe" before "pain or suffering", to delete the words "based on discrimination of any kind", and to delete the second sentence "It does not include pain or suffering arising only from, inherent in or incidental to lawful sanctions." With regard to article 4, paragraph 1, the Soviet Union proposed to add the words "irrespective of the reasons, purposes and motives for which they were committed" after the words "all acts of torture" (doc. A/C.3/39/L.64). Regarding article 18, paragraph 2(b), the Byelorussian delegation proposed to replace "a majority vote" by "consensus" (doc. A/C.3/39/L.67). As far as article 20 was concerned, this same delegation proposed in document A/C.3/39/L.66 to insert, after article 27, a new article 28, reading as follows:

> "*Article 28*
>
> 1. Each State may, at the time of signature or ratification of this Convention or accession thereto, declare that it does not recognize the competence of the Committee provided for in article 20.
>
> 2. Any State Party having made a reservation in accordance with the preceding paragraph may, at any time, withdraw this reservation by notification to the Secretary-General of the United Nations."

This last proposal of the Byelorussian delegation (which had not co-sponsored the amendment L. 50) was particularly interesting since it represented a step in the direction of those delegations who wished to give article 20 a mandatory character.

As the time drew near when the Third Committee would formally deal with draft resolution L.40, the sponsors of this draft had to make a choice between two basic options: either to choose confrontation or to pursue consensus.

Two arguments militated against the road of confrontation. First of all, if the draft resolution were voted upon as it stood, it would probably be adopted with a number of negative votes (mainly of the Soviet Union and the other Socialist States) and a great number of abstentions (mainly of African and Asian States). This would diminish the chances for worldwide adherence to the future convention. In the second place, it might even happen that the draft resolution would not be put to the vote at all, if a procedural motion to defer action on L. 40 to the next session of the General Assembly would obtain a majority in the Third Committee. Such deferral would probably lead to the reopening of the discussion on many provisions of the draft convention and might eventually result in the adoption of a seriously weakened version.

On the other hand, if consensus were the aim it would not be possible to incorporate in the convention all amendments proposed by the Soviet Union and other Socialist States. Some of these amendments were plainly unacceptable to the sponsors of L. 40; others were attractive to most sponsors but would cause problems with other delegations, in particular Islamic delegations, and this would jeopardize the chance for consensus adoption of the convention. At the same time, the sponsors had to adjust the text of article 20 to take into account the principal concerns expressed by Third World delegations in the course of the consultations.

With these considerations in mind, the sponsors decided to seek consensus on the basis of the Byelorussian proposal contained in document L. 66.

The Third Committee dealt with draft resolution L. 40 in its morning session of 5 December. Mr Hamer announced that the sponsors, in a spirit of compromise, could agree to a number of changes. They were prepared to modify article 20, paragraph 1, by replacing "information" by "reliable information", by replacing "reliable indications" by "well-founded indications" and by inserting the words "to co-operate in the examination of the information and to this end" after the words "the Committee shall invite that State Party". They were further prepared to modify article 20, paragraph 5, by inserting at the end of the first sentence "and at all stages of the proceedings the co-operation of the State Party shall be sought" and by replacing in the second sentence the words "at its discretion" by the words "after consultations with the State Party concerned". They were also prepared to accept the new article 28, proposed by Byelorussia in document L. 66, and to delete the words "or suggestions" from article 19, paragraphs 3 and 4. Mr Hamer announced, however, that those modifications were strictly conditional upon withdrawal of all other amendments.

The Yugoslav delegation proposed that a decision on the draft resolution be postponed to enable delegations to consult with their missions. The delegates of Morocco and Senegal appealed to the Yugoslav delegate not to insist on his proposal. They considered it of vital importance that the Committee should adopt the draft resolution at this meeting. The Yugoslav delegation thereupon withdrew its proposal. In the light of the urgent pleas by Morocco and Senegal, the delegation of Kuwait refrained from tabling a procedural motion it had prepared to defer taking a decision on draft resolution L. 40 to the next session of the General Assembly.

After a brief suspension of the meeting the Soviet delegation announced that the sponsors of the amendments contained in the documents L.50, L.63

and L.64 had agreed to withdraw them. The representative of the Byelorussian SSR asked whether the sponsors of the draft resolution would accept insertion of the word "general" before "comments" in article 19, paragraphs 3 and 4. Mr Hamer replied that the sponsors had no objection to this provided that the amendment contained in document L. 67 was withdrawn; the Byelorussian delegate then agreed to withdraw the last-mentioned amendment. Thereupon draft resolution L. 40, as orally revised, was adopted by the Third Committee without a vote. The tension that had been building up during the last two weeks broke in spontaneous applause.

In the afternoon meeting several delegations made statements in explanation of vote. The Syrian delegation said it would have preferred postponement of a decision until the next session of the General Assembly and expressed reservations concerning any provision which might contravene Syrian national legislation. The Turkish delegation reserved its position on certain points which, although minor, reflected deficiencies because fundamental norms of international law had not been adequately taken into account. The Japanese delegation stated that the draft convention contained certain provisions whose implications would require further study. The Tunisian delegation reserved the right to express its views on the draft convention at a later stage. The delegate of Bangladesh stated that the fact that he had joined in adopting the draft resolution without a vote in no way implied that his country had agreed entirely with all provisions of the draft convention. Some parts of the text might in fact be in conflict with the national laws of Bangladesh and with the Islamic *Sharia*. According to the Romanian delegation it would have been preferable to continue seeking agreement on all parts of the draft convention with the aim of making it acceptable to all States. This delegation therefore reserved its position until the competent Romanian authorities had had the opportunity to examine the convention in depth.

On 10 December 1984 the plenary General Assembly adopted without a vote the draft resolution as submitted to it by the Third Committee.[45] After the adoption the delegations of the Netherlands, Sweden, Colombia, the United States, Israel, Mexico and the Soviet Union took the floor. These delegations expressed no reservations with regard to the newly adopted *Convention against Torture and Other Cruel, Inhuman or Degrading Treatment or Punishment*. The Israeli delegation observed that it had joined the consensus on the understanding that the new *Convention* would not supersede the 1949 *Geneva Conventions* as regards their applicability to armed conflicts. The Swedish delegation, speaking on behalf of the five Nordic countries, recalled the initiative Sweden had taken in 1977 and underlined the importance of making the *Convention* enter into force as early as possible and of making it

[45] UNGA resolution 39/46. The text of this resolution is reproduced in Appendix 14.

effective by universal adherence. Most speakers gave special attention to the fact that the date of 10 December is celebrated as Human Rights Day.

12. Signature and entry into force of the Convention

After the General Assembly had formally decided to open the *Convention* for signature, the UN Secretariat needed some time to prepare the documents to be signed in the six authentic languages in conformity with the final version adopted by the Assembly. Moreover, the governments intending to sign the *Convention* had to go through certain internal procedures before they could provide their representatives with the necessary full powers. Therefore, the first signatures were actually made on 4 February 1985 during a ceremony at UN headquarters which was chaired by the Under-Secretary-General for Political and General Assembly Affairs, William B. Buffum.

Up to 1 January 1988 the *Convention* was signed by the following States:

Afghanistan	4 February 1985
Argentina	4 February 1985
Belgium	4 February 1985
Bolivia	4 February 1985
Costa Rica	4 February 1985
Denmark	4 February 1985
Dominican Republic	4 February 1985
Ecuador	4 February 1985
Finland	4 February 1985
France	4 February 1985
Greece	4 February 1985
Iceland	4 February 1985
Italy	4 February 1985
Netherlands	4 February 1985
Norway	4 February 1985
Portugal	4 February 1985
Senegal	4 February 1985
Spain	4 February 1985
Sweden	4 February 1985
Switzerland	4 February 1985
Uruguay	4 February 1985
Venezuela	15 February 1985
Luxembourg	22 February 1985
Panama	22 February 1985
Austria	14 March 1985
United Kingdom	15 March 1985
Mexico	18 March 1985
Sierra Leone	18 March 1985

Colombia	10 April 1985
Nicaragua	15 April 1985
Peru	29 May 1985
Liechtenstein	27 June 1985
Canada	23 August 1985
Brazil	23 September 1985
Cyprus	9 October 1985
Gambia	23 October 1985
Indonesia	23 October 1985
Algeria	26 November 1985
Australia	10 December 1985
Union of Soviet Socialist Republics	10 December 1985
Byelorussian Soviet Socialist Republic	19 December 1985
Morocco	8 January 1986
Poland	13 January 1986
New Zealand	14 January 1986
Gabon	21 January 1986
Cuba	27 January 1986
Ukrainian Soviet Socialist Republic	27 February 1986
German Democratic Republic	7 April 1986
Guinea	30 May 1986
Sudan	4 June 1986
Bulgaria	10 June 1986
Czechoslovakia	8 September 1986
Federal Republic of Germany	13 October 1986
Israel	22 October 1986
Hungary	28 November 1986
China	12 December 1986
Togo	25 March 1987
Tunisia	26 August 1987
Chile	23 September 1987

Declarations in accordance with article 28, paragraph 1, concerning non-recognition of the Committee's competence under article 20 were made at the time of signature by Bulgaria, the Byelorussian SSR, Chile, China, Czechoslovakia, the German Democratic Republic, Hungary, Morocco, Poland, the Soviet Union and the Ukrainian SSR.

Declarations in accordance with article 30, paragraph 2, concerning not being bound by the first paragraph of that article were made at the time of signature by Bulgaria, the Byelorussian SSR, Chile, China, Czechoslovakia, the German Democratic Republic, Hungary, Morocco, Poland, the Soviet Union and the Ukrainian SSR.

Chile, the Federal Republic of Germany, Togo, Tunisia and the United Kingdom declared upon signature that they reserved the right to formulate declarations or reservations when ratifying the *Convention*. The Federal Republic of Germany referred in this context especially to the applicability of article 3 of the *Convention*.

Up to 1 January 1988 the *Convention* was ratified or acceded to by the following States:

Sweden	8 January 1986
Mexico	23 January 1986
France	18 February 1986
Belize (*accession*)	17 March 1986
Philippines (*accession*)	18 June 1986
Egypt (*accession*)	25 June 1986
Norway	9 July 1986
Senegal	21 August 1986
Argentina	24 September 1986
Uruguay	24 October 1986
Uganda (*accession*)	3 November 1986
Switzerland	2 December 1986
Bulgaria	16 December 1986
Cameroon (*accession*)	19 December 1986
Ukrainian Soviet Socialist Republic	24 February 1987
Union of Soviet Socialist Republics	3 March 1987
Byelorussian Soviet Socialist Republic	13 March 1987
Afghanistan	1 April 1987
Hungary	15 April 1987
Denmark	27 May 1987
Canada	24 June 1987
Austria	29 July 1987
Panama	24 August 1987
German Democratic Republic	9 September 1987
Luxembourg	29 September 1987
Spain	21 October 1987
Togo	18 November 1987
Colombia	8 December 1987

The declarations in accordance with article 28, paragraph 1, and article 30, paragraph 2, which several of the ratifying States had made upon signature, were confirmed by them when they ratified the *Convention*. Moreover, France and Panama declared upon ratification, in accordance with article 30, paragraph 2, that they would not be bound by the first paragraph of that article. Afghanistan made a similar declaration upon ratification and further declared in accordance with article 28, paragraph 1, that it did not recognize the Committee's competence under article 20.

On the other hand, Argentina, Austria, Denmark, France, Luxembourg,

Norway, Spain, Sweden, Switzerland and Togo declared upon ratification that they recognized the Committee's competence under articles 21 and 22.

Declarations on other matters were made upon ratification by Austria, the German Democratic Republic and Luxembourg.

The Austrian declaration read:

> "1. Austria will establish its jurisdiction in accordance with article 5 of the Convention irrespective of the laws applying to the place where the offence occurred, but in respect of paragraph 1 (c) only if prosecution by a State having jurisdiction under paragraph 1 (a) or paragraph 1 (b) is not to be expected.
> 2. Austria regards article 15 of the Convention as the legal basis for the inadmissibility provided therein of the use of statements which are established to have been made as a result of torture."

The declaration of the German Democratic Republic read:

> "The German Democratic Republic declares that it will bear its share only of those expenses in accordance with article 17, paragraph 7, and article 18, paragraph 5, of the Convention arising from activities under the competence of the Committee as recognized by the German Democratic Republic."

The declaration of Luxembourg read:

> "The Grand Duchy of Luxembourg declares that the only sanctions that it recognizes as 'lawful sanctions' as used in article 1 are those that are recognized as such equally under domestic law as under international law."

Since twenty instruments of ratification or accession had been deposited by 27 May 1987, the *Convention* entered into force in accordance with article 27, paragraph 1, on 26 June 1987.

In accordance with article 21, paragraph 2, and article 22, paragraph 8, this entry into force equally applied to the provisions of articles 21 and 22 with regard to the States which had recognized the Committee's competence under those articles.

13. First meeting of the States Parties and election of the Committee against Torture

The first meeting of the States Parties was held on 26 November 1987, five months after the entry into force of the *Convention*.[46] At that date, twenty-six

[46] The summary record of this meeting is contained in United Nations document CAT/SP/SR.1.

States were Parties to the *Convention*. Representatives of twenty-five of these States took part in the meeting; Belize was not represented. The representatives attending the meeting elected the members of the Committee against Torture and took care of some procedural matters, in particular the question of the responsibilities of the States Parties for the expenses incurred in connection with the implementation of the *Convention*.

Jan Mårtenson, Under-Secretary-General for Human Rights and Director-General of the United Nations Office at Geneva, opened the meeting on behalf of the Secretary-General. Alejandro L. Despouys of Argentina was chosen as chairman of the meeting.

The main purpose of the meeting was to elect ten experts to serve in their personal capacity on the Committee against Torture, in accordance with article 17 of the *Convention*. Candidates had originally been nominated by the governments of Argentina, Austria, Bulgaria, Cameroon, Canada, Denmark, Egypt, France, the German Democratic Republic, Mexico, Norway, Panama, the Philippines, Switzerland, Uganda and the Union of Soviet Socialist Republics. However, the German Democratic Republic, Norway and Panama withdrew their candidatures before the election. From among the remaining thirteen candidates, the following experts were elected at the meeting of the States Parties in one round of voting as members of the Committee against Torture:

Alfredo R.A. BENGZON	(Philippines)
Peter Thomas BURNS	(Canada)
Christine CHANET	(France)
Socorro DIAZ PALACIOS	(Mexico)
Alexis DIPANDA MOUELLE	(Cameroon)
Ricardo GIL LAVEDRA	(Argentina)
Yuri A. KHITRIN	(Soviet Union)
Dimitar Nikolov MIKHAILOV	(Bulgaria)
Bent SØRENSEN	(Denmark)
Joseph VOYAME	(Switzerland)

Immediately after the election, the experts from Bulgaria, Cameroon, Denmark, Switzerland and the Soviet Union were chosen by lot, in accordance with article 17, paragraph 5, to serve terms which will expire at the end of two years. The States Parties agreed that the members of the Committee would assume office on 1 January 1988.

Before the meeting an informal consensus had been worked out between representatives of States Parties relating to equitable distribution by region. According to this "gentleman's agreement", the Committee would consist of two members from Africa, one from Asia, two from Eastern Europe, two from Latin America and three from Western Europe. Following the election, the representatives of Senegal, Egypt, Cameroon and the Philippines expressed their concern that this informal consensus had not been followed.

Furthermore, the meeting considered the question of the financial responsibilities of the States Parties under article 17, paragraph 7, and article 18, paragraph 5, of the *Convention.* Under the terms of article 17, paragraph 7, "States Parties shall be responsible for the expenses of the members of the Committee while they are in performance of Committee duties". Under the terms of article 18, paragraph 5, "the States Parties shall be responsible for expenses incurred in connection with the holding of meetings of the States Parties and of the Committee, including reimbursement to the United Nations for any expenses, such as the cost of staff and facilities, incurred by the United Nations pursuant to paragraph 3 of this article".

For the purpose of the consideration of this matter by the meeting, the Secretary-General had prepared a detailed document relating to programme budget implications on an annual basis and to the apportionment of annual expenses among the States Parties (document CAT/SP/4 of 2 November 1987). Herein the Secretary-General proposed for consideration the following three alternative methods for apportioning the annual expenses:

(a) equally,

(b) proportionately, on the basis of the scale of assessments for apportioning the United Nations regular budget,

(c) fifty per cent equally and fifty per cent proportionately.

Representatives of States Parties had already discussed this question in informal consultations prior to the meeting. At their meeting of 26 November, the States Parties decided that the estimated annual expenses related to measures of implementation of the *Convention* shall be apportioned proportionately on the basis of the United Nations scale of assessments, it being understood that in no case the share of a single State Party shall be in excess of 25% of the expenses estimated for that year.

This decision was laid down in a resolution proposed by the chairman which was adopted by consensus. The same resolution contained a number of related decisions which may be summarized as follows.

The estimated annual expenses as submitted by the Secretary-General were approved, it being understood that the estimates for the expenses of the first meeting of the Committee should be based on the assumption that the Committee would be able to conclude its business within five working days.

The estimates on the expenses of meetings of the Committee should be based on the assumption that the Committee would decide on English, French, Russian and Spanish as its official and working languages and on English, French and Spanish as the languages of its summary records.

As to their own meetings, the States Parties decided that the official and working languages shall be English, French, Russian and Spanish, and that the summary records shall appear in English, French and Spanish.

The first financial period for activities under the *Convention* would run from 26 June 1987 to 31 December 1988 and subsequent financial periods would run according to calendar year. As from 1 January 1989, the apportionment of estimated annual expenses should be based each year on the actual number of States Parties at that time.

A State Party would be considered in arrears if payment of its assessed contribution is not made within 60 days from the date of the assessment notice. In view of the financial crisis which continued to affect the United Nations, activities envisaged under the *Convention*, including meetings of the Committee against Torture, would not take place until sufficient funds have been collected from the States Parties.

Finally, the meeting requested the Secretary-General to inform the States Parties on the status of the payments of contributions by each State Party within six months after the transmittal of the assessment notices and subsequently whenever the situation of financial resources so required.

After the resolution containing the above decisions had been adopted, some statements were made in connection with the declaration which the German Democratic Republic had made upon ratification with regard to its share in the expenses of the Committee.[47]

The representative of Sweden observed that in the view of the Nordic countries the *Convention* provided no grounds for restricting the joint responsibility of States Parties for the Committee's expenses. He expressed the hope that the German Democratic Republic would reconsider its position, and that this position would not create a precedent. The representative of Canada stated that his government did not regard the declaration as consistent with the spirit of the *Convention* or with the obligations of the States Parties to provide the necessary support for the machinery established for its implementation. The representative of Switzerland spoke in the same sense as the two previous speakers.

The representative of the German Democratic Republic observed that his government's reservation relating to article 20 and the non-applicability of articles 21 and 22 to his country were in accordance with the *Convention*. Therefore, the reservation by his government to the effect that it would not fund the activities of the Committee under these articles was in conformity with the *Convention*.

Following this discussion the meeting of the States Parties was closed.

[47] See *supra* p. 110.

Chapter IV

Annotations on the provisions of the Convention

1. Annotations on Part I: Substantive provisions

Article 1

1. For the purposes of this Convention, the term "torture" means any act by which severe pain or suffering, whether physical or mental, is intentionally inflicted on a person for such purposes as obtaining from him or a third person information or a confession, punishing him for an act he or a third person has committed or is suspected of having committed, or intimidating or coercing him or a third person, or for any reason based on discrimination of any kind, when such pain or suffering is inflicted by or at the instigation of or with the consent or acquiescence of a public official or other person acting in an official capacity. It does not include pain or suffering arising only from, inherent in or incidental to lawful sanctions.

2. This article is without prejudice to any international instrument or national legislation which does or may contain provisions of wider application.

As has been set out in Chapter II, section 2, prohibitions of torture have been included in a number of international instruments, in particular the *Universal Declaration of Human Rights* of 1948, the four *Geneva Conventions* of 1949 on the humanitarian rules which apply to armed conflicts and the two *Additional Protocols* thereto of 1977, the European *Convention for the Protection of Human Rights and Fundamental Freedoms* of 1950, the *International Covenant on Civil and Political Rights* of 1966, the *American Convention on Human Rights* of 1969 and the *African Charter on Human and Peoples' Rights* of 1981. In most of these instruments the prohibition also applies to other cruel, inhuman or degrading treatment or punishment.

Although all these instruments are clear in their condemnation of torture, in none of them has an attempt been made to define torture. However, in its *Report in the Greek case*, adopted on 5 November 1969, the European Commission of Human Rights had given certain indications about how it interpreted the terms "torture", "inhuman treatment" and "degrading treatment", as they appear in article 3 of the *European Convention.* The European Commission stated as follows (Chapter IV, paragraphs 1-2, of its Report):

> "1. Article 3 of the Convention provides that: 'No one shall be subjected to torture or to inhuman or degrading treatment or punishment'.
> 2. It is plain that there may be treatment to which all these descriptions apply, for all torture must be inhuman and degrading treatment, and

> inhuman treatment also degrading. The notion of inhuman treatment covers at least such treatment as deliberately causes severe suffering, mental or physical, which, in the particular situation, is unjustifiable.
>
> The word 'torture' is often used to describe inhuman treatment, which has a purpose, such as the obtaining of information or confessions, or the infliction of punishment, and it is generally an aggravated form of inhuman treatment. Treatment or punishment of an individual may be said to be degrading if it grossly humiliates him before others or drives him to act against his will or conscience."

These indications gave some guidance to those who proposed the text of a definition for inclusion in the *Declaration on the Protection of All Persons from Being Subjected to Torture and Other Cruel, Inhuman or Degrading Treatment or Punishment*, adopted by the UN General Assembly on 9 December 1975.[1] It is easy to see that some of the elements in the European Comission's Report also appear in the 1975 *Declaration*, whose article 1 reads as follows:

> "1. For the purpose of this Declaration, torture means any act by which severe pain or suffering, whether physical or mental, is intentionally inflicted by or at the instigation of a public official on a person for such purposes as obtaining from him or a third person information or confession, punishing him for an act he has committed or is suspected of having committed, or intimidating him or other persons. It does not include pain or suffering arising only from, inherent in or incidental to, lawful sanctions to the extent consistent with the Standard Minimum Rules for the Treatment of Prisoners.
>
> 2. Torture constitutes an aggravated and deliberate form of cruel, inhuman or degrading treatment or punishment."

In the case of Ireland *versus* the United Kingdom, the European Commission of Human Rights and the European Court of Human Rights were faced with interpreting article 3 of the European *Convention* in relation to five "interrogation techniques" which had been used against detainees in Northern Ireland. In the Court's judgment of 18 January 1978, these five techniques are described as follows:

> "(a) *wall-standing*: forcing the detainees to remain for periods of some hours in a 'stress position', described by those who underwent it as being 'spreadeagled against the wall, with their fingers put high above the head against the wall, the legs spread apart and the feet back, causing them to stand on their toes with the weight of the body mainly on the fingers';
>
> (b) *hooding*: putting a black or navy coloured bag over the detainees'

[1] *Cf.* Chapter II, section 3, concerning the preparation and the contents of the 1975 *Declaration*. The text of the *Declaration* is reproduced in Appendix 2.

heads and, at least initially, keeping it there all the time except during interrogation;
(c) *subjection to noise*: pending their interrogations, holding the detainees in a room where there was a continuous loud and hissing noise;
(d) *deprivation of sleep*: pending their interrogations, depriving the detainees of sleep;
(e) *deprivation of food and drink*: subjecting the detainees to a reduced diet during their stay at the centre and pending interrogations."

The Commission considered unanimously that the combined use of these five techniques in the cases before it constituted a practice of inhuman treatment and of torture in breach of article 3 of the *European Convention*. The Court, on the other hand, considered that the techniques did not attain the severity implied in the concept of torture. In its judgment, it set out its reasoning as follows:

"167. The five techniques were applied in combination, with premeditation and for hours at a stretch; they caused, if not actual bodily injury, at least intense physical and mental suffering to the persons subjected thereto and also led to acute psychiatric disturbances during interrogation. They accordingly fell into the category of inhuman treatment within the meaning of Article 3. The techniques were also degrading since they were such as to arouse in their victims feelings of fear, anguish and inferiority capable of humiliating and debasing them and possibly breaking their physical or moral resistance.

On these two points, the Court is of the same view as the Commission.

In order to determine whether the five techniques should also be qualified as torture, the Court must have regard to the distinction, embodied in Article 3, between this notion and that of inhuman or degrading treatment.

In the Court's view, this distinction derives principally from a difference in the intensity of the suffering inflicted.

The Court considers in fact that, whilst there exists on the one hand violence which is to be condemned both on moral grounds and also in most cases under the domestic law of the Contracting States but which does not fall within Article 3 of the Convention, it appears on the other hand that it was the intention that the Convention, with its distinction between 'torture' and 'inhuman or degrading treatment', should by the first of these terms attach a special stigma to deliberate inhuman treatment causing very serious and cruel suffering.

Moreover, this seems to be the thinking lying behind Article 1 *in fine* of Resolution 3452 (XXX) adopted by the General Assembly of the United Nations on 9 December 1975, which declares:

'Torture constitutes an *aggravated* and deliberate form of cruel, inhuman or degrading treatment or punishment'.

Although the five techniques, as applied in combination, undoubtedly amounted to inhuman and degrading treatment, although their object was the extraction of confessions, the naming of others and/or information and although they were used systematically, they did not occasion suffering of the particular intensity and cruelty implied by the word torture as so understood.

168. The Court concludes that recourse to the five techniques amounted to a practice of inhuman and degrading treatment, which practice was in breach of Article 3."

After the present *Convention* was adopted in 1984, the *Inter-American Convention to Prevent and Punish Torture* was signed at Cartagena de Indias in Colombia on 9 December 1985.[2] In its article 2, it contains a definition of torture which is influenced by, but not identical to, the definition in the present *Convention*. Article 2 of the *Inter-American Convention* reads as follows:

"For the purposes of this Convention, torture shall be understood to be any act intentionally performed whereby physical or mental pain or suffering is inflicted on a person for purposes of criminal investigation, as a means of intimidation, as personal punishment, as a preventive measure, as a penalty, or for any other purpose. Torture shall also be understood to be the use of methods upon a person intended to obliterate the personality of the victim or to diminish his physical or mental capacities, even if they do not cause physical pain or mental anguish.

The concept of torture shall not include physical or mental pain or suffering that is inherent in or solely the consequence of lawful measures, provided that they do not include the performance of the acts or use of the methods referred to in this article."

As regards the definition of torture in *paragraph 1* of article 1 of the present *Convention*, the following remarks may be made.

The act of torture is defined as being the *infliction of severe pain or suffering*, whether physical or mental. The most characteristic and easily distinguishable case is that of infliction of physical pain by beating, kicking or similar acts. In many cases, the pain is inflicted with the help of objects such as canes, knives, cigarettes or metal objects which transmit electrical shocks. In order to constitute torture, the act must cause *severe* pain. Alternative wordings, such as *extreme* or *extremely severe* pain, were suggested during the *travaux préparatoires*, but the phrase "severe pain" was considered sufficient to convey the idea that only acts of a certain gravity shall be considered to constitute torture. A proposal that it should be added as a further criterion that the pain was inflicted systematically was not reflected in the final text of the article,

---

[2] *Cf. supra* p. 29. The text of this *Inter-American Convention* is reproduced in Appendix 18.

which means that even a single, isolated act can be considered to constitute torture.

The acts inflicting severe *mental* pain or suffering can be of very different kinds. One category consists of acts which imply threats or which create fear in the victim. Examples are that the victim is made to believe that he will be killed or that reprisals will be taken against his wife or his children if he does not co-operate. Another category is where the victim is forced to witness events such as the execution or the torture of other detainees or of his own family members. The fact of not satisfying certain basic needs of a person could also, in some circumstances, constitute torture. Examples of this are deprivation of food or water or of sleep, prolonged isolation, perhaps even in darkness, etc. In all of these cases, however, the act concerned can only be described as torture if the pain or suffering inflicted is severe.

Normally, what constitutes torture is a positive act, and the definition in article 1 only refers to acts and not to omissions. This does not exclude, however, that in special cases an omission should be assimilated to an act. The intentional failure to provide a prisoner with food or drink could be a case in point.

Article 1 does not expressly refer to *medical or scientific experiments* being carried out on a prisoner against his will and without any therapeutic purpose. This does not exclude, however, that subjecting a person to such experiments could in some cases amount to torture, provided, of course, that the experiments could be said to have resulted in severe pain or suffering. In this respect, it may be recalled that article 7 of the *International Covenant on Civil and Political Rights* does mention medical or scientific experimentation as a characteristic example of acts violating the prohibition of torture and inhuman or degrading treatment or punishment.

According to the definition in article 1, torture must be an *intentional* act. It follows that where pain or suffering is the result of an accident or of mere negligence, the criteria for regarding the act as torture are not fulfilled.

During the *travaux préparatoires*, there were different views as to whether the definition should include a reference to the purposes for which severe pain or suffering is intentionally inflicted. The result was a compromise: the most common purposes are indicated, but the list of purposes is not exhaustive. Just like the list in article 1 of the 1975 *Declaration*, it is preceded by the words "such purposes as". There could be other purposes as well; however, these cannot be understood as "any other purpose" as mentioned in article 2 of the 1985 *Inter-American Convention.* The words "such ... as" imply that the other purposes must have something in common with the purposes expressly listed.

This requirement does not necessarily mean that the purposes must be illegitimate. Several purposes of the list, in particular obtaining information or a confession, punishing or even intimidating and coercing, may be perfectly legitimate on condition that legitimate methods are used to achieve them. In principle, the common element of the purposes referred to in the definition should rather be understood to be the existence of some – even remote – connection with the interests or policies of the State and its organs. It is important to note, in this context, that the primary objective of the *Convention* is to eliminate torture committed by or under the responsibility of public officials for purposes connected with their public functions. Precisely because the public interest is sometimes seen in such cases as a justification, the authorities may be reluctant to suppress these practices. The provisions of the *Convention* are intended to ensure that torture does not occur in such cases or that, if it occurs, action is taken against the offender.

If the purposes referred to in article 1 must be understood as having some connection with the interests or policies of the State and its organs, it could be argued that torture committed by a public official without any such purposes but for purely sadistic or otherwise private motives would fall outside the scope of the *Convention*. It should be observed, however, that even where a sadistic motive is predominating, there is normally also an element of punishment or intimidation which would bring the act under the definition in article. 1 Moreover, it can often be assumed that where a public official performs such an act, there is also to some extent a public policy to tolerate or to acquiesce in such acts. Only in exceptional cases should it therefore be possible to conclude that the infliction of severe pain or suffering by a public official would not constitute torture as meant in the definition on the ground that he acted for purely private reasons.

Finally, if severe pain or suffering is inflicted in the course of a fully justified medical treatment, it is obvious that this cannot constitute torture as defined in article 1. In the first place, the purpose would belong to a different category. In the second place, the severe pain or suffering would not be inflicted "intentionally" in the sense of the definition. On the contrary, such pain or suffering would be an unintended side-effect of the treatment, which the performers of the treatment would endeavour to reduce as far as possible. A similar line of reasoning may be applied to other situations where severe pain or suffering would be caused by a deliberate act but where nonetheless the element of "intentional infliction" would be lacking.

Among the purposes mentioned in article 1 the most typical one is that of obtaining information or a confession. While normally the intention is to obtain the information or the confession from the person who is tortured, it is also possible that a third person is the one whom the torturer wishes to make speak (for example, the wife is tortured in order to make the husband speak). Other purposes mentioned are those of punishment, intimidation, coercion and discrimination.

Another question which caused some discussion during the *travaux préparatoires* was whether or not an act of the kind referred to in article 1 should be regarded as torture *irrespective of who committed the act*. The conclusion was, however, that only torture for which the authorities could be held responsible should fall within the article's definition. If torture is committed without any involvement of the authorities, but as a criminal act by private persons, it can be expected that the normal machinery of justice will operate and that prosecution and punishment will follow under the normal conditions of the domestic legal system.

The problem with which the *Convention* was meant to deal was that of torture in which the authorities of a country were themselves involved and in respect of which the machinery of investigation and prosecution might therefore not function normally. A typical case is torture inflicted by a policeman or an officer of the investigating or prosecuting authority. But many variations are conceivable. It could be that the torturer is not directly connected with any public authority but that the authorities have hired him to help gather information or have at least accepted or tolerated his act. All such situations where the responsibility of the authorities is somehow engaged are supposed to be covered by the rather wide phrase appearing in article 1: "inflicted by or at the instigation of or with the consent or acquiescence of a public official or other person acting in an official capacity".

If torture is performed by a public agency, such as the security police, the government of the country has no defence under the *Convention* in saying that it was unaware of the act or even disapproved of it once it was informed.

Whereas article 1 specifies the category of persons bearing responsibility for the acts of inflicting severe pain or suffering, namely public officials and other persons acting in an official capacity, the definition contains no particulars as to the victims of these acts. Instead, it simply refers to pain or suffering being inflicted "on a person". The same holds true for the definition set out in the 1975 *Declaration*. However, this does not imply that the category of victims is indefinite. The history of the *Declaration* and the *Convention* make it clear that the victims must be understood to be persons who are deprived of their liberty or who are at least under the factual power or control of the person inflicting the pain or suffering.

The 1975 *Declaration* was drawn up by the Fifth UN Congress on the Prevention of Crime and the Treatment of Offenders in response to a request from the General Assembly "to include, in the elaboration of the Standard Minimum Rules for the Treatment of Prisoners, rules for the protection of *all persons subjected to any form of detention or imprisonment* (italics added) against torture and other cruel, inhuman or degrading treatment or punishment". Two years after the adoption of the 1975 *Declaration*, the General Assembly requested the Commission on Human Rights to draw up a draft convention "in the light of the principles embodied in the Declaration". All work undertaken in the framework of the Commission for preparing the present *Convention* was performed under an agenda item reading "Question of the human rights of *all persons subjected to any form of detention or imprisonment* (italics added)". The connection between the phenomenon of torture as dealt with in the *Convention* and deprivation of liberty is also apparent from articles 10 and 11 which explicitly refer to persons "subjected to any form of arrest, detention or imprisonment".

Ignoring this connection might lead to interpretations of the *Convention* that its authors never had in mind. Any use of armed force by the military or by the police in the exercise of such functions as the defence of the country, the maintenance of law and order and the arrest of criminals would come under the formula of intentional infliction of severe pain or suffering by public officials for coercive purposes. Yet this would not constitute torture in the sense of the *Convention.* The fact that the use of armed force for military and police purposes does not by itself constitute torture is particularly relevant in the light of article 2, paragraph 2, of the *Convention* which states that no exceptional circumstances whatsoever, whether a state of war or a threat of war, internal political instability or any other public emergency, may be invoked as a justification of torture.

The second sentence of paragraph 1 of article 1 is probably the most controversial element of the whole article. It provides that torture does not include pain or suffering arising only from, inherent in or incidental to lawful sanctions. It has often been said that this is a too far-reaching exception, since it might be interpreted so as to allow a State to practise methods which would normally be regarded as torture, by making them lawful sanctions under its own legal system. On the other hand, it has been argued that while the *Convention* was intended to strengthen the already existing prohibition of torture in international law, it was not intended to lead to a reform of the system of penal sanctions in different States and that, if that had been the intention, the *Convention* would have been unacceptable to a number of countries.

In the original Swedish proposal for the text of the *Convention*, the exception for lawful sanctions, as was also the case in the 1975 *Declaration*, was limited to such sanctions as were consistent with the *Standard Minimum Rules for the Treatment of Prisoners.*[3] These *Rules*, which were adopted by the First UN Congress on the Prevention of Crime and the Treatment of Offenders, held at Geneva in 1955, and subsequently approved by the Economic and Social Council, are not a binding international treaty, and for that reason it was considered inappropriate to refer to them in a binding instrument as the *Convention against Torture.* At the same time, no binding international instrument existed which indicated with any precision which penal sanctions are so harsh and severe as being contrary to international standards.

There was a certain divergence of opinion between those who thought that the *Convention* should exclusively deal with acts of torture which were also illegal under national law and those who considered that there must be a limit

[3] *Cf.* articles 31 to 34 of the *Standard Minimum Rules*, reproduced in Appendix 15.

beyond which sanctions provided for by national law are so cruel as to constitute torture.

The second sentence of paragraph 1 of article 1 does not resolve this controversy in a unequivocal manner. It is true that it makes a general exception for lawful sanctions, but it does not make it clear whether, in order to be lawful, a sanction must also be consistent with international law under which cruel, inhuman or degrading treatment or punishment is prohibited. It may therefore be argued that various forms of corporal punishment, including those involving mutilation, are not covered by the exception in the second sentence, but this is undoubtedly a view which is not shared by everyone.

In this context it is appropriate to observe that, although we have referred to paragraph 1 of article 1 as containing a "definition" of torture, it should not be understood as a definition in the strict sense of penal law. Unlike earlier international instruments which simply refer to the concept of "torture", the 1975 *Declaration* as well as the present *Convention* elucidate what the concept implies by listing a number of constitutive elements. In this way paragraph 1 gives a *description* of torture for the purpose of understanding and implementing the *Convention* rather than a legal definition for direct application in criminal law and criminal procedure. This explains, for instance, why the authors could decide to include in this description a non-exhaustive list of purposes by using the formula "for such purposes as" in accordance with the example given by the *Declaration*. In national penal law, the definition of a crime by using an open-ended list of purposes might give rise to the objection that this would run counter to a strict application of the principle *"nullum crimen sine lege"*.

Paragraph 2 of article 1 makes it clear that the definition of torture in no way affects the protection which can be derived from other international instruments or from national legislation of wider application. In other words, insofar as other international instruments or national laws give the individual a better protection, he shall be entitled to benefit from it; however, other international instruments or national law can never restrict the protection which the individual enjoys under the present *Convention*.

It should be observed that article 1 contains no definition of cruel, inhuman or degrading treatment or punishment, although, according to the title of the *Convention*, it also deals with such treatment or punishment. In fact, it has been found impossible to find any satisfactory definition of this general concept, whose application to a specific case must be assessed on the basis of all the particularities of the concrete situation. It may also be appropriate to point out that, although the definition of torture in article 1 may give the impression of being a very precise and detailed one, one of the basic concepts which it contains, namely "severe pain or suffering", is in fact a rather vague concept, on the application of which to a specific case there may be very different views. It would not be surprising if the opinions of different persons on this matter would be influenced by their legal background and by the role humanitarian considerations play within their own societies. Nevertheless, it was not the intention of those who drafted the *Convention* that the content of the concept of torture should vary from country to country. One of the basic tasks of those who are to apply the *Convention*, and in particular of the Committee against Torture set up under its article 17, should be to determine a uniform level above which pain or suffering becomes so severe that the infliction of it constitutes torture.

Article 2

1. Each State Party shall take effective legislative, administrative, judicial or other measures to prevent acts of torture in any territory under its jurisdiction.

2. No exceptional circumstances whatsoever, whether a state of war or a threat of war, internal political instability or any other public emergency, may be invoked as a justification of torture.

3. An order from a superior officer or a public authority may not be invoked as a justification of torture.

This article contains the general but basic obligation of each State Party to promote the objectives of the *Convention*. According to *paragraph 1* of the article, which generally speaking corresponds to article 4 of the 1975 *Declaration*, each State Party shall take *effective measures to prevent torture*. The character of these measures is left to the discretion of the State concerned. It is merely indicated that the measures may be legislative, administrative, judicial or of some other kind, but in any case they must be effective. The paragraph should also be compared with article 4 of the *Convention*, which specifically requires legislative measures in order to make all acts of torture criminal offences punishable by appropriate penalties which take into account their grave nature.

The obligation under article 2 is not only to prohibit but to *prevent* acts of torture. This further emphasizes that the measures shall be effective: a formal prohibition is not sufficient, but the acts shall actually be prevented.

This does not mean, of course, that a State can guarantee that no act of torture will ever be committed in its territory. It is sufficient that the State does what can reasonably be expected from it in order to prevent such acts from occurring. If nevertheless such acts occur, other obligations under the *Convention* become applicable, and the State may then be obliged under article 2, paragraph 1, to take further effective measures in order to prevent a repetition. Such measures may include changes of personnel in a certain unit, stricter supervision, the issue of new instructions, etc.

The obligation under paragraph 1 relates to any *territory under the jurisdiction* of the State concerned. This expression is intended to include not only the actual land territory of the State and its territorial sea, but also ships flying its flag and aircraft registered in the State concerned as well as platforms and other installations on its continental shelf.

Paragraph 2 of article 2 makes it clear that the *prohibition of torture is absolute* and without exception. No exceptional situation, such as a state of war or internal instability, can ever justify torture. The same rule is laid down in the second sentence of article 3 of the 1975 *Declaration.*

The background is that, while under several human rights conventions States are allowed to derogate from their obligations in time of war or in other emergencies, no such derogation is allowed in respect of a few fundamental rights of the individual, including the right not to be subjected to torture or other inhuman or degrading treatment or punishment (articles 4, paragraph 2, and 7 of the *International Covenant on Civil and Political Rights*, articles 3 and 15, paragraph 2, of the European *Convention for the Protection of Human Rights and Fundamental Freedoms*, and articles 5, paragraph 2, and 27, paragraph 2, of the *American Convention on Human Rights).* In this context it should also be noted that the prohibitions of torture included in the 1949 *Geneva Conventions* and their *Additional Protocols* of 1977 are expressly meant to apply in situations of armed conflict.

The absolute character of the prohibition of torture is further reaffirmed by *paragraph 3* of article 3, according to which an *order from a superior* or a public authority may not be invoked as a justification of torture. This is an important element in making the prohibition of torture effective, since in many cases torturers act under the authority of superiors. The Nuremberg principles made it clear that superior orders cannot justify the commission of particularly serious crimes under international law, and it is important that this rule is strictly applied to as serious a crime as torture. It was discussed in the course of the *travaux préparatoires* whether the order of a superior, although not being a justification, could still be an extenuating fact justifying a milder penalty. This cannot be excluded, although it would be contrary to the spirit of the *Convention* if the penalty was so lenient as not to take into account the very serious nature of the offence.

Article 3

1. No State Party shall expel, return ("refouler") or extradite a person to another State where there are substantial grounds for believing that he would be in danger of being subjected to torture.

2. For the purpose of determining whether there are such grounds, the competent authorities shall take into account all relevant considerations including, where applicable, the existence in the State concerned of a consistent pattern of gross, flagrant or mass violations of human rights.

This article has no equivalent in the 1975 *Declaration*, and it is generally seen as providing significant additional protection in comparison with previous human rights instruments. It makes it clear that a State is not only responsible for what happens in its own territory, but it must also refrain from exposing an individual to serious risks outside its territory by handing him or her over to another State from which treatment contrary to the *Convention* might be expected.

To some extent the article is based on article 33 of the 1951 Geneva *Convention Relating to the Status of Refugees*, which provides that "No Contracting State shall expel or return ("refouler") a refugee in any manner whatsoever to the frontiers of territories where his life or freedom would be threatened on account of his race, religion, nationality, membership of a particular social group or political opinion". However, the scope of the two provisions is different. In the *Refugee Convention*, protection is given to refugees, i.e. to persons who are persecuted in their country of origin for a special reason, whereas article 3 of the present *Convention* applies to any person who, for whatever reason, is in danger of being subjected to torture if handed over to another country.

The article had been inspired by the case-law of the European Commission of Human Rights with regard to article 3 of the *European Convention on Human Rights*. The Commission has considered that the prohibition of torture and inhuman or degrading treatment in article 3 of the *European Convention* does not only oblige a State to prevent torture within its own territory, but also to refrain from handing a person over to another State where he might, with some degree of probability, be subjected to such treatment.

The European Commission has developed an extensive case-law on this point. It has frequently pointed out that, while no right of residence and no right of asylum are guaranteed by the *European Convention*, a person's expulsion or extradition might nevertheless, in exceptional cases, give rise to a question of a possible violation of article 3 of that *Convention*. The Commission has stated, for instance (European Commission of Human Rights, *Decisions and Reports*, Vol. 36, pages 231-232):

> "However, according to established case-law, extradition may under certain exceptional circumstances constitute treatment prohibited by Article 3 of the Convention. This is the case, for example, where the person concerned is in danger of being subjected in the State to which he is to be extradited, to torture or any treatment contrary to Article 3."

The Commission has also recognized that an issue under article 3 of the *European Convention* may arise where extradition to a country is contemplated in which "due to the very nature of the régime of that country or to a particular situation in that country, basic human rights, such as are guaranteed by the Convention, might be either grossly violated or entirely suppressed" (*Yearbook of the European Convention on Human Rights*, Vol. 6, page 480).

Paragraph 1 of article 3 of the present *Convention* refers to three ways of handing a person over to another State: expulsion, return ("refoulement") and extradition. The original Swedish draft only referred to expulsion and extradition, but a reference to return ("refoulement") was added in order to make the provision more complete and with article 33 of the *Refugee Convention* as an obvious source of inspiration. As it now reads, the article is intended to cover all measures by which a person is physically transferred to another State.

In the course of the discussions regarding this article, it became clear that the extradition of persons for the purpose of criminal prosecution or the serving of a sentence may in some cases give rise to special problems. This is so because extradition is frequently governed by bilateral or multilateral agreements under which a State may have special obligations to extradite under circumstances as defined in the treaties concerned. It is therefore conceivable that the prohibition of extradition in the present *Convention* is, in some cases, in conflict with an obligation to extradite under an extradition treaty. The question then arises of just how such a conflict should be resolved.

When extradition to a State is contemplated which is also a Party to the present *Convention*, the extradition treaty may well be considered to have been supplemented between the two States concerned by the exception provided for in article 3 of this *Convention*. This would mean that extradition could be refused if the conditions in article 3 are fulfilled, without any resulting breach of an obligation under the extradition treaty.

Moreover, the problem of conflicting obligations should only arise in relation to extradition treaties concluded before the State which contemplated extradition became a party to the present *Convention*. With regard to any subsequent extradition treaties, a State which is already a Party to the present *Convention* cannot undertake any obligations in the field of extradition which are in conflict with article 3 of this *Convention*.

A conflict between the undertaking in article 3 of the present *Convention* and existing extradition treaties may arise, however, where the obligations under these treaties are so absolute that they allow of no exception even in the special circumstances envisaged in the said article. Even in such a case it might be argued that the obligation in article 3 is so fundamental that it can be said to have its basis in customary and generally accepted human rights law, and if that is so, compliance with the obligation could be considered not to constitute a breach of another international obligation under the extradition treaty. However, such an argument might not be generally accepted, and during the *travaux préparatoires* considerable attention was given to the problem of conflicts with existing treaty obligations.

When paragraph 1 of article 3 was first adopted by the Working Group set up by the Commission on Human Rights, it was agreed to add the following remark in the report (doc. E/CN.4/1367, paragraph 18):

> "Some delegations indicated that their States might wish, at the time of signature or ratification of the Convention or accession thereto, to declare that they did not consider themselves bound by Article 3 of the Convention, in so far as that article might not be compatible with obligations towards States not Party to the Convention under extradition treaties concluded before the date of the signature of the Convention."

The same remark again appears in subsequent reports of the Working Group, including the last report of 1984 (doc. E/CN.4/1984/72, paragraph 12). It therefore seems reasonable to assume that a reservation or a declaration along these lines would be legally permissible, if made by a State in connection with its signature or ratification of the *Convention*, or its accession thereto.

It should further be observed that the obligation on a State Party under article 3 concerns expulsion, return and extradition to any other State, i.e. also a State which is not a Party to the present Convention. It could even be said that the undertaking under article 3 is especially important as to the transfer of a person to a State which is not a Party to the *Convention*, since such a State, unlike the States Parties to the *Convention*, may not have made any internationally binding undertaking to suppress torture in its territory.

A condition under article 3 is that there are *substantial* grounds for believing that the person concerned *would* be in danger of being subjected to torture, if handed over to the other State. In the original Swedish draft, it was proposed that there should be *reasonable* grounds to believe that he or she *might* be in danger of being subjected to torture, but the present wording was proposed by the United Kingdom as being more precise than the original text (doc. E/CN.4/1314, paragraph II 8).

The question as to whether or not such substantial grounds exist in a given case must be assessed in the light of the particular circumstances of that case. It may be of great importance, for instance, whether it can be established that the person concerned belonged to a certain opposition group in his home country or whether he was a member of a persecuted minority group of some kind. In such matters, questions of evidence may often be difficult, and while the affirmations of the person concerned must have some credible appearance in order to be accepted, it would often be unreasonable and contrary to the spirit of the *Convention* to require full proof of the truthfulness of the alleged facts.

In addition to the facts of the specific case, it is important also to take into account what is known about the general human rights situation in the country concerned and about the way relevant minority or opposition groups are treated in that country. This aspect is particularly addressed in *paragraph 2* of article 3 which provides that, for the purpose of determining whether such grounds as referred to in paragraph 1 exist in a given case, all relevant circumstances shall be taken into account, including the existence of a consistent pattern of gross, flagrant or mass violations of human rights in the State concerned.

The original Swedish draft contained no provision of this kind. However, the Soviet Union proposed in 1979 an additional paragraph according to which, in considering whether a danger of torture existed in a given case, special regard should be had to the existence of a situation "characterized by flagrant and massive violations of human rights brought about when *apartheid*, racial discrimination or genocide, the suppression of national liberation movements, aggression or the occupation of foreign territory are made State policy".[4]

The Soviet proposal gave rise to a lively discussion. A number of delegations were firmly opposed to an enumeration of this kind, whereas others considered that it should be further extended by also referring to state policies of colonialism or neo-colonialism. The compromise which was reached consisted of deleting the enumeration of specific situations while maintaining a reference to situations characterized by a consistent pattern of gross, flagrant or mass violations of human rights.[5]

The existence of such a serious human rights situation in a country should serve as a warning to other States which might consider the possibility of expelling, returning or extraditing a person to that country. However, paragraph 2 does not exclude the possibility of handing over a person to that country, if the State taking the decision is satisfied that in that specific case no risk of torture exists. Nor does paragraph 2 mean that a person may always be handed over to a State where there is no consistent pattern of human rights violations. It may be that, nevertheless, in the specific case a risk of torture exists, for instance because the person concerned belongs to a specific group, or has committed a specific act, which might give rise to special risks for him in the country concerned. Insofar as paragraph 2 refers to the existence in a State of a consistent pattern of gross, flagrant or mass violations of human rights, the provision is neither absolute nor exhaustive. Expulsion, return or extradition may sometimes be permitted even if such a general situation exists, and on the other hand, expulsion, return or extradition may sometimes be prohibited under the general rule of article 3 even if there is no such consistent pattern of human rights violations. The general rule is the one indicated in the first part of paragraph 2, namely that the existence of substantial grounds for believing in a risk of torture shall be assessed in the light of *all relevant circumstances*.

---

[4] *Cf. supra* p. 51.

[5] Cf. *supra* pp. 93–94 concerning the explanatory statements made on behalf of the USSR and the USA after the adoption of this compromise by the Working Group.

Article 4

1. Each State Party shall ensure that all acts of torture are offences under its criminal law. The same shall apply to an attempt to commit torture and to an act by any person which constitutes complicity or participation in torture.

2. Each State Party shall make these offences punishable by appropriate penalties which take into account their grave nature.

This article makes it clear that torture must be a punishable offence under the criminal law of each State Party to the *Convention* (paragraph 1). Moreover, the punishment provided for under the domestic law of a State Party must not be trivial or disproportionate, but it must take into account the grave nature of the offence (paragraph 2). This means that torture must be punishable by severe penalties.

However, it was not possible to indicate in the *Convention* any particular penalty which should be applied, such as imprisonment above a certain minimum. In fact, the practice with regard to criminal sanctions differs very much from country to country, and the severity of a penalty must therefore be assessed in relation to the severity of the sanctions which are generally applied in a particular country. What is considered severe in a country which generally applies mild punishments may well be considered mild in a country where criminal sanctions are normally harsh. In applying article 4 it seems reasonable to require, however, that the punishment for torture should be close to the penalties applied to the most serious offences under the domestic legal system. Nevertheless, the *Convention*, being a human rights instrument, should not be invoked as justification for the application of the death penalty.

The requirement that torture shall be a criminal offence under domestic law does not mean that there must be a specific, separate offence corresponding to torture under article 1 of the *Convention*. What is important is that all acts of torture should be criminal offences under domestic law, and that they are punishable by sufficiently severe penalties. However, each State Party is free to decide for itself whether to deal with torture as a separate offence or to include acts of torture in one or more wider categories of offences, such as ill-treatment, infliction of bodily harm, assault, unlawful compulsion, or the like. Whatever solution is adopted, the criminal law must cover all cases falling within the definition in article 1 of the *Convention*. It is not sufficient, for instance, to penalize acts which involve physical ill-treatment, but mental torture must also fall within the ambit of the criminal law.

Paragraph 1 makes it clear that the obligation to make torture a criminal offence also applies to any act which constitutes an attempt to commit torture or complicity or participation in torture. It is important, in particular, that different forms of complicity or participation are punishable, since the torturer who inflicts pain or suffering often does not act alone, but his act is made possible by the support or encouragement which he receives from other persons. In many cases the torturer is merely a tool in the hands of someone else, and although this does not relieve him of criminal responsibility, the person or persons who instructed him should also be punished. In the definition of torture in article 1, reference is made to cases where pain or suffering is inflicted "at the instigation or with the consent or acquiescence of a public official or other person acting in an official capacity". Such instigation, consent or acquiescence should be considered to be included in the term "complicity or participation" in article 4.

It should be recalled that article 4 is inspired by similar articles in the *Conventions* regarding hijacking, sabotage against aircraft, attacks on diplomats and the taking of hostages. These *Conventions* provide that the acts concerned shall be offences under domestic law and that they shall be punishable either by severe penalties (article 2 of the *Convention for the Suppression of Unlawful Seizure of Aircraft* and article 3 of the *Convention for the Suppression of Unlawful Acts against the Safety of Civil Aviation)* or by appropriate penalties which take into account the grave nature of the offences concerned (article 2, paragraph 2, of the *Convention on the Prevention and Punishment of Crimes against Internationally Protected Persons, including Diplomatic Agents* and article 2 of the *International Convention against the Taking of Hostages).* They also make it clear that not only the primary offence but also attempts to commit that offence and acts which constitute complicity in the offence shall be punishable and subject to appropriate penalties (article 1 (b) of the *Convention for the Suppression of Unlawful Seizure of Aircraft*, article 1, paragraph 2, of the *Convention for the Suppression of Unlawful Acts against the Safety of Civil Aviation*, article 2, paragraph 1 (d) and (e) of the *Convention on the Prevention and Punishment of Crimes against Internationally Protected Persons, including Diplomatic Agents*, and article 1, paragraph 2, of the *International Convention against the Taking of Hostages).*

Article 5

1. Each State Party shall take such measures as may be necessary to establish its jurisdiction over the offences referred to in article 4 in the following cases:

(a) When the offences are committed in any territory under its jurisdiction or on board a ship or aircraft registered in that State;

(b) When the alleged offender is a national of that State;

(c) When the victim is a national of that State if that State considers it appropriate.

2. Each State Party shall likewise take such measures as may be necessary to establish its jurisdiction over such offences in cases where the alleged offender is present in any territory under its jurisdiction and it does not extradite him pursuant to article 8 to any of the States mentioned in paragraph 1 of this article.

3. This Convention does not exclude any criminal jurisdiction exercised in accordance with internal law.

This article must be seen as a cornerstone in the *Convention*, an essential purpose of which is to ensure that a torturer does not escape the consequences of his acts by going to another country. As with previous conventions against terrorism, in particular the *Convention for the Suppression of Unlawful Seizure of Aircraft*, the *Convention for the Suppression of Unlawful Acts against the Safety of Civil Aviation*, the *Convention on the Prevention and Punishment of Crimes against Internationally Protected Persons, including Diplomatic Agents* and the *International Convention against the Taking of Hostages*, the present *Convention* is also based on the principle "*aut dedere aut punire*"; in other words, the country where the suspected offender happens to be shall either extradite him for the purpose of prosecution or proceed against him on the basis of its own criminal law. To be in a position to bring criminal proceedings against the offender, the State concerned must have jurisdiction over the offence, and this is what article 5 seeks to ensure.

Paragraph 1 of article 5 deals with a number of specific grounds of jurisdiction. Under *sub-paragraph (a)* a State Party to the Convention shall be obliged to establish its jurisdiction over offences of torture, including attempts to commit torture and complicity or participation in torture, on the basis of the criterion of territoriality. This means, first of all, that the State shall have jurisdiction over the offence when it has been committed in its territory. Under international or national law, there may be certain limited exceptions to this rule, e.g. in regard to foreign diplomats, foreign troops, parliament members or other categories benefiting from special immunities, and such immunities may be accepted insofar as they apply to criminal acts in general and are not unduly extensive.

However, sub-paragraph 1 does not only apply to offences committed in the territory of a certain State, but to offences committed in any territory under its jurisdiction. This is in fact a wider concept. It means that the obligation to establish jurisdiction is not limited to a State's land territory, its territorial sea and the airspace over its land and sea territory, but it also applies to territories under military occupation, to colonial territories and to any other territories over which a State has factual control. To a limited extent it is also applicable to certain maritime areas outside the territorial sea over which a State has limited jurisdiction. If, for instance, torture is committed on an oil-rig or other installation placed on the continental shelf of a State Party, that State should be required to have jurisdiction over the offence.

Sub-paragraph *(a)* also mentions, specifically, offences committed on board ships and aircraft over which the State in which the ship or the aircraft is registered must likewise establish jurisdiction.

According to *sub-paragraph (b)* of article 5, the nationality of the offender is another criterion on the basis of which States must establish jurisdiction over torture offences. This criterion is common under the domestic laws of many countries. There are some countries, however, in particular those having an Anglo-Saxon legal tradition, where territoriality is, with regard to most offences, the only ground of jurisdiction. Such countries must therefore, when they become parties to the *Convention*, extend their jurisdiction in respect of torture offences.

The question may arise as to whether the obligation to establish jurisdiction on the basis of the nationality of the offender also applies to cases where the alleged offender acquired the nationality of the State concerned after the offence was committed. When considering this question, one should take into account the general purpose of the *Convention* which is to make it possible in all situations to prosecute torturers. Therefore it could not be accepted that a State, by granting a suspected torturer its nationality, would in fact give him at the same time immunity from criminal jurisdiction in respect of the offence. It may be that the grant of a new nationality becomes a bar to extradition, since many States do not extradite their own citizens, but in such cases it would be contrary to the *Convention* if it was not possible for the State whose nationality the alleged offender has acquired to bring criminal proceedings against him. However, this problem of interpretation in relation to paragraph 1 *(b)* becomes less important in view of paragraph 2, which provides for a general duty to establish jurisdiction over an offence where the alleged offender is present in a territory under the jurisdiction of a State Party and that State does not extradite him to another State having jurisdiction under paragraph 1.

One further ground of jurisdiction, i.e. the nationality of the victim, appears in *paragraph 1 (c)*. While this ground of jurisdiction is to be found in some legal systems and is also reflected in, for instance, article 6, paragraph 2 (d), of the *International Convention against the Taking of Hostages*, it is in no way generally recognized and cannot be said to have the same firm basis in different legal systems as the grounds mentioned in sub-paragraphs *(a)* and *(b)*. For that reason, the wording of sub-paragraph *(c)* contains no more than a reminder that States might find it desirable to establish jurisdiction also on this ground. However, there is no obligation to do so, since sub-paragraph *(c)* only requires jurisdiction to be established on the basis of the victim's nationality if the State concerned *considers it appropriate*.

Paragraph 2 provides that, whether or not any of the grounds of jurisdiction dealt with in paragraph 1 exist, a State Party shall have jurisdiction over offences of torture in all cases where the alleged offender is present in a territory under its jurisdiction and it does not extradite him to a State which has jurisdiction under paragraph 1. In view of paragraph 2, the *Convention* can be said to be based on the principle of universal jurisdiction. It should be noted, however, that a State Party is only required under paragraph 2 to establish its jurisdiction where the alleged offender is present in a territory under its jurisdiction. If the offender is not present in such a territory, the State is under no obligation to establish jurisdiction upon which a request for extradition could be based.

The jurisdiction which a State is required to establish under paragraph 2 may be conditional in the sense that it may be limited to cases where the State does not extradite the alleged offender. Nevertheless, it may be natural for many countries to make the jurisdiction general while limiting its exercise to cases where no extradition takes place (cf. article 7 of the *Convention*). However, it is also permissible for a State to make the jurisdiction as such conditional on the fact that the alleged offender is not extradited. If that is done, it is clear that there must be jurisdiction in a case where an extradition request has been made but rejected. The question arises, however, as to whether or not there must also be jurisdiction in a case where no extradition request has been made at all. During the negotiations regarding the *Convention* initially different opinions emerged on this point. There were delegations which considered that jurisdiction should be dependent on an extradition request having been made but refused. However, this was not the predominating opinion, and not the opinion which was reflected in the *Convention*.

The same question also arises in a more acute form in regard to article 7 of the *Convention* which makes the obligation to exercise jurisdiction dependent on whether the alleged offender is not extradited. The reasoning related to that article applies *mutatis mutandis* to article 5, and it therefore seems correct to conclude that jurisdiction must be established also for cases where no extradition request is made by any other State. During the *travaux préparatoires* it was suggested that jurisdiction should exist after a certain time had elapsed without extradition having been requested, but no such time-limit appears in the text of the *Convention*. Each State is therefore free to determine, within reasonable limits, at what stage it is justified to conclude that no extradition request will be made.

Like in paragraph 1 *(a)*, the expression "any territory under its jurisdiction" in paragraph 2 refers to all territories under the factual control of a State, including territories under military occupation.

In *paragraph 3* it is made clear that article 5 must not be interpreted *a contrario* so as to exclude the application of any further ground of jurisdiction which may exist in domestic law.

Article 6

1. Upon being satisfied, after an examination of information available to it, that the circumstances so warrant, any State Party in whose territory a person alleged to have committed any offence referred to in article 4 is present shall take him into custody or take other legal measures to ensure his presence. The custody and other legal measures shall be as provided in the law of that State but may be continued only for such time as is necessary to enable any criminal or extradition proceedings to be instituted.

2. Such State shall immediately make a preliminary inquiry into the facts.

3. Any person in custody pursuant to paragraph 1 of this article shall be assisted in communicating immediately with the nearest appropriate representative of the State of which he is a national, or, if he is a stateless person, with the representative of the State where he usually resides.

4. When a State, pursuant to this article, has taken a person into custody, it shall immediately notify the States referred to in article 5, paragraph 1, of the fact that such person is in custody and of the circumstances which warrant his detention. The State which makes the preliminary inquiry contemplated in paragraph 2 of this article shall promptly report its findings to the said States and shall indicate whether it intends to exercise jurisdiction.

In order to ensure that an alleged offender can be prosecuted or extradited, it may be necessary to detain him or take other measures to ensure his presence. Provisions to this effect are also contained in article 6 of the *Convention for the Suppression of Unlawful Seizure of Aircraft*, article 6 of the *Convention for the Suppression of Unlawful Acts against the Safety of Civil Aviation*, article 6 of the *Convention on the Prevention and Punishment of Crimes against Internationally Protected Persons, including Diplomatic Agents* and article 6 of the *International Convention against the Taking of Hostages*. The provisions of article 6 of the present *Convention* are similar to the corresponding provisions of the previous *Conventions*.

According to *paragraph 1* of article 6 of the present *Convention*, a State Party shall take a suspected torturer into custody or take other legal measures to ensure his presence, when it is "satisfied, after an examination of information available to it, that the circumstances so warrant". This statement implies that, in principle, each State Party is obliged to take measures of this kind. However, each State has a wide degree of freedom to assess whether or not the circumstances warrant such a measure. In assessing this, a State may examine whether the conditions laid down in its national law relating, in particular, to the degree of suspicion required and to the existence of a danger of flight are fulfilled. Under domestic law there may also be certain time-limits which apply to custody or other measures restricting individual freedoms, and as long as such time-limits do not render the general obligation to extradite or prosecute illusory, they should be considered to be acceptable under the *Convention*. The second sentence of paragraph 1 also gives a general indication of the need to keep the duration of such measures as short as possible by providing that they "may be continued only for such time as is necessary to enable any criminal or extradition proceedings to be instituted".

The "other legal measures" to which paragraph 1 refers may include restrictions of the freedom of movement (e.g. prohibition to leave the country or obligation to stay at a certain place or in a certain area) as well as an obligation to report regularly to the police or other authorities.

Paragraph 2 gives a further indication of the importance of proceeding quickly and with care once a person has been detained or subjected to other restrictions of his personal liberty. It provides that the State which has imposed such a measure shall *immediately* make a preliminary inquiry into the facts. This obligation is clear when it is the detaining State itself which intends to bring criminal proceedings against the detained person. However, the situation is somewhat different when a person is detained exclusively for the purpose of extradition. In that instance, it is the requesting State which primarily makes an inquiry into the facts and which provides the detaining State with such material as is necessary to justify extradition. However, the necessity, in such cases, of keeping detention as short as possible is usually reflected in time-limits provided by extradition treaties and by national laws.

The right of an alien taken into custody according to this article to communicate with a diplomatic or consular mission of his State of nationality is dealt with in *paragraph 3*. The rule is similar to, but less detailed than, the provisions of article 36 of the *Vienna Convention on Consular Relations*. However, paragraph 3 contains an additional element insofar as it also deals with the problem of stateless persons who shall have the right to communicate with a representative of the country where they have their habitual residence.

Paragraph 3 is intended to give protection to a detained person who may decide himself whether or not to make use of that protection. However, the paragraph does not grant the authorities of his country of nationality or residence the right to communicate with the detained person against his will.

When a State Party has taken an alleged offender into custody, it must immediately, according to *paragraph 4* of article 6, notify those States Parties which have or may have jurisdiction over the offence on any of the grounds mentioned in article 5, paragraph 1, i.e. the State in a territory under whose jurisdiction the offence was committed as well as the States of nationality of the offender and the victim. The obligation to notify these States is of a general character, and notification shall therefore be made even where there is already a firm intention to prosecute the person concerned in the State where he was arrested. The States referred to in article 5, paragraph 1, may have an interest not only in considering the possibility of an extradition request but also in receiving information on action taken by another State in respect of an offence over which they themselves also have jurisdiction. Consequently, even where the detaining State is one of the States having jurisdiction under article 5, paragraph 1, it shall inform the other State or States which also have jurisdiction under that paragraph.

It further follows from the second sentence of paragraph 4 of article 6 that the detaining State shall promptly report the results of its inquiry to the States referred to in article 5, paragraph 1, and shall at the same time indicate whether it intends to exercise jurisdiction. It is important that this is done as quickly as possible, since it makes it clear to these other States whether there is any reason for them to request the extradition of the alleged offender or whether any preparations for such a request should be pursued.

Article 7

1. The State Party in the territory under whose jurisdiction a person alleged to have committed any offence referred to in article 4 is found shall in the cases contemplated in article 5, if it does not extradite him, submit the case to its competent authorities for the purpose of prosecution.

2. These authorities shall take their decision in the same manner as in the case of any ordinary offence of a serious nature under the law of that State. In the cases referred to in article 5, paragraph 2, the standards of evidence required for prosecution and conviction shall in no way be less stringent than those which apply in the cases referred to in article 5, paragraph 1.

3. Any person regarding whom proceedings are brought in connection with any of the offences referred to in article 4 shall be guaranteed fair treatment at all stages of the proceedings.

Article 7 expresses one of the fundamental principles upon which the *Convention* is based, i.e. the principle according to which an alleged torturer shall either be extradited to another country for prosecution or be brought to trial in the country where he is present. The basic obligation of the States Parties either to extradite or to prosecute is laid down in article 7. While article 5 obliges States Parties to establish jurisdiction over offences of torture on the basis of different criteria, article 7 deals with the exercise of that jurisdiction in any case where an alleged torturer is present in a territory under the jurisdiction of a State Party. As regards the meaning of the expression "territory under the jurisdiction of a State Party", reference is made to the comments under article 5.

According to *paragraph 1* of article 7, the obligation of a State Party, if it does not extradite the alleged offender, is to bring the case to its competent authorities for the purpose of prosecution. The wording is similar to that which appears in article 7 of the *Convention for the Suppression of Unlawful Seizure of Aircraft*, article 7 of the *Convention for the Suppression of Unlawful Acts against the Safety of Civil Aviation*, article 7 of the *Convention on the Prevention and Punishment of Crimes against Internationally Protected Persons, including Diplomatic Agents* and article 8 of the *International Convention against the Taking of Hostages*.

It has been argued that a State basing its jurisdiction exclusively on article 5, paragraph 2, should not be obliged to prosecute, unless it has first refused extradition to one of the States referred to in article 5 paragraph 1. During the *travaux préparatoires* regarding the *Convention*, proposals were made to include specific provisions to this effect in the Convention. However, these proposals were not accepted and most States did not consider this to be a satisfactory solution.

In fact, it would considerably weaken the effectiveness of the *Convention* if the obligation to prosecute was dependent on whether an extradition request had been made and rejected. In many cases, the only State having jurisdiction under article 5, paragraph 1, is the State whose authorities have accepted, or at least tolerated, that torture occurred in its territory and which may accordingly be most reluctant to ask for the extradition of the offenders to bring them to trial. If a request for extradition from such a State was a condition for the exercise of the jurisdiction of the State in whose territory the alleged offender is present, the principle *aut dedere aut judicare* would only have a very limited application and the effectiveness of the *Convention* would be considerably weakened.

Moreover, the actual wording of article 7, paragraph 1, ("if it does not extradite him") also supports the interpretation that the mere fact that extradition does not take place, whether the reason is that no extradition request is made or that such a request is refused, is a sufficient basis for creating the obligation to submit the case to the prosecuting authorities of the State which has jurisdiction under article 5, paragraph 2.

The question arises, however, as to how long the State in whose territory the alleged offender is present is entitled to wait for a possible extradition request to arrive, before taking measures itself for the purpose of prosecution. In this respect, a certain discretion must be given to the State concerned to decide at what stage it can conclude that no request for extradition is likely to arrive. However, this discretion must naturally be exercised in a reasonable manner, and in most cases the situation will become clear without much delay. It will frequently appear from the general situation in the State or States having jurisdiction under article 5, paragraph 1, or from the reactions or attitudes of that State or those States, that no extradition request is to be expected, and the obligation to proceed to prosecution will then arise at an early stage. If there is some doubt, it is also possible for the State having jurisdiction under article 5, paragraph 2, to try to clarify the situation by putting questions, through diplomatic channels or otherwise, to the State or States having jurisdiction under article 5, paragraph 1. In any case, it would not be consistent with the general purpose of the *Convention* to defer prosecution for a long time under the pretext that it is still uncertain whether an extradition request will be made.

The obligation under article 7, paragraph 1, is not to prosecute but to "submit the case to its competent authorities for the purpose of prosecution". Under *paragraph 2* these authorities shall take their decision "in the same manner as in the case of any ordinary offence of a serious nature under the law of that State". This means that the normal procedures relating to serious offences as well as the normal standards of evidence shall be applied. It is specifically indicated in the second sentence of paragraph 2 that the standards of evidence shall in no way be less stringent than those applicable in the cases referred to in article 5, paragraph 1. The lack of evidence may frequently be a serious obstacle to bringing proceedings in a country other than that in which the torture took place. It may be difficult to call witnesses and collect other evidence, in particular where the State in which the offences were committed is not willing to co-operate in investigating the case. The second sentence makes it clear, however, that although the principle of universal jurisdiction has been regarded as an essential element in making the Convention an effective instrument, there has been no intention to have the alleged offenders prosecuted or convicted on the basis of insufficient or inadequate evidence.

Paragraph 3 contains rules aimed at safeguarding the fundamental rights of the person who is accused of torture. He must be given "fair treatment at all stages of the proceedings", which means that he must himself in no circumstances be subjected to torture or to inhuman or degrading treatment and he must get a fair trial before an impartial tribunal. The general human rights standards reflected in instruments such as the *Universal Declaration of Human Rights* and the *International Covenant on Civil and Political Rights* must apply also to him.

Article 8

1. The offences referred to in article 4 shall be deemed to be included as extraditable offences in any extradition treaty existing between States Parties. States Parties undertake to include such offences as extraditable offences in every extradition treaty to be concluded between them.

2. If a State Party which makes extradition conditional on the existence of a treaty receives a request for extradition from another State Party with which it has no extradition treaty, it may consider this Convention as the legal basis for extradition in respect of such offences. Extradition shall be subject to the other conditions provided by the law of the requested State.

3. States Parties which do not make extradition conditional on the existence of a treaty shall recognize such offences as extraditable offences between themselves subject to the conditions provided by the law of the requested State.

4. Such offences shall be treated, for the purpose of extradition between States Parties, as if they had been committed not only in the place in which they occurred but also in the territories of the States required to establish their jurisdiction in accordance with article 5, paragraph 1.

Even where a request for extradition is made, there is never any obligation to extradite under the *Convention*. It follows from article 7 that the requested State always has a choice between extradition and criminal proceedings in its own territory. Nevertheless, extradition is an essential element in the system of the *Convention*, and it is therefore important that all States Parties have the legal possibility of extraditing alleged torturers in all cases where they would find it desirable and appropriate to do so.

Article 8 is intended to remove, as far as possible, any legal obstacles to extradition, and in this respect it corresponds to article 8 of the *Convention for the Suppression of Unlawful Seizure of Aircraft*, article 8 of the *Convention for the Suppression of Unlawful Acts against the Safety of Civil Aviation*, article 8 of the *Convention on the Prevention and Punishment of Crimes against Internationally Protected Persons, including Diplomatic Agents* and article 10 of the *International Convention against the Taking of Hostages*.

Paragraph 1 of article 8 deals with the relation between the *Convention* and any existing or future extradition treaties, whether bilateral or multilateral, between States Parties. With regard to existing treaties, paragraph 1 provides that offences of torture shall be deemed to be included as extraditable offences in such treaties. Consequently, the fact that such offences may not already be covered by such treaties shall not be an obstacle to extradition. With regard to future extradition treaties between States Parties, paragraph 1 makes it compulsory to include offences of torture as extraditable offences.

According to the legal principles applied in some States, extradition cannot take place in the absence of a treaty. *Paragraph 2* deals with the case where a State Party belonging to this category receives a request for extradition regarding an offence of torture from another State Party with which it has no extradition treaty. It is indicated that in such a case the *Convention may* be the legal basis of extradition. During the *travaux préparatoires* it was discussed whether the word "may" or the word "shall" should be used in this context, but as in the end preference was given to "may", it remains to be seen to what extent the States concerned will in fact accept the *Convention* as the basis of extradition.

Those States which do not require treaties as a condition for extradition can, in the absence of such a treaty, decide on the basis of their domestic legislation whether or not to extradite for a specific offence. There is good reason to presume that offences of torture, in view of their seriousness, are already extraditable under most national extradition laws. Nevertheless, *paragraph 3* of article 8 provides an additional guarantee insofar as States Parties which do not require extradition treaties undertake to recognize torture offences as extraditable between themselves. However, the conditions provided by the law of the requested State shall apply, which means that there may be specific exceptions in national law which, if applicable, may prevent extradition.

In some extradition treaties and national laws, a condition for extradition is that the offence has been committed in the territory of the requesting State. *Paragraph 4* of article 8 provides, however, that for the purpose of extradition between States Parties offences of torture shall be treated as having been committed also in the territories of the States required to establish their jurisdiction in accordance with article 5, paragraph 1. This means that even a State which applies the principle of territoriality in extradition matters should be able to extradite an alleged torturer to the State of which he is a national (article 5, paragraph 1 *(b)*), just as if the offence had occurred in that State.

It may be more doubtful whether paragraph 4 is also intended to refer to article 5, paragraph 1 (c), in view of the fact that there is no real obligation under that sub-paragraph for a State to establish its jurisdiction on the basis of the nationality of the victim, this only being done "if that State considers it appropriate". A reasonable interpretation would be, however, that where a State Party has established its jurisdiction over torture offences on the basis of that criterion, another State Party shall, for the purpose of extradition, regard the offence concerned as also having been committed in the territory of the State of nationality of the victim.

Article 9

1. States Parties shall afford one another the greatest measure of assistance in connection with criminal proceedings brought in respect of any of the offences referred to in article 4, including the supply of all evidence at their disposal necessary for the proceedings.

2. States Parties shall carry out their obligations under paragraph 1 of this article in conformity with any treaties on mutual judicial assistance that may exist between them.

According to *paragraph 1* of this article, States Parties undertake to give one another legal assistance in connection with criminal proceedings brought in respect of torture offences. In cases where proceedings are brought against the alleged offender in a State other than that in whose territory the acts of torture were committed, it may be of the utmost importance to receive assistance from the latter State in obtaining evidence and information on various matters. In some cases, witnesses from that other country should be heard at the trial, and the assistance which States Parties are obliged to give under this article may include measures to facilitate the hearing of such witnesses.

In the course of the *travaux préparatoires* the United Kingdom delegation raised the question as to whether the provisions of article 9 might require the supplying of evidence that might be considered inadmissible in the requested State. There was no dissent from the opinion expressed by some delegations that the law of the requested State would apply to determine such matters.[6] When the national law of a State Party lays down special legal requirements for the supply of legal assistance to other States, or provides for special procedures to be applied in the determination of matters of international legal assistance, such conditions or procedures cannot normally be considered to be contrary to article 9. However, the undertaking of the States Parties to give one another "the greatest measure of assistance" seems to imply that States should not apply rules or procedures which are unduly burdensome, or which might make it virtually impossible to obtain the evidence or the information which is required in order to conduct an inquiry or a trial in a satisfactory way.

In the instance where two States Parties are also parties to a treaty on mutual legal assistance, it is clear, and expressly stated in *paragraph 2* of article 9, that the provisions of that treaty shall be respected when the States Parties carry out their obligations under paragraph 1 of that article.

Article 10

1. Each State Party shall ensure that education and information regarding the prohibition against torture are fully included in the training of law enforcement personnel, civil or military, medical personnel, public officials and other persons who may be involved in the custody, interrogation or treatment of any individual subjected to any form of arrest, detention or imprisonment.

2. Each State Party shall include this prohibition in the rules or instructions issued in regard to the duties and functions of any such persons.

In reading article 10 of the *Convention* one should bear in mind that, in accordance with article 16, paragraph 1, its provisions apply not only to torture but also to other acts of cruel, inhuman or degrading treatment or punishment when such acts are committed by or at the instigation of or with the consent or acquiescence of a public official or other person acting in an official capacity. As to the categories of persons who may be victims of such acts, the reader is referred to the comments made under article 16.

While in some cases torture or other acts of cruel, inhuman or degrading treatment or punishment are ordered, encouraged or tolerated by the higher

[6] *Cf.* paragraph 40 of the 1982 report of the Working Group.

authorities of a country, there are other cases where such acts occur exclusively or mainly as a result of initiatives by individual police or prison officers or other persons involved in the treatment of people who are deprived of their liberty. The provisions of article 10 are of vital importance with a view to preventing such practices in both types of situations.

Paragraph 1 of article 10, read together with paragraph 1 of article 16, provides that education and information regarding the prohibition of torture and other acts of cruel, inhuman or degrading treatment or punishment shall be part of the training of all categories of people who may be involved in the custody, interrogation or treatment of arrested, detained or imprisoned persons. The categories which are specifically mentioned are law enforcement personnel, whether civil or military, as well as medical personnel; however, the enumeration is not exhaustive: other public officials and other persons who may have to deal with detainees are also included.

It is not sufficient that such education and information are included in training courses given by governmental agencies to governmental personnel. Each State Party is obliged to ensure that, where required, such education and information are also included in training courses given by non-governmental agencies and in training courses for non-governmental personnel.

In order to create respect for the prohibition of torture and other acts of cruel, inhuman or degrading treatment or punishment, this issue should not be treated with brevity or as a formality. Extensive information should be given about the international efforts to combat these practices and about the results of these efforts, in particular the 1975 *Declaration* and the present *Convention*, as well as the *Code of Conduct for Law Enforcement Officials*[7] and the *Principles of Medical Ethics*[8], adopted by the United Nations General Assembly in 1979 and 1982 respectively. Of course, information should also be given about the severe penalties to which everyone guilty of torture may be subjected.

Paragraph 2 of article 10 is of no lesser importance than paragraph 1. Read together with article 16, paragraph 1, it provides that the prohibition against torture and other acts of cruel, inhuman or degrading treatment or punishment shall be included in the rules and instructions issued with regard to the duties and functions of all categories of officials and other persons who may be involved in the custody, interrogation or treatment of people who are deprived of their liberty.

The authors of the *Convention* considered it essential that the prohibition of these practices should not be embodied only in general norms perhaps unfamiliar to many of the persons concerned, but that it should also form part

[7] *Cf.* Chapter II, section 4, sub-section (c). The text of article 5 of the *Code* is reproduced in Appendix 16.

[8] *Cf.* Chapter II, section 4, sub-section (d). The text of the *Principles* is reproduced in Appendix 17.

of the specific rules and instructions given to those directly involved in the treatment of prisoners and detainees. The prohibition should be set out in unequivocal terms, taking into account applicable international standards, such as those contained in the *Code of Conduct for Law Enforcement Officials* and the *Principles of Medical Ethics*. The incorporation of this prohibition in the specific rules and instructions may be expected to minimize the chances that individual police, prison or military personnel will commit such acts on their own initiative. At the same time it may be expected to make it highly difficult for the higher authorities to order, encourage or tolerate such practices. In this connection it is important that the rules and instructions make it clear, in accordance with article 2, paragraph 3, of the *Convention*, that an order from a superior officer or a public authority may not be invoked as a justification of torture. It is also desirable that they mention explicitly that no exceptional circumstances whatsoever, whether a state of war or a threat of war, internal political instability or any other public emergency, may be invoked as a justification of torture, as laid down in article 2, paragraph 2, of the *Convention*.

Article 11

Each State Party shall keep under systematic review interrogation rules, instructions, methods and practices as well as arrangements for the custody and treatment of persons subjected to any form of arrest, detention or imprisonment in any territory under its jurisdiction, with a view to preventing any cases of torture.

This article applies both to torture and to other acts of cruel, inhuman or degrading treatment or punishment, in virtue of article 16, paragraph 1. It provides for a systematic review of rules and practices regarding interrogation and detention, with a view to preventing all such acts.

Article 10 is the only provision in the *Convention* which mentions interrogation explicitly. Interrogation is, of course, mentioned implicitly in article 1 where this refers to the obtaining of information or a confession as one of the purposes of torture. Experience shows that, among the situations in which torture may occur, interrogation is the most important. Moreover, interrogation methods can also involve other acts of cruel, inhuman or degrading treatment. In this connection reference may be made to the findings of the European Court of Human Rights, quoted above in the comments under article 1.

The term "systematic review" indicates that it is not sufficient once only to lay down such rules and instructions and to establish such methods, practices and arrangements which in themselves exclude torture and other acts of cruel, inhuman or degrading treatment or punishment, but that each State Party is obliged to follow the actual situation continuously. If cases of torture or other cruel, inhuman or degrading treatment or punishment are detected, it is necessary to take further steps to revise the rules etc. in order to improve the protection against all such acts.

The comments made with regard to article 10 also have some bearing on the present article. It may be desirable, for instance, whenever the risk of torture or other cruel, inhuman or degrading treatment or punishment is found to exist, to improve the education and information of the personnel concerned, to make the rules and instructions given to this personnel even more specific, and to emphasize the severe sanctions which follow upon any breach of the prohibition against all such acts.

As regards the meaning of the term "territory under the jurisdiction of a State Party", reference is made to the comments under article 5.

Article 12

Each State Party shall ensure that its competent authorities proceed to a prompt and impartial investigation, wherever there is reasonable ground to believe that an act of torture has been committed in any territory under its jurisdiction.

As in the two preceding articles, article 12 applies both to torture and to other acts of cruel, inhuman or degrading treatment or punishment, pursuant to article 16, paragraph 1. While all such acts are formally prohibited in virtually all countries, they still occur in many places. This clearly shows that a formal prohibition is not sufficient, and that action must also be taken against those who violate that prohibition. In order to make the prohibition effective, it is essential that any suspicion of such acts having taken place gives rise to an investigation. According to the present article, each State Party undertakes to ensure that its authorities proceed to such investigations.

An investigation must be instituted irrespective of any complaint. In fact, the victim, for instance of torture, is often unable to complain, or he may refrain from making a complaint because of the risk of reprisals against him. Article 12 therefore only requires that there is reasonable ground to believe that an act of torture (or an act of cruel, inhuman or degrading treatment or punishment as referred to in article 16, paragraph 1) has been committed, and it is without importance where the information behind this suspicion comes from.

It is important that suspicions regarding any such acts give rise to investigations, as otherwise the officials concerned may be given the impression that their superiors are prepared to accept such acts, or at least are not anxious to combat them in an effective way.

Article 12 adds two requirements as regards the investigation to be made: it shall be "prompt" and "impartial". Both these elements are important. Promptness is essential not only in the interest of the victim but also in many cases to prevent the acts from occurring again, whether against the same person or against someone else. Impartiality is important, since any investigation which proceeds from the assumption that no such acts have occurred, or in which there is a desire to protect the suspected officials, cannot be considered effective. In order to ensure impartiality, it is necessary to avoid entrusting the investigation to persons who have close personal or professional links with the persons suspected of having committed such acts, or who may have an interest in protecting these persons or the particular unit to which they belong.

With regard to the meaning of the term "territory under the jurisdiction of a State Party", reference is again made to the comments under article 5.

Article 13

Each State Party shall ensure that any individual who alleges he has been subjected to torture in any territory under its jurisdiction has the right to complain to, and to have his case promptly and impartially examined by, its competent authorities. Steps shall be taken to ensure that the complainant and witnesses are protected against all ill-treatment or intimidation as a consequence of his complaint or any evidence given.

As with the three preceding articles, article 13 applies both to torture and to other acts of cruel, inhuman or degrading treatment or punishment, in virtue of article 16, paragraph 1. While under article 12 a State Party is obliged to proceed to an investigation as soon as there is reasonable ground to believe that any such act has been committed, article 13 provides that any person who claims to be the victim of such an act shall have a right of complaint to the competent authorities. Moreover, his complaint shall be examined promptly and impartially by these authorities. As regards the requirements of promptness and impartiality, reference is made to the comments made in connection with article 12.

Even if there is, according to article 12, a general duty of each State Party to proceed *ex officio* to an investigation when there is a reasonable suspicion of any such act having been committed, it is nevertheless important that the person who alleges to be the victim of such an act has a formal right of complaint and a right to have his complaint properly examined. The right of complaint implies that if the person concerned is in detention, the officials responsible for his detention must forward his complaint to the competent authorities, and these authorities, in their turn, must look into the matter seriously and must not reject the complaint unless it appears, on the basis of reliable facts, to be unfounded.

In many cases a victim of such an act may be afraid of lodging a complaint, because this may expose him to a risk of further ill-treatment or other reprisals. The second sentence of article 13 therefore requires a State Party to take steps to eliminate this risk. Different kinds of steps may be envisaged depending on the circumstances: the complainant's removal to another place of detention, change of the personnel responsible for him during his detention, the presence of a witness during further interrogations, or the like.

In the course of examining a complaint of torture or other cruel, inhuman or degrading treatment or punishment, the authorities may hear witnesses. It is important for the truthfulness of their evidence and for their own safety that they are not exposed to any risk of reprisals as a result of the statements made. The second sentence of article 13 therefore requires the State Party also to take steps to protect such witnesses.

The obligations of a State Party under this article relate to allegations of torture or other cruel, inhuman or degrading treatment or punishment "in any territory under its jurisdiction". The meaning of this term has been explained in the comments under article 5.

Article 14

1. Each State Party shall ensure in its legal system that the victim of an act of torture obtains redress and has an enforceable right to fair and adequate compensation, including the means for as full rehabilitation as possible. In the event of the death of the victim as a result of an act of torture, his dependants shall be entitled to compensation.

2. Nothing in this article shall affect any right of the victim or other persons to compensation which may exist under national law.

According to *paragraph 1* of this article, a victim of torture shall, under the legal system of each State Party, be able to obtain redress and have an enforceable right to compensation. While redress seems to refer primarily to an official recognition of the wrong that has been done to the person concerned, the compensation is of a material (and primarily pecuniary) nature. Moreover, there shall be a legal right to compensation in domestic law. It is not sufficient that compensation can be granted as an *ex gratia* measure in appropriate cases.

Paragraph 1 does not give any clear indication of how the compensation shall be calculated. It states, however, that the compensation shall be fair and adequate.

In these circumstances, it must be accepted that compensation may differ a great deal from country to country. Such differences may depend on the general income level and standard of living in the country concerned as well as on its legal practice in regard to the level of compensation for damage in general.

However, the requirement that the compensation shall be fair and adequate excludes purely symbolic amounts of compensation. The compensation to which the torture victim is entitled must be substantial. In the first place, it must be required that compensation be paid for any costs which the victim may have had for medical or psychological treatment. In the second place, the non-material damage which he suffered as a consequence of the torture must also be compensated in a significant way.

It is expressly mentioned that compensation shall include the means for as full rehabilitation as possible. This means that where there is a need for medical or psychological treatment or for special mechanical aids, such treatment or such aids shall be provided so far as they are available.

The second sentence of paragraph 1 deals with the situation which arises when a person dies as a result of torture. In such a case, the dependants shall be entitled to compensation. A wife, a husband and/or minor children can normally be considered as dependants. Other relatives can be considered to belong in this category when they depended for their support upon financial help from the deceased person.

The right of the dependants to compensation is an independent right intended to compensate the loss that the dependants themselves have suffered. This could include material as well as non-material damage. The article gives no indication of how the compensation is to be calculated, and there is not even a requirement that it should be fair and adequate. Consequently, it can be assumed that the State Parties enjoy a particularly wide discretion in determining the amounts of compensation in cases of this kind.

Paragraph 2 indicates that where there is a wider right to compensation under domestic law, this right shall not be affected by the provisions of article 14. It may be, for instance, that under some legal systems a victim of torture enjoys a right to considerably higher amounts of compensation than can reasonably be derived from the *Convention*, and it is also possible that persons who have assisted a victim of torture could be compensated for their expenses under certain national laws. Any such rights remain unaffected by article 14.

Article 15

Each State Party shall ensure that any statement which is established to have been made as a result of torture shall not be invoked as evidence in any proceedings, except against a person accused of torture as evidence that the statement was made.

Article 12 of the 1975 *Declaration* provides that "Any statement which is established to have been made as a result of torture or other cruel, inhuman or degrading treatment or punishment may not be invoked as evidence against the person concerned or against any other person in any proceedings". Unlike this provision of the *Declaration*, article 15 of the present *Convention* applies exclusively to torture.

The rule laid down in article 15 would seem to be based on two different considerations. First of all, it is clear that a statement made under torture is often an unreliable statement, and it could therefore be contrary to the principle of "fair trial" to invoke such a statement as evidence before a court. Even in countries whose court procedures are based on a free evaluation of all evidence, it is hardly acceptable that a statement made under torture should be allowed to play any part in court proceedings.

In the second place, it should be recalled that torture is often aimed at ensuring evidence in judicial proceedings. Consequently, if a statement made under torture cannot be invoked as evidence, an important reason for using torture is removed, and the prohibition against the use of such statements as evidence before a court can therefore have the indirect effect of preventing torture.

While article 12 of the 1975 *Declaration* provides that such statements may not be invoked as evidence against any persons in any proceedings, article 15 of the *Convention* adds an exception to this principle. The rule that evidence of this kind cannot be accepted does not apply if the statement is invoked against the alleged torturer in order to prove that the statement was made.

However, when the statement is invoked in such a manner, the intention is not to prove that the statement is a true statement. The purpose is rather to prove that a specific statement was made under torture and presumably that the tortured person would not otherwise have made the same statement, because it was untrue or because it disclosed certain information which he would not otherwise have been prepared to disclose. Consequently, the exception is more apparent than real. It does not affect the validity of the principle that the facts appearing from a statement made under torture should not be invoked in court proceedings as if they were true facts.

Article 16

1. Each State Party shall undertake to prevent in any territory under its jurisdiction other acts of cruel, inhuman or degrading treatment or punishment which do not amount to torture as defined in article 1, when such acts are committed by or at the instigation of or with the consent or acquiescence of a public official or other person acting in an official capacity. In particular, the obligations contained in articles 10, 11, 12 and 13 shall apply with the substitution for references to torture of references to other forms of cruel, inhuman or degrading treatment or punishment.

2. The provisions of this Convention are without prejudice to the provisions of any other international instrument or national law which prohibits cruel, inhuman or degrading treatment or punishment or which relates to extradition or expulsion.

The United Nations General Assembly instructed the Commission on Human Rights, in its resolution 32/62 of 1977, to draw up a draft convention against torture and other cruel, inhuman or degrading treatment or punishment. The request was repeated in several subsequent resolutions.

When the Working Group set up by the Commission studied this question, it found first of all that, while the concept of torture could be defined in reasonably precise terms, it was impossible to draft a precise definition of other cruel, inhuman or degrading treatment or punishment. Secondly, since the convention was to impose upon the States Parties many binding legal obligations which would be reflected in the penal and procedural laws of these States, it was hardly possible to attach these obligations to a vague concept like cruel, inhuman or degrading treatment or punishment.

On the other hand, the Working Group admitted that the convention should also contain some obligations of a more general character which could be made applicable both to torture and to other cruel, inhuman or degrading treatment or punishment. There were, however, different opinions within the Working Group as to which undertakings in the convention should also apply to such treatment and punishment.

In *paragraph 1* of article 16, the States Parties first make a general undertaking to prevent in any territories under their jurisdiction acts of cruel, inhuman or degrading treatment or punishment not amounting to torture, where such acts are committed by or at the instigation of or with the consent or acquiescence of a public official or other person acting in an official capacity. This provision corresponds basically to the general obligation in article 2, paragraph 1, to take effective measures to prevent acts of torture; and as in article 1, paragraph 1, only acts for which the public authorities can be held responsible are included in the undertakings of the States Parties. As regards the interpretation of the term "territory under the jurisdiction of a State Party", the same considerations apply as with regard to article 5.

Whereas article 16 specifies the category of persons bearing responsibility for the acts of cruel, inhuman or degrading treatment or punishment in the same sense as article 1 with regard to those responsible for torture, namely public officials or other persons acting in an official capacity, the text does not contain any particulars as to the victims of these acts. In this respect, too, it resembles article 1. However, this does not mean that the category of victims is indefinite. In view of the history of the *Convention*, the victims of acts referred to in article 16 must be understood as consisting of persons who are deprived of their liberty or who are otherwise under the factual power or control of the person responsible for the treatment or punishment. The reasons for this interpretation are the same as those set out in the foregoing comments under article 1 with regard to the victims of torture.[9]

Although the meaning of article 16 corresponds to the purport of article 1 in this respect, there is an important difference between the two articles in another respect. Unlike in the definition of torture in article 1, no reference is made to the purpose of the act in the provision dealing with other cruel, inhuman or degrading treatment or punishment. It therefore seems justified to conclude that the purpose of the act is irrelevant in determining whether or not the act should be considered to constitute cruel, inhuman or degrading treatment or punishment.

In the second sentence of paragraph 1, it is indicated that, in particular, the obligations in articles 10, 11, 12 and 13 shall also apply to other cruel, inhuman or degrading treatment or punishment. During the *travaux préparatoires*, there were for some time different views on whether or not the obligations in articles 3, 14 and 15 should also apply to such treatment and punishment. In the end it was decided not to include any reference to these articles.

In *paragraph 2*, it is made clear that a wider protection in international instruments or national law shall not be affected by the limited protection which the *Convention* gives against other cruel, inhuman or degrading treatment or punishment. A similar clarification is included with regard to international instruments or national law relating to extradition or expulsion. Consequently, insofar as it might be possible to derive from other international or national legal instruments a prohibition against extradition or expulsion to a country where the extradited or expelled person might be exposed to cruel, inhuman or degrading treatment or punishment falling short of torture, the fact that article 3 of the present *Convention* only deals with torture should not be interpreted as limiting the prohibition against extradition or expulsion which follows from such other instruments.

2. Annotations on Part II: Implementation provisions

Part II, consisting of articles 17 to 24, contains provisions regarding international supervision of the implementation of the *Convention.* In establishing a special body for this purpose, the Committee against Torture, the *Convention* follows the example of other human rights treaties concluded under the aegis of the United Nations, in particular the 1965 *International Convention on the Elimination of All Forms of Racial Discrimination* (the *CERD Convention*), the 1966 *International Covenant on Civil and Political Rights*, and the 1979 *Convention on the Elimination of All Forms of Discrimination against Women* (the *CEDAW Convention*), which provided for the creation of, respectively, the

[9] See *supra* pp. 120–121.

Committee on the Elimination of Racial Discrimination (CERD), the Human Rights Committee, and the Committee on the Elimination of Discrimination agaist Women (CEDAW). Many elements of the implementation system set out in Part II have been borrowed from these three treaties. On the other hand, the system includes several elements which are new in comparison with those earlier treaties. In particular, the procedure regarding inquiries dealt with in article 20 has no precedent in other human rights treaties of the UN.

The basic rules concerning the composition and the *modus operandi* of the Committee against Torture are contained in articles 17 and 18. These articles have been modelled after the relatively simple articles 8 and 10 of the *CERD Convention* and articles 17, 19 and 20 of the *CEDAW Convention*, rather than after the more complicated provisions contained in articles 28 to 39 of the *Covenant on Civil and Political Rights*. At the same time, the authors of the present *Convention* incorporated in the formulation of these rules several minor modifications which they considered preferable from the point of view of logic and consistency.

Article 17

1. There shall be established a Committee against Torture (hereinafter referred to as the Committee) which shall carry out the functions hereinafter provided. The Committee shall consist of ten experts of high moral standing and recognized competence in the field of human rights, who shall serve in their personal capacity. The experts shall be elected by the States Parties, consideration being given to equitable geographical distribution and to the usefulness of the participation of some persons having legal experience.

2. The members of the Committee shall be elected by secret ballot from a list of persons nominated by States Parties. Each State Party may nominate one person from among its own nationals. States Parties shall bear in mind the usefulness of nominating persons who are also members of the Human Rights Committee established under the International Covenant on Civil and Political Rights and who are willing to serve on the Committee against Torture.

3. Elections of the members of the Committee shall be held at biennial meetings of States Parties convened by the Secretary-General of the United Nations. At those meetings, for which two thirds of the States Parties shall constitute a quorum, the persons elected to the Committee shall be those who obtain the largest number of votes and an absolute majority of the votes of the representatives of States Parties present and voting.

4. The initial election shall be held no later than six months after the date of the entry into force of this Convention. At least four months before the date of each election, the Secretary-General of the United Nations shall address a letter to the

States Parties inviting them to submit their nominations within three months. The Secretary-General shall prepare a list in alphabetical order of all persons thus nominated, indicating the States Parties which have nominated them, and shall submit it to the States Parties.

5. The members of the Committee shall be elected for a term of four years. They shall be eligible for re-election if renominated. However, the term of five of the members elected at the first election shall expire at the end of two years; immediately after the first election the names of these five members shall be chosen by lot by the chairman of the meeting referred to in paragraph 3 of this article.

6. If a member of the Committee dies or resigns or for any other cause can no longer perform his Committee duties, the State Party which nominated him shall appoint another expert from among its nationals to serve for the remainder of his term, subject to the approval of the majority of the States Parties. The approval shall be considered given unless half or more of the States Parties respond negatively within six weeks after having been informed by the Secretary-General of the United Nations of the proposed appointment.

7. States Parties shall be responsible for the expenses of the members of the Committee while they are in performance of Committee duties.

This article regulates the composition of the Committee against Torture, the election of its members, the terms of office of these members, and the filling of casual vacancies.

According to *paragraph 1* the Committee shall consist of ten members. This is considerably less than the membership of the Human Rights Committee (eighteen members), the CERD (eighteen members) and the CEDAW (initially eighteen and eventually twenty-three members). A total of ten members was considered sufficient because the subject-matter to be dealt with by the Committee is more specific than the wide range of problems which the other committees have to handle. Just like the members of those other committees, the members "shall serve in their personal capacity", which means that they shall exercise their functions as Committee members on the basis of their own knowledge, experience and judgement and that they shall not act on behalf of the government which nominated them or on behalf of the country of their nationality. The members are described as "experts", as are the members of the CERD and the CEDAW. The requirement that they should be persons "of high moral standing and recognized competence in the field of human rights" is identical with a formula contained in article 28 of the *Covenant* regarding the members of the Human Rights Committee. The same applies to the provision that consideration shall be given to "the usefulness of the participation of some persons having legal experience". The requirement that consideration shall be given to "equitable geographical distribution" corresponds with similar provisions in article 8 of the *CERD Convention*, article 31 of the *Covenant* and article 17 of the *CEDAW Convention*. On the other hand, these three treaties provide, in the same context, that consideration shall also be given to the representation of "the different forms of civilization" and of "the principal legal systems". This provision has not been taken over in the present *Convention*.

The first two sentences of *paragraph 2* are identical with the corresponding provisions of the *CERD* and *CEDAW Conventions*. The third sentence, concerning the usefulness of nominating persons who are also members of the Human Rights Committee, represents a new element which has the following background. During the elaboration of the *Convention*, Sweden had initially proposed to entrust the task of supervising its implementation to the existing Human Rights Committee.[10] This set-up met with objections, in particular on the part of the Legal Counsel of the UN.[11] Sweden then submitted new proposals whereby the *Convention* would establish a special body for this purpose, the Committee against Torture, which should be composed of nationals of the States Parties and, so far as possible, of persons who were also members of the Human Rights Committee.[12] During the discussion in the Working Group this requirement was considered too stringent by several delegations. This led to the less obligatory formula that "States Parties shall bear in mind the usefulness of nominating persons who are also members of the Human Rights Committee".

Good co-ordination between the activities of the Committee against Torture and the Human Rights Committee is desirable at any rate, in particular to avoid differences of interpretation in respect of the concepts of torture and other cruel, inhuman or degrading treatment or punishment. This applies to the consideration of States Parties' reports on measures they have taken as well as to the consideration of communications of States or individuals under the optional complaint procedures.

The election system set out in the next three paragraphs is essentially similar to that of the *Covenant* and the *CERD* and *CEDAW Conventions*. However, the authors of the present *Convention* have tried to formulate this system in a more convenient manner.

Paragraph 3 contains general rules on the election meetings of the States Parties. In the other three treaties the corresponding rules are preceded by other provisions, *inter alia* regarding the initial meeting. Moreover, those treaties do not state explicitly that the election meetings are biennial; this only follows implicitly from the provisions concerning the terms of office of the committee members. In contrast with these treaties, the present *Convention* does not provide that the election meetings shall be held at UN headquarters.

Paragraph 4 mentions time-limits which conform to the corresponding

---

[10] See Appendix 6, articles 16 to 21.
[11] *Cf. supra* p. 76.
[12] See Appendix 10, article 17.

provisions of the *Covenant* and differ slightly from those of the *CERD* and *CEDAW Conventions*. The latter *Conventions* provide that the initial meeting shall be held *six* months after the entry into force of the Convention, and that the Secretary-General shall invite the States Parties at least *three* months before the date of each election to submit their nominations within *two* months.

Paragraph 5 makes it clear that the Committee members serve for a term of four years according to a scheme under which half of the membership is elected every two years. A similar alternating scheme applies to the Human Rights Committee as well as to the CERD and the CEDAW. In this way a considerable degree of continuity in the work of these bodies is ensured, since the new members can always benefit from the experience of at least half the membership. Just like the *Covenant*, the present *Convention* specifies that the members are eligible for re-election if renominated. This paragraph also conforms to the Covenant in providing that, after the first election, the chairman of the election meeting shall choose by lot the members who will serve for two years instead of four years, and not the chairman of the Committee as stated in the *CERD* and *CEDAW Conventions.*

Paragraph 6 concerning the filling of vacancies occurring during a term of office differs from the corresponding provisions of the *Covenant* as well as the *CERD* and *CEDAW Conventions*. Although the authors of the present *Convention* agreed that an elaborate system, as contained in articles 33 and 34 of the *Covenant*, was not necessary for the Committee against Torture, they did not want simply to copy the provision contained in article 8, paragraph 5 (b), of the *CERD Convention* and article 17, paragraph 7, of the *CEDAW Convention*. Unlike that provision, the present *Convention* does not use the term "casual vacancies" but circumscribes this concept, and does not make replacement subject to the approval of the Committee but makes it subject to the approval of the majority of the States Parties. The last sentence of paragraph 6 makes sure that this requirement will not lead to undue delays.

Paragraph 7 is identical with article 8, paragraph 6, of the *CERD Convention*. It does not mean that the expenses of an individual Committee member shall be borne by the State Party which has nominated him, but that all the States Parties shall be collectively responsible for the joint expenses of all the Committee members. The way of apportionment of these costs among the States Parties is left open. During the drafting of the present *Convention* this matter was discussed on the basis of a more elaborate formula proposed by the chairman-rapporteur of the Working Group.[13] His proposal was deemed too specific by several delegations. After various alternatives had been discussed, the Group eventually decided to make the text conform to the corresponding provision of the *CERD Convention*. It was not possible to turn to the

[13] See Appendix 12, article 17, paragraph 7.

Covenant or to the *CEDAW Convention* for guidance in this matter, because neither of them provides for any financial responsibility of the States Parties for the expenses of the supervisory body, all such expenses being borne by the United Nations.

After the entry into force of the *Convention*, the States Parties decided at their first meeting that the expenses shall be apportioned among the States Parties proportionately on the basis of the United Nations scale of assessment, it being understood that in no case the share of a single State Party shall be in excess of 25% of the expenses estimated for the year concerned.[14]

Article 18

1. The Committee shall elect its officers for a term of two years. They may be re-elected.

2. The Committee shall establish its own rules of procedure, but these rules shall provide, inter alia, that:

(a) Six members shall constitute a quorum;

(b) Decisions of the Committee shall be made by a majority vote of the members present.

3. The Secretary-General of the United Nations shall provide the necessary staff and facilities for the effective performance of the functions of the Committee under this Convention.

4. The Secretary-General of the United Nations shall convene the initial meeting of the Committee. After its initial meeting, the Committee shall meet at such times as shall be provided in its rules of procedure.

5. The States Parties shall be responsible for expenses incurred in connection with the holding of meetings of the States Parties and of the Committee, including reimbursement to the United Nations for any expenses, such as the cost of staff and facilities, incurred by the United Nations pursuant to paragraph 3 of this article.

This article deals with the internal procedures of the Committee, with its staff and other facilities and with the responsibility for expenses relating to its election and functioning. In contrast with the *CERD* and *CEDAW Conventions*, which deal with the internal procedures and the staff and other facilities of the respective Committees in provisions that follow after an article on the reporting obligations of the States Parties, the authors of the present *Convention* thought it more appropriate to place such provisions before the

---

[14] See *supra* Chapter III, section 13.

articles concerning specific implementation procedures such as the system of reporting by the States Parties.

Paragraphs 1, 2, 3 and *4* are modelled on article 39, paragraphs 1 and 2, article 36 and article 37, paragraphs 1 and 2, of the *Covenant*. On the other hand, *paragraph 5* has no precedent in other human rights treaties of the United Nations. The *Covenant* and the *CEDAW Convention* make the United Nations responsible for all costs incurred in connection with those treaties, both by the UN itself and by the bodies established under those treaties. In the case of the *CERD Convention*, the expenses of CERD members incurred in performance of Committee duties have to be borne by the States Parties, but the expenses incurred by the UN in providing services to the Committee and the meetings of the States Parties are borne by the UN. According to the present *Convention*, all such expenses shall be reimbursed to the UN by the States Parties.

After the entry into force of the *Convention*, the States Parties decided at their first meeting that the expenses shall be apportioned among the States Parties proportionately on the basis of the United Nations scale of assessment, it being understood that in no case the share of a single State Party shall be in excess of 25% of the expenses estimated for the year concerned.[15]

Article 19

1. The States Parties shall submit to the Committee, through the Secretary-General of the United Nations, reports on the measures they have taken to give effect to their undertakings under this Convention, within one year after the entry into force of the Convention for the State Party concerned. Thereafter the States Parties shall submit supplementary reports every four years on any new measures taken and such other reports as the Committee may request.

2. The Secretary-General of the United Nations shall transmit the reports to all States Parties.

3. Each report shall be considered by the Committee which may make such general comments on the report as it may consider appropriate and shall forward these to the State Party concerned. That State Party may respond with any observations it chooses to the Committee.

4. The Committee may, at its discretion, decide to include any comments made by it in accordance with paragraph 3 of this article, together with the observations thereon received from the State Party concerned, in its annual report made in accordance with article 24. If so requested by the State Party concerned, the

---

[15] See *supra* Chapter III, section 13.

Committee may also include a copy of the report submitted under paragraph 1 of this article.

This article regulates the States Parties' obligations to submit reports on the implementation of the *Convention*, and lays down what action the Committee shall or may undertake in relation to those reports. The article is the result of extensive discussions which even continued up to the very last moment before the Third Committee of the General Assembly decided on the definitive text of the *Convention.*

Comparable reporting procedures are included in the *Covenant*[16] and in the *CERD* and *CEDAW Conventions*. Each of these treaties provides for the submission of a first report within one year after the entry into force of the treaty for the State Party concerned. The *CERD Convention* obliges the States Parties thereafter to submit further reports every two years and whenever the CERD so requests. The *CEDAW Convention* obliges the States Parties to submit further reports at least every four years and whenever the CEDAW so requests. On the other hand, the *Covenant* does not provide expressly for a system of periodic reporting; it only provides that the States Parties shall submit reports within one year of the entry into force and thereafter whenever the Human Rights Committee so requests. Meanwhile, the Human Rights Committee decided in 1981 that the States Parties to the *Covenant* shall regularly submit reports every five years.

Paragraph 1 of article 19 provides for a four-year reporting cycle, but unlike the *Covenant* and the *CERD* and *CEDAW Conventions* it makes it clear that the regular supplementary reports are not of the same character as the comprehensive initial report since such reports will only relate to "any new measures taken". A further difference is that under those treaties the States Parties shall submit their reports to the Secretary-General of the UN, for consideration by the respective Committees, whereas under the present *Convention* the States Parties shall submit their reports to the Committee itself, through the Secretary-General of the UN.

According to paragraph 1, each State Party shall submit a report within one year after the *Convention* entered into force for it. This report shall relate to the measures the State Party has taken to give effect to its undertakings under the *Convention*. This formula should not be misunderstood as if referring solely to measures which the State concerned has adopted with the express purpose of implementing the *Convention*. As a matter of course it covers all measures which in fact give effect to undertakings under the *Convention*, whatever the time at which they were adopted and whatever the reasons underlying their adoption.

---

[16] Besides the *International Covenant on Civil and Political Rights*, a system of reporting by States Parties is also included in the *International Covenant on Economic, Social and Cultural Rights.*

Paragraph 1 does not elaborate on the kinds of measures to be reported on. In particular it does not refer to "legislative, judicial, administrative or other measures" as is done in article 9 of the *CERD Convention* and article 18 of the *CEDAW Convention*. Following the example of article 40 of the *Covenant*, the paragraph simply refers to "measures". This is certainly not meant to be narrower in scope than the formula used in the *CERD* and *CEDAW Conventions*. In this context it should be recalled that article 2, paragraph 1, of the present *Convention* itself refers to "effective legislative, administrative, judicial or other measures". Furthermore, the fact that the text refers to measures taken by the States Parties does not mean that it only relates to measures taken by the central government of the State Party concerned. Reports under this article may include information on measures taken by local authorities or by public officials and public bodies which are independent of the central government. Whereas the term "measures" should be interpreted in a wide sense, it should also be noted that the present *Convention* does not ask explicitly for information on the "progress" made in its implementation, as is done in the *Covenant* and in the *CEDAW Convention*.

Paragraph 2 stipulates that the Secretary-General shall transmit the reports to all States Parties. The *Covenant* and the *CERD* and *CEDAW Conventions* do not contain a similar provision.

According to *paragraph 3* the reports shall be considered by the Committee. Like the other treaties, the present *Convention* does not specify a procedure for the consideration of the reports. It is up to the Committee to decide whether it will follow the practice established by the CERD and the Human Rights Committee, which orally discuss each report with representatives of the State Party concerned in meetings that are open to the public. On the other hand, paragraph 3 explicitly provides for a written dialogue between the Committee and a specific reporting State, a provision that is not found in equally unambiguous terms in earlier UN treaties on human rights.

Under article 40 of the *Covenant* the Human Rights Committee, after having studied the reports submitted by the States Parties, may transmit to the States Parties "its reports" (obviously its own reports concerning its study of the States Parties' reports) and "such general comments as it may consider appropriate", and the States Parties may submit to the Committee observations on its comments. Under article 9 of the *CERD Convention* and article 21 of the *CEDAW Convention*, the CERD and the CEDAW may make "suggestions and general recommendations based on the examination of reports and information received from the States Parties", and such suggestions and general recommendations may be commented upon by the States Parties. It is a moot point whether or not these provisions allow the respective Committees to address comments or suggestions to a specific State Party. The present *Convention* leaves no doubt on this question in its formulation of paragraph 3 of article 19, since this paragraph refers to comments "on the report" (singular) and to the forwarding of such comments "to the State Party concerned" (singular). Those comments are defined as "general" in accordance with the example of the *Covenant.*

It will be up to the Committee to determine the confines of the concept "general comments". On the one hand it will bear in mind that the General Assembly substituted this term for the expression "comments or suggestions" on which no agreement had been reached in the Commission on Human Rights. On the other hand the text of paragraph 3 presupposes that such general comments relate to a specific report of a specific State Party. In view of the wording of this paragraph, it could even be argued that the Committee would not be authorized to address comments to all States Parties collectively based on the examination of a number of reports. This is certainly not something the authors of the *Convention* intended.

Paragraph 4 represent another innovative element in the implementation system of the *Convention.* The reader of this provision should be aware of the fact that the annual reports of the Committee, made in accordance with article 24, are public reports. Consequently, the Committee is authorized to *publish* the general comments which it has addressed to an individual State Party. The words "at its discretion" make it clear that the Committee is free to decide whether or not to use this possibility. However, if it decides to publish such comments, it is obliged also to publish the observations received thereon from the State Party concerned. On the other hand, the Committee is not obliged to include in its own annual report a copy of the State Party's report, even if this State so requests in accordance with the last sentence of the paragraph. In this connection one should take into account that all reports of States Parties under paragraph 1 may be expected anyhow to be published separately, in accordance with the practice followed so far with regard to the State reports submitted under the *Covenant* and the *CERD* and *CEDAW Conventions.*

Article 20

1. If the Committee receives reliable information which appears to it to contain well-founded indications that torture is being systematically practised in the territory of a State Party, the Committee shall invite that State Party to co-operate in the examination of the information and to this end to submit observations with regard to the information concerned.

2. Taking into account any observations which may have been submitted by the State Party concerned, as well as any other relevant information available to it, the Committee may, if it decides that this is warranted, designate one or more of its members to make a confidential inquiry and to report to the Committee urgently.

3. If an inquiry is made in accordance with paragraph 2 of this article, the

Committee shall seek the co-operation of the State Party concerned. In agreement with that State Party, such an inquiry may include a visit to its territory.

4. After examining the findings of its member or members submitted in accordance with paragraph 2 of this article, the Committee shall transmit these findings to the State Party concerned together with any comments or suggestions which seem appropriate in view of the situation.

5. All the proceedings of the Committee referred to in paragraphs 1 to 4 of this article shall be confidential, and at all stages of the proceedings the co-operation of the State Party shall be sought. After such proceedings have been completed with regard to an inquiry made in accordance with paragraph 2, the Committee may, after consultations with the State Party concerned, decide to include a summary account of the results of the proceedings in its annual report made in accordance with article 24.

Article 20 represents the most important new element in the implementation system of the *Convention* and has been the object of much controversy during the last stages of the preparatory work. It has no precedent in earlier human rights treaties. Agreement with regard to this article was only achieved on the day the Third Committee of the General Assembly was to decide on the definitive text of the *Convention.* This agreement included the insertion of a new provision in the *Convention*, in the form of article 28, which makes it possible for States Parties to opt out of the application of article 20.

Article 20 authorizes the Committee to institute, at its own initiative, an inquiry into the occurrence of a systematic practice of torture in the territory of a State Party. It should be noted that the procedure set out in article 20 only applies to torture and not to other cruel, inhuman or degrading treatment or punishment. The idea of including such an inquiry procedure in the *Convention* was inspired to some degree by the procedure set out in resolution 1503 of the Economic and Social Council of the United Nations. By that resolution, adopted in 1970, the Council authorized the UN Commission on Human Rights under certain conditions, in connection with communications received from non-governmental sources, to examine particular situations which appear to reveal a consistent pattern of gross and reliably attested violations of human rights. All actions undertaken under this resolution shall remain confidential until such time as the Commission may decide to make recommendations to the Council. More than once the Commission has made use of this method of "going public" if it considered that a country under examination clearly failed to co-operate during the confidential stage of the procedure.

The text of article 20, as it developed in the course of the discussions in Geneva and New York, provides for a step-by-step approach which gives ample opportunity to the State Party concerned to make its views on the matter known to the Committee. An important feature of the procedure is that the matter is dealt with from the outset on a confidential basis. However, this requirement of confidentiality is not maintained up to the very last stage. At the end of the procedure the Committee may decide to publish some information relating to the inquiry and its follow-up.

According to *paragraph 1* the procedure is set in motion if the Committee receives reliable information which appears to it to contain well-founded indications that torture is being systematically practised in the territory of a State Party. The text contains no specifications as to the sources of such information. In principle any kind of source may come under consideration as long as the information provided can be deemed reliable. The Committee will have to assess first of all this question of reliability. In the second place it will have to determine whether or not the information appears to contain well-founded indications of the existence of a systematic practice of torture in the territory of a State Party. The consideration of these two questions represents the first step of the procedure. If the Committee concludes that the information is reliable and that it appears to contain well-founded indications of the purport mentioned above, it is not free to let the matter rest: the Committee is then obliged to move to the second step of the procedure. This step consists of giving the State Party concerned an opportunity to co-operate in the examination of the information and to submit observations thereon. When the Committee informs the State Party about the information received, it is, of course, not obliged to divulge the identity of its sources if this might entail serious risks on their part.

Paragraph 2 describes the third step of the procedure. After having given the State Party concerned an opportunity to submit its observations, the Committee may designate one or more of its members to make a confidential inquiry. The Committee may only do so if it has decided that this is warranted, in view of all the relevant information available to it. Paragraph 2 opens by mentioning the observations which may have been submitted by the State Party concerned, in this way underlining the particular importance of this category of information. As a rule one may expect that a State Party will respond to an invitation of the Committee in accordance with paragraph 1. Nevertheless, if the State Party fails to do so this cannot prevent the Committee from exercising its competence under paragraph 2.

Paragraph 3 deals with the fourth step of the procedure, namely the inquiry itself. In this context the Committee shall again seek the co-operation of the State Party concerned. In agreement with that State the inquiry may include a visit to its territory. If the State Party concerned refuses to co-operate, this will make the inquiry more difficult to carry out. On the other hand, such a refusal will not be helpful to dispel the suspicion that the indications were well-founded. After the inquiry has been completed, the member or members having conducted it shall submit a report to the Committee in accordance with the last part of paragraph 2.

Paragraph 4 deals with the fifth and the sixth step of the procedure. The fifth step consists of the examination by the Committee of the findings of the inquiry and the formulation of comments or suggestions if the Committee considers this appropriate. Suggestions by the Committee will be called for particularly should the inquiry confirm that systematic torture did occur. After the completion of the fifth step the Committee is again not free to let the matter rest. It is obliged to transmit the findings of the inquiry to the State Party concerned, together with its comments or suggestions. This is the sixth step of the procedure.

Paragraph 5 lays down first of all that all the proceedings under the previous paragraphs shall be confidential. It emphasizes once again that the co-operation of the State Party concerned shall be sought at all stages of the proceedings. In the final stage it will of course be particularly relevant in what way the State Party concerned has reacted to the findings of the inquiry and to the comments or suggestions of the Committee.

The second sentence of paragraph 5 deals with the seventh step of the procedure. This step consists of a decision by the Committee as to whether or not it will publish a summary account of the results of the proceedings in its annual report. Such an account will necessarily have to disclose that there existed well-founded indications concerning systematic torture and that a confidential inquiry was undertaken. The results of the proceedings comprise more than just the findings of the inquiry: they may include the comments or suggestions of the Committee as well as the reaction thereto of the State Party concerned. It is possible that this reaction was positive and included the taking of effective measures to remedy the situation. It is also possible that the reaction was negative. By having the option of "going public" the Committee disposes of an important means of pressure in order to induce the State Party concerned to co-operate and to end the practice of torture, if such a practice really exists. The Committee may "reward" such co-operation by deciding to keep the entire matter confidential.

Before the Committee decides on publishing a summary account in its annual report, it is obliged to conduct consultations with the State Party concerned, but it is not obliged to refrain from such publication if that State objects to it. On the other hand, if the State agrees the Committee can normally be expected to proceed to publishing the account. The State Party concerned may have itself an interest in such publication, for instance if suspicions of torture practices in its territory had already become widely known and if the inquiry had established that those suspicions were unfounded or if the State has taken satisfactory measures to make an end to such practices.

Finally, it should be recalled that article 20 has to be read in conjunction with article 28 which enables States to declare, at the time they become Parties to the *Convention*, that they do not recognize the competence of the Committee provided for in article 20.

Article 21

1. A State Party to this Convention may at any time declare under this article that it recognizes the competence of the Committee to receive and consider communications to the effect that a State Party claims that another State Party is not fulfilling its obligations under this Convention. Such communications may be received and considered according to the procedures laid down in this article only if submitted by a State Party which has made a declaration recognizing in regard to itself the competence of the Committee. No communication shall be dealt with by the Committee under this article if it concerns a State Party which has not made such a declaration. Communications received under this article shall be dealt with in accordance with the following procedure:

(a) If a State Party considers that another State Party is not giving effect to the provisions of this Convention, it may, by written communication, bring the matter to the attention of that State Party. Within three months after the receipt of the communication the receiving State shall afford the State which sent the communication an explanation or any other statement in writing clarifying the matter, which should include, to the extent possible and pertinent, reference to domestic procedures and remedies taken, pending or available in the matter;

(b) If the matter is not adjusted to the satisfaction of both States Parties concerned within six months after the receipt by the receiving State of the initial communication, either State shall have the right to refer the matter to the Committee, by notice given to the Committee and to the other State;

(c) The Committee shall deal with a matter referred to it under this article only after it has ascertained that all domestic remedies have been invoked and exhausted in the matter, in conformity with the generally recognized principles of international law. This shall not be the rule where the application of the remedies is unreasonably prolonged or is unlikely to bring effective relief to the person who is the victim of the violation of this Convention;

(d) The Committee shall hold closed meetings when examining communications under this article;

(e) Subject to the provisions of subparagraph (c), the Committee shall make available its good offices to the States Parties concerned with a view to a friendly solution of the matter on the basis of respect for the obligations provided for in this Convention. For this purpose, the Committee may, when appropriate, set up an ad hoc conciliation commission;

(f) In any matter referred to it under this article, the Committee may call upon the States Parties concerned, referred to in subparagraph (b), to supply any relevant information;

(g) The States Parties concerned, referred to in subparagraph (b), shall have the

right to be represented when the matter is being considered by the Committee and to make submissions orally and/or in writing;

(h) The Committee shall, within twelve months after the date of receipt of notice under subparagraph (b), submit a report:

(i) If a solution within the terms of subparagraph (e) is reached, the Committee shall confine its report to a brief statement of the facts and of the solution reached;

(ii) If a solution within the terms of subparagraph (e) is not reached, the Committee shall confine its report to a brief statement of the facts; the written submissions and record of the oral submissions made by the States Parties concerned shall be attached to the report.

In every matter, the report shall be communicated to the States Parties concerned.

2. The provisions of this article shall come into force when five States Parties to this Convention have made declarations under paragraph 1 of this article. Such declarations shall be deposited by the States Parties with the Secretary-General of the United Nations, who shall transmit copies thereof to the other States Parties. A declaration may be withdrawn at any time by notification to the Secretary-General. Such a withdrawal shall not prejudice the consideration of any matter which is the subject of a communication already transmitted under this article; no further communication by any State Party shall be received under this article after the notification of withdrawal of the declaration has been received by the Secretary-General, unless the State Party concerned has made a new declaration.

This article provides for a procedure for dealing with complaints of States Parties concerning non-fulfilment of obligations under the *Convention* on the part of other States Parties. The procedure is modelled after similar State complaint procedures in the *CERD Convention* and the *Covenant*. Comparable State complaint procedures are also included in the European *Convention for the Protection of Human Rights and Fundamental Freedoms*, the *American Convention on Human Rights* and the *African Charter on Human and Peoples' Rights*. As is the case with all these treaties the present *Convention* does not use the word "complaint" as such.

The procedure is optional, like the State complaint procedure of the *Covenant* but unlike the mandatory State complaint procedure of the *CERD Convention*. The optional character is laid down in the opening phrase of paragraph 1, providing that a State Party may at any time declare that it recognizes the competence of the Committee under this article, and in the third phrase of paragraph 2, providing that such a declaration may be withdrawn at any time. This optional system is based on reciprocity: a State Party having made such a declaration only undertakes to accept consideration by the Committee of complaints brought by a State Party which has itself also declared that it recognizes the competence of the Committee under this article.

Most of the text of the article has been borrowed from the corresponding article 41 of the *Covenant*. Apart from purely editorial changes, article 21 deviates on the following points from the system set out in the *Covenant*.

Subparagraph (c) of paragraph 1 waives the requirement of exhaustion of domestic remedies not only where the application of the remedies is unreasonably prolonged but also where it "is unlikely to bring effective relief to the person who is the victim of the violation of this Convention".

Subparagraph (e) of paragraph 1 refers to a friendly solution on the basis of "respect for the obligations provided for in this Convention". The *Convention* does not include elaborate provisions concerning the establishment and *modus operandi* of an *ad hoc* conciliation commission as contained in article 42 of the *Covenant*. Instead, the possibility of setting up such a commission is summarily mentioned in the second sentence of this subparagraph.

Paragraph 2 makes the application of article 21 dependent on the acceptance of the competence of the Committee under this article by at least five States Parties.

Article 22

1. A State Party to this Convention may at any time declare under this article that it recognizes the competence of the Committee to receive and consider communications from or on behalf of individuals subject to its jurisdiction who claim to be victims of a violation by a State Party of the provisions of the Convention. No communication shall be received by the Committee if it concerns a State Party which has not made such a declaration.

2. The Committee shall consider inadmissible any communication under this article which is anonymous or which it considers to be an abuse of the right of submission of such communications or to be incompatible with the provisions of this Convention.

3. Subject to the provisions of paragraph 2, the Committee shall bring any communications submitted to it under this article to the attention of the State Party of this Convention which has made a declaration under paragraph 1 and is alleged to be violating any provisions of the Convention. Within six months, the receiving State shall submit to the Committee written explanations or statements clarifying the matter and the remedy, if any, that may have been taken by that State.

4. The Committee shall consider communications received under this article in the light of all information made available to it by or on behalf of the individual and by the State Party concerned.

5. The Committee shall not consider any communications from an individual under this article unless it has ascertained that:

(a) The same matter has not been, and is not being, examined under another procedure of international investigation or settlement;

(b) The individual has exhausted all available domestic remedies; this shall not be the rule where the application of the remedies is unreasonably prolonged or is unlikely to bring effective relief to the person who is the victim of the violation of this Convention.

6. The Committee shall hold closed meetings when examining communications under this article.

7. The Committee shall forward its views to the State Party concerned and to the individual.

8. The provisions of this article shall come into force when five States Parties to this Convention have made declarations under paragraph 1 of this article. Such declarations shall be deposited by the States Parties with the Secretary-General of the United Nations, who shall transmit copies thereof to the other States Parties. A declaration may be withdrawn at any time by notification to the Secretary-General. Such a withdrawal shall not prejudice the consideration of any matter which is the subject of a communication already transmitted under this article; no further communication by or on behalf of an individual shall be received under this article after the notification of withdrawal of the declaration has been received by the Secretary-General, unless the State Party has made a new declaration.

This article sets out a procedure for dealing with complaints of or on behalf of individuals who claim to be victims of a violation of the *Convention* by a State Party. The procedure is modelled after similar individual complaint procedures in the *CERD Convention* and in the *Optional Protocol* to the *Covenant*. Comparable individual complaint procedures are also included in the European *Convention for the Protection of Human Rights and Fundamental Freedoms*, the *American Convention on Human Rights* and the *African Charter on Human and Peoples' Rights*. Like all these treaties the present *Convention* does not use the word "complaint" as such.

The procedure is optional, like the individual complaint procedures contained in the *CERD Convention* and the *Optional Protocol.* The optional character appears from the opening phrase of paragraph 1, providing that a State Party may at any time declare that it recognizes the competence of the Committee under this article, and from the third phrase of paragraph 8, providing that such a declaration may be withdrawn at any time.

Most of the text of the article has been borrowed from the *Optional Protocol* which embodies the procedure for individual complaints relating to the Covenant. Apart from purely editorial changes, article 22 deviates on the following points from the system set out in the *Protocol.*

Paragraph 1 authorizes the Committee to receive and consider communications "from or on behalf of" individuals who claim to be victims of a violation, whereas article 1 of the *Protocol* only refers to communications "from" individuals who claim to be victims of a violation. The paragraph does not specify who is competent to submit a communication on behalf of an individual. It can be assumed, however, that where an individual is personally unable to complain, a communication can be submitted on his behalf, for instance, by a close relative. It is also possible that in certain circumstances a non-governmental organization could be entitled to act on behalf of the individual directly affected.

Pursuant to *paragraph 4*, the Committee is entitled also to take account of information which has not been made available in writing, whereas article 5 of the Protocol only refers to "written information". The formula of the *Convention* is an important improvement which enables the Committee, for example, to hear witnesses and experts when considering a complaint.

Pursuant to *paragraph 5*, subparagraph (a), the Committee is not allowed to consider complaints if the same matter is being examined under another procedure of international investigation or settlement and the same applies if the matter has already "been examined" under such a procedure. The latter limitation is not found in the corresponding article 5, paragraph 2, subparagraph (a) of the *Protocol*, which only refers to the case that the same matter is "being examined" under such a procedure. This limitation implies, *inter alia*, that the Committee is not allowed to consider a complaint on a matter which has already been dealt with in substance by the Human Rights Committee or by the European Commission of Human Rights. If, however, a complaint to another international body has been rejected on a purely formal ground, there is probably no obstacle to a new examination under the present *Convention*.

It should also be noted that an investigation under ECOSOC resolution 1503[17] should not prevent a subsequent individual complaint from being examined by the Committee against Torture, since under the said resolution the investigation concerns a *situation* and not the violation of an individual's right as such.

Paragraph 5, subparagraph (b), waives the requirement of exhaustion of domestic remedies not only where the application of the remedies is unreasonably prolonged but also where it "is unlikely to bring effective relief to the person who is the victim of the violation of this Convention".

Paragraph 8 makes the application of article 22 dependent on acceptance of the competence of the Committtee under this article by at least five States Parties.

[17] *Cf. supra* p. 37.

Article 23

The members of the Committee and of the ad hoc conciliation commissions which may be appointed under article 21, paragraph 1(e), shall be entitled to the facilities, privileges and immunities of experts on mission for the United Nations as laid down in the relevant sections of the Conventions on the Privileges and Immunities of the United Nations.

This article conforms with article 43 of the *Covenant*.

Article 24

The Committee shall submit an annual report on its activities under this Convention to the States Parties and to the General Assembly of the United Nations.

The *Covenant* and the *CERD* and *CEDAW Conventions* also provide that the supervisory bodies established under these instruments shall report annually on their activities to the General Assembly of the United Nations, but do not expressly provide for submission of these reports to the States Parties. The authors of the present *Convention* considered that the responsibility of the Committee against Torture towards the States Parties which have elected it should come first and foremost.

Like the reports of those other supervisory bodies, the annual reports of the Committee are public reports. This is especially relevant in connection with the provisions of article 19, paragraph 4, and article 20, paragraph 5.

3. Annotations on Part III: Final provisions

Article 25

1. This Convention is open for signature by all States.

2. This Convention is subject to ratification. Instruments of ratification shall be deposited with the Secretary-General of the United Nations.

Article 26

This Convention is open to accession by all States. Accession shall be effected by the deposit of an instrument of accession with the Secretary-General of the United Nations.

Article 27

1. This Convention shall enter into force on the thirtieth day after the date of the deposit with the Secretary-General of the United Nations of the twentieth instrument of ratification or accession.

2. For each State ratifying this Convention or acceding to it after the deposit of the twentieth instrument of ratification or accession, the Convention shall enter into force on the thirtieth day after the date of the deposit of its own instrument of ratification or accession.

The reader may be referred to Chapter II for an explanation of the terms "signature", "ratification" and "accession".[18] In conformity with the practice followed in similar treaties concluded under the aegis of the UN, the *Convention* remains open for signature after it has entered into force, whereas on the other hand States are free to accede to the *Convention* even before its entry into force. This implies that, both before and after the entry into force of the *Convention*, States may choose between the option of first signing it and undertaking a binding commitment at a later date by ratification, and the option of undertaking such a commitment immediately by accession.

Article 28

1. Each State may, at the time of signature or ratification of this Convention or accession thereto, declare that it does not recognize the competence of the Committee provided for in article 20.

2. Any State Party having made a reservation in accordance with paragraph 1 of this article may, at any time, withdraw this reservation by notification to the Secretary-General of the United Nations.

This article embodies the opting-out clause proposed by the Byelorussian Soviet Socialist Republic during the consideration of the draft convention at the General Assembly, this being the clause which made agreement possible with regard to article 20. The clause goes less far than making the procedure under article 20 fully optional like the procedures under articles 21 and 22. First of all, States Parties are not bound by articles 21 or 22 as long as they have not positively declared that they accept the application of those articles, whereas States Parties are bound automatically by article 20 unless they have expressly excluded the application of that article. In the second place, a declaration in accordance with article 28 excluding the application of article

[18] See *supra* p. 8.

20 cannot be made at a later time than that of ratification or accession. Consequently, once having bound themselves to the *Convention* without making such a reservation, States Parties can never divest themselves of the competence of the Committee under article 20. The same applies for a State which has made such a reservation but has later withdrawn it in accordance with article 28, paragraph 2. On the other hand, as regards the procedures of article 21 and article 22 States Parties may in principle opt in and out as often as they please.

Article 29

1. Any State Party to this Convention may propose an amendment and file it with the Secretary-General of the United Nations. The Secretary-General shall thereupon communicate the proposed amendment to the States Parties with a request that they notify him whether they favour a conference of States Parties for the purpose of considering and voting upon the proposal. In the event that within four months from the date of such communication at least one third of the States Parties favours such a conference, the Secretary-General shall convene the conference under the auspices of the United Nations. Any amendment adopted by a majority of the States Parties present and voting at the conference shall be submitted by the Secretary-General to all the States Parties for acceptance.

2. An amendment adopted in accordance with paragraph 1 of this article shall enter into force when two thirds of the States Parties to this Convention have notified the Secretary-General of the United Nations that they have accepted it in accordance with their respective constitutional processes.

3. When amendments enter into force, they shall be binding on those States Parties which have accepted them, other States Parties still being bound by the provisions of this Convention and any earlier amendments which they have accepted.

The text of this article is based on article 51 of the *Covenant*, with some editorial changes. There are two differences as compared with the *Covenant* which are more than editorial: the insertion of the words "within four months from the date of such communication" in paragraph 1 and the omission of the requirement of approval by the UN General Assembly in paragraph 2.

Article 30

1. Any dispute between two or more States Parties concerning the interpretation or application of this Convention which cannot be settled through negotiation shall, at the request of one of them, be submitted to arbitration. If within six months from the date of the request for arbitration the Parties are unable to agree on the organization of the arbitration, any one of those Parties may refer the dispute to the International Court of Justice by request in conformity with the Statute of the Court.

2. Each State may, at the time of signature or ratification of this Convention or accession thereto, declare that it does not consider itself bound by paragraph 1 of this article. The other States Parties shall not be bound by paragraph 1 of this article with respect to any State Party having made such a reservation.

3. Any State Party having made a reservation in accordance with paragraph 2 of this article may at any time withdraw this reservation by notification to the Secretary-General of the United Nations.

The text of this article conforms to that of article 29 of the *CEDAW* Convention, apart from some editorial changes.

Article 31

1. A State Party may denounce this Convention by written notification to the Secretary-General of the United Nations. Denunciation becomes effective one year after the date of receipt of the notification by the Secretary-General.

2. Such a denunciation shall not have the effect of releasing the State Party from its obligations under this Convention in regard to any act or omission which occurs prior to the date at which the denunciation becomes effective, nor shall denunciation prejudice in any way the continued consideration of any matter which is already under consideration by the Committee prior to the date at which the denunciation becomes effective.

3. Following the date at which the denunciation of a State Party becomes effective, the Committee shall not commence consideration of any new matter regarding that State.

Unlike the *Covenant* and the *CEDAW Convention* which do not contain any provisions on this question, the present *Convention* has an explicit article on denunciation. Paragraph 1 conforms to article 21 of the *CERD Convention.* Paragraph 2 sets out two additional provisions with a view to limiting the effects of denunciation. The second of these provisions has a precedent in article 12, paragraph 2, of the *Optional Protocol* to the *Covenant*, but its formulation is more precise because it makes it clear, when read together with paragraph 3, that only if the Committee has already commenced consideration of a specific matter such consideration may continue after the denunciation becomes effective.

Article 32

The Secretary–General of the United Nations shall inform all members of the United Nations and all States which have signed this Convention or acceded to it of the following:

(a) Signatures, ratifications and accessions under articles 25 and 26;
(b) The date of entry into force of this Convention under article 27 and the date of the entry into force of any amendments under article 29;
(c) Denunciations under article 31.

Although this may be considered a standard final clause for treaties of which the Secretary-General of the UN is the depositary, a similar provision is not found in, for example, the *CEDAW Convention.*

Article 33

1. This Convention, of which the Arabic, Chinese, English, French, Russian and Spanish texts are equally authentic, shall be deposited with the Secretary-General of the United Nations.

2. The Secretary-General of the United Nations shall transmit certified copies of this Convention to all States.

This is a customary final clause of treaties concluded under the auspices of the United Nations.

Epilogue

In addition to the information which this book is intended to convey on the origins and the contents of the *Convention against Torture and Other Cruel, Inhuman or Degrading Treatment or Punishment*, some comments should be made on its significance.

The entry into force of this *Convention* should be seen as a major step forward on the road towards eradicating the evil of torture. At the same time, one should place the importance of this step in proper perspective. It will probably take a long time before the large majority of States will have adhered to the *Convention*. Even then one cannot expect that the existence of the *Convention* will by itself be sufficient to make torture completely disappear. Much more will be required before all public authorities are really convinced that torture cannot be tolerated under any circumstances.

In the struggle for the protection of human rights it is necessary to be both a sceptic and a believer. In 1975 the adoption of the United Nations *Declaration* was welcomed by many as a tremendous success in the fight against torture. However, during the second half of the nineteen-seventies, that is after the adoption of the *Declaration*, torture may well have been perpetrated in this world on an even larger scale than during the first half. And yet, this is no reason for despair.

In the struggle for human rights, documents are not sufficient. But they are by no means unimportant.

In this connection we should like to recall another epoch in the struggle for human rights, namely the era of Enlightenment in the eighteenth and the first part of the nineteenth century.

All too often torture is referred to as a "medieval" practice. However, this may not be entirely fair to the Middle Ages. In fact, the two centuries immediately following the close of the Middle Ages were a period of remarkable cruelty in the treatment of alleged offenders. It was a period during which capital punishment was applied to an ever-increasing number of offences. It was also a period during which torture was a standard element of criminal procedure in most European countries.

If we compare the situation in Europe at the end of the seventeenth century with the situation at the end of the nineteenth century from the perspective of the occurrence of systematic torture, they are as different as night and day. At the end of the nineteenth century, torture had virtually disappeared in Europe. This radical change was not brought about by forces of nature, but by the dedicated and persevering work of men.

In the course of the eighteenth century, a growing number of individuals in many European countries began to protest against the cruelty which then characterized the administration of criminal justice. It is natural to mention in particular the Italian scholar Cesare Beccaria, whose famous work *Dei delitti e delle pene (On Crimes and Punishments)* made an enormous impact. Many other books and pamphlets were published; associations were founded. The fight against torture was one of the principal elements of the human rights movement which developed in the era of Enlightenment. And this fight *was* successful!

It should be recalled that an important part of this fight concentrated on standard-setting. As a result, national laws were changed in most European countries. The human rights movement brought about a change in mental attitudes, a change in actual practices, and a change in legislation. All these developments went hand-in-hand and mutually reinforced each other.

However, such changes are not irreversible. In the first half of the present century, régimes came to power in some European countries which deliberately used torture on a wide scale as an instrument of policy. This experience was one of the roots of the second human rights movement which was born at about the same time as the United Nations. Under the impact of this new movement an impressive number of international standards have come into being, of which this *Convention* is one of the latest examples.

Of course, one should never think that the final victory has been won, one should always realize that new lapses into cruelty and oppression are possible. But the message conveyed by the experience of 200 years ago is that action for the promotion and protection of human rights is *not* useless, even if its results are not perennial. The fight against torture is an important fight, and standard-setting is an important and indispensable part of that fight. This gives the proper perspective for assessing the significance of the *Convention against Torture and Other Cruel, Inhuman or Degrading Treatment or Punishment.*

Appendices

APPENDIX 1

Convention against Torture and Other Cruel, Inhuman or Degrading Treatment or Punishment

Adopted by the United Nations General Assembly on 10 December 1984 (resolution 39/46)

The States Parties to this Convention,

Considering that, in accordance with the principles proclaimed in the Charter of the United Nations, recognition of the equal and inalienable rights of all members of the human family is the foundation of freedom, justice and peace in the world,

Recognizing that those rights derive from the inherent dignity of the human person,

Considering the obligation of States under the Charter, in particular Article 55, to promote universal respect for, and observance of, human rights and fundamental freedoms,

Having regard to article 5 of the Universal Declaration of Human Rights and article 7 of the International Covenant on Civil and Political Rights, both of which provide that no one shall be subjected to torture or to cruel, inhuman or degrading treatment or punishment,

Having regard also to the Declaration on the Protection of All Persons from Being Subjected to Torture and Other Cruel, Inhuman or Degrading Treatment or Punishment, adopted by the General Assembly on 9 December 1975,

Desiring to make more effective the struggle against torture and other cruel, inhuman or degrading treatment or punishment throughout the world,

Have agreed as follows:

PART I

Article 1

1. For the purposes of this Convention, the term "torture" means any act by which severe pain or suffering, whether physical or mental, is intentionally inflicted on a person for such purposes as obtaining from him or a third person information or a confession, punishing him for an act he or a third person has committed or is suspected of having committed, or intimidating or coercing him or a third person, or for any reason based on discrimination of any kind, when such pain or suffering is inflicted by or at the instigation of or with the consent or acquiescence of a public official or other person acting in an official

capacity. It does not include pain or suffering arising only from, inherent in or incidental to lawful sanctions.

2. This article is without prejudice to any international instrument or national legislation which does or may contain provisions of wider application.

Article 2

1. Each State Party shall take effective legislative, administrative, judicial or other measures to prevent acts of torture in any territory under its jurisdiction.

2. No exceptional circumstances whatsoever, whether a state of war or a threat of war, internal political instability or any other public emergency, may be invoked as a justification of torture.

3. An order from a superior officer or a public authority may not be invoked as a justification of torture.

Article 3

1. No State Party shall expel, return ("*refouler*") or extradite a person to another State where there are substantial grounds for believing that he would be in danger of being subjected to torture.

2. For the purpose of determining whether there are such grounds, the competent authorities shall take into account all relevant considerations including, where applicable, the existence in the State concerned of a consistent pattern of gross, flagrant or mass violations of human rights.

Article 4

1. Each State Party shall ensure that all acts of torture are offences under its criminal law. The same shall apply to an attempt to commit torture and to an act by any person which constitutes complicity or participation in torture.

2. Each State Party shall make these offences punishable by appropriate penalties which take into account their grave nature.

Article 5

1. Each State Party shall take such measures as may be necessary to establish its jurisdiction over the offences referred to in article 4 in the following cases:

(*a*) When the offences are committed in any territory under its jurisdiction or on board a ship or aircraft registered in that State;

(*b*) When the alleged offender is a national of that State;

(*c*) When the victim is a national of that State if that State considers it appropriate.

2. Each State Party shall likewise take such measures as may be necessary to establish its jurisdiction over such offences in cases where the alleged offender is present in any territory under its jurisdiction and it does not extradite him pursuant to article 8 to any of the States mentioned in paragraph 1 of this article.

3. This Convention does not exclude any criminal jurisdiction exercised in accordance with internal law.

Article 6

1. Upon being satisfied, after an examination of information available to it, that the circumstances so warrant, any State Party in whose territory a person alleged to have committed any offence referred to in article 4 is present shall take him into custody or take other legal measures to ensure his presence. The custody and other legal measures shall be as provided in the law of that State but may be continued only for such time as is necessary to enable any criminal or extradition proceedings to be instituted.

2. Such State shall immediately make a preliminary inquiry into the facts.

3. Any person in custody pursuant to paragraph 1 of this article shall be assisted in communicating immediately with the nearest appropriate representative of the State of which he is a national, or, if he is a stateless person, with the representative of the State where he usually resides.

4. When a State, pursuant to this article, has taken a person into custody, it shall immediately notify the States referred to in article 5, paragraph 1, of the fact that such person is in custody and of the circumstances which warrant his detention. The State which makes the preliminary inquiry contemplated in paragraph 2 of this article shall promptly report its findings to the said States and shall indicate whether it intends to exercise jurisdiction.

Article 7

1. The State Party in the territory under whose jurisdiction a person alleged to have committed any offence referred to in article 4 is found shall in the cases contemplated in article 5, if it does not extradite him, submit the case to its competent authorities for the purpose of prosecution.

2. These authorities shall take their decision in the same manner as in the case of any ordinary offence of a serious nature under the law of that State. In the cases referred to in article 5, paragraph 2, the standards of evidence required for prosecution and conviction shall in no way be less stringent than those which apply in the cases referred to in article 5, paragraph 1.

3. Any person regarding whom proceedings are brought in connection with

any of the offences referred to in article 4 shall be guaranteed fair treatment at all stages of the proceedings.

Article 8

1. The offences referred to in article 4 shall be deemed to be included as extraditable offences in any extradition treaty existing between States Parties. States Parties undertake to include such offences as extraditable offences in every extradition treaty to be concluded between them.

2. If a State Party which makes extradition conditional on the existence of a treaty receives a request for extradition from another State Party with which it has no extradition treaty, it may consider this Convention as the legal basis for extradition in respect of such offences. Extradition shall be subject to the other conditions provided by the law of the requested State.

3. States Parties which do not make extradition conditional on the existence of a treaty shall recognize such offences as extraditable offences between themselves subject to the conditions provided by the law of the requested State.

4. Such offences shall be treated, for the purpose of extradition between States Parties, as if they had been committed not only in the place in which they occurred but also in the territories of the States required to establish their jurisdiction in accordance with article 5, paragraph 1.

Article 9

1. States Parties shall afford one another the greatest measure of assistance in connection with criminal proceedings brought in respect of any of the offences referred to in article 4, including the supply of all evidence at their disposal necessary for the proceedings.

2. States Parties shall carry out their obligations under paragraph 1 of this article in conformity with any treaties on mutual judicial assistance that may exist between them.

Article 10

1. Each State Party shall ensure that education and information regarding the prohibition against torture are fully included in the training of law enforcement personnel, civil or military, medical personnel, public officials and other persons who may be involved in the custody, interrogation or treatment of any individual subjected to any form of arrest, detention or imprisonment.

2. Each State Party shall include this prohibition in the rules or instructions issued in regard to the duties and functions of any such persons.

Article 11

Each State Party shall keep under systematic review interrogation rules, instructions, methods and practices as well as arrangements for the custody and treatment of persons subjected to any form of arrest, detention or imprisonment in any territory under its jurisdiction, with a view to preventing any cases of torture.

Article 12

Each State Party shall ensure that its competent authorities proceed to a prompt and impartial investigation, wherever there is reasonable ground to believe that an act of torture has been committed in any territory under its jurisdiction.

Article 13

Each State Party shall ensure that any individual who alleges he has been subjected to torture in any territory under its jurisdiction has the right to complain to, and to have his case promptly and impartially examined by, its competent authorities. Steps shall be taken to ensure that the complainant and witnesses are protected against all ill-treatment or intimidation as a consequence of his complaint or any evidence given.

Article 14

1. Each State Party shall ensure in its legal system that the victim of an act of torture obtains redress and has an enforceable right to fair and adequate compensation, including the means for as full rehabilitation as possible. In the event of the death of the victim as a result of an act of torture, his dependants shall be entitled to compensation.

2. Nothing in this article shall affect any right of the victim or other persons to compensation which may exist under national law.

Article 15

Each State Party shall ensure that any statement which is established to have been made as a result of torture shall not be invoked as evidence in any proceedings, except against a person accused of torture as evidence that the statement was made.

Article 16

1. Each State Party shall undertake to prevent in any territory under its jurisdiction other acts of cruel, inhuman or degrading treatment or punishment which do not amount to torture as defined in article 1, when such acts are committed by or at the instigation of or with the consent or acquiescence of a public official or other person acting in an official capacity. In particular,

the obligations contained in articles 10, 11, 12 and 13 shall apply with the substitution for references to torture of references to other forms of cruel, inhuman or degrading treatment or punishment.

2. The provisions of this Convention are without prejudice to the provisions of any other international instrument or national law which prohibits cruel, inhuman or degrading treatment or punishment or which relates to extradition or expulsion.

PART II

Article 17

1. There shall be established a Committee against Torture (hereinafter referred to as the Committee) which shall carry out the functions hereinafter provided. The Committee shall consist of ten experts of high moral standing and recognized competence in the field of human rights, who shall serve in their personal capacity. The experts shall be elected by the States Parties, consideration being given to equitable geographical distribution and to the usefulness of the participation of some persons having legal experience.

2. The members of the Committee shall be elected by secret ballot from a list of persons nominated by States Parties. Each State Party may nominate one person from among its own nationals. States Parties shall bear in mind the usefulness of nominating persons who are also members of the Human Rights Committee established under the International Covenant on Civil and Political Rights and who are willing to serve on the Committee against Torture.

3. Elections of the members of the Committee shall be held at biennial meetings of States Parties convened by the Secretary-General of the United Nations. At those meetings, for which two thirds of the States Parties shall constitute a quorum, the persons elected to the Committee shall be those who obtain the largest number of votes and an absolute majority of the votes of the representatives of States Parties present and voting.

4. The initial election shall be held no later than six months after the date of the entry into force of this Convention. At least four months before the date of each election, the Secretary-General of the United Nations shall address a letter to the States Parties inviting them to submit their nominations within three months. The Secretary-General shall prepare a list in alphabetical order of all persons thus nominated, indicating the States Parties which have nominated them, and shall submit it to the States Parties.

5. The members of the Committee shall be elected for a term of four years. They shall be eligible for re-election if renominated. However, the term of five of the members elected at the first election shall expire at the end of two years; immediately after the first election the names of these five members shall be

chosen by lot by the chairman of the meeting referred to in paragraph 3 of this article.

6. If a member of the Committee dies or resigns or for any other cause can no longer perform his Committee duties, the State Party which nominated him shall appoint another expert from among its nationals to serve for the remainder of his term, subject to the approval of the majority of the States Parties. The approval shall be considered given unless half or more of the States Parties respond negatively within six weeks after having been informed by the Secretary-General of the United Nations of the proposed appointment.

7. States Parties shall be responsible for the expenses of the members of the Committee while they are in performance of Committee duties.

Article 18

1. The Committee shall elect its officers for a term of two years. They may be re-elected.

2. The Committee shall establish its own rules of procedure, but these rules shall provide, *inter alia*, that:

(*a*) Six members shall constitute a quorum;

(*b*) Decisions of the Committee shall be made by a majority vote of the members present.

3. The Secretary-General of the United Nations shall provide the necessary staff and facilities for the effective performance of the functions of the Committee under this Convention.

4. The Secretary-General of the United Nations shall convene the initial meeting of the Committee. After its initial meeting, the Committee shall meet at such times as shall be provided in its rules of procedure.

5. The States Parties shall be responsible for expenses incurred in connection with the holding of meetings of the States Parties and of the Committee, including reimbursement to the United Nations for any expenses, such as the cost of staff and facilities, incurred by the United Nations pursuant to paragraph 3 of this article.

Article 19

1. The States Parties shall submit to the Committee, through the Secretary-General of the United Nations, reports on the measures they have taken to give effect to their undertakings under this Convention, within one year after the entry into force of the Convention for the State Party concerned. Thereafter the States Parties shall submit supplementary reports every four years on any new measures taken and such other reports as the Committee may request.

2. The Secretary-General of the United Nations shall transmit the reports to all States Parties.

3. Each report shall be considered by the Committee which may make such general comments on the report as it may consider appropriate and shall forward these to the State Party concerned. That State Party may respond with any observations it chooses to the Committee.

4. The Committee may, at its discretion, decide to include any comments made by it in accordance with paragraph 3 of this article, together with the observations thereon received from the State Party concerned, in its annual report made in accordance with article 24. If so requested by the State Party concerned, the Committee may also include a copy of the report submitted under paragraph 1 of this article.

Article 20

1. If the Committee receives reliable information which appears to it to contain well-founded indications that torture is being systematically practised in the territory of a State Party, the Committee shall invite that State Party to co-operate in the examination of the information and to this end to submit observations with regard to the information concerned.

2. Taking into account any observations which may have been submitted by the State Party concerned, as well as any other relevant information available to it, the Committee may, if it decides that this is warranted, designate one or more of its members to make a confidential inquiry and to report to the Committee urgently.

3. If an inquiry is made in accordance with paragraph 2 of this article, the Committee shall seek the co-operation of the State Party concerned. In agreement with that State Party, such an inquiry may include a visit to its territory.

4. After examining the findings of its member or members submitted in accordance with paragraph 2 of this article, the Committee shall transmit these findings to the State Party concerned together with any comments or suggestions which seem appropriate in view of the situation.

5. All the proceedings of the Committee referred to in paragraphs 1 to 4 of this article shall be confidential, and at all stages of the proceedings the co-operation of the State Party shall be sought. After such proceedings have been completed with regard to an inquiry made in accordance with paragraph 2, the Committee may, after consultations with the State Party concerned, decide to include a summary account of the results of the proceedings in its annual report made in accordance with article 24.

Article 21

1. A State Party to this Convention may at any time declare under this article that it recognizes the competence of the Committee to receive and consider communications to the effect that a State Party claims that another State Party is not fulfilling its obligations under this Convention. Such communications may be received and considered according to the procedures laid down in this article only if submitted by a State Party which has made a declaration recognizing in regard to itself the competence of the Committee. No communication shall be dealt with by the Committee under this article if it concerns a State Party which has not made such a declaration. Communications received under this article shall be dealt with in accordance with the following procedure:

(*a*) If a State Party considers that another State Party is not giving effect to the provisions of this Convention, it may, by written communication, bring the matter to the attention of that State Party. Within three months after the receipt of the communication the receiving State shall afford the State which sent the communication an explanation or any other statement in writing clarifying the matter, which should include, to the extent possible and pertinent, reference to domestic procedures and remedies taken, pending or available in the matter;

(*b*) If the matter is not adjusted to the satisfaction of both States Parties concerned within six months after the receipt by the receiving State of the initial communication, either State shall have the right to refer the matter to the Committee, by notice given to the Committee and to the other State;

(*c*) The Committee shall deal with a matter referred to it under this article only after it has ascertained that all domestic remedies have been invoked and exhausted in the matter, in conformity with the generally recognized principles of international law. This shall not be the rule where the application of the remedies is unreasonably prolonged or is unlikely to bring effective relief to the person who is the victim of the violation of this Convention;

(*d*) The Committee shall hold closed meetings when examining communications under this article;

(*e*) Subject to the provisions of subparagraph (*c*), the Committee shall make available its good offices to the States Parties concerned with a view to a friendly solution of the matter on the basis of respect for the obligations provided for in this Convention. For this purpose, the Committee may, when appropriate, set up an *ad hoc* conciliation commission;

(*f*) In any matter referred to it under this article, the Committee may call upon the States Parties concerned, referred to in subparagraph (*b*), to supply any relevant information;

(*g*) The States Parties concerned, referred to in subparagraph (*b*), shall have the right to be represented when the matter is being considered by the Committee and to make submissions orally and/or in writing;

(*h*) The Committee shall, within twelve months after the date of receipt of notice under subparagraph (*b*), submit a report:

(i) If a solution within the terms of subparagraph (*e*) is reached, the Committee shall confine its report to a brief statement of the facts and of the solution reached;

(ii) If a solution within the terms of subparagraph (*e*) is not reached, the Committee shall confine its report to a brief statement of the facts; the written submissions and record of the oral submissions made by the States Parties concerned shall be attached to the report.

In every matter, the report shall be communicated to the States Parties concerned.

2. The provisions of this article shall come into force when five States Parties to this Convention have made declarations under paragraph 1 of this article. Such declarations shall be deposited by the States Parties with the Secretary-General of the United Nations, who shall transmit copies thereof to the other States Parties. A declaration may be withdrawn at any time by notification to the Secretary-General. Such a withdrawal shall not prejudice the consideration of any matter which is the subject of a communication already transmitted under this article; no further communication by any State Party shall be received under this article after the notification of withdrawal of the declaration has been received by the Secretary-General, unless the State Party concerned has made a new declaration.

Article 22

1. A State Party to this Convention may at any time declare under this article that it recognizes the competence of the Committee to receive and consider communications from or on behalf of individuals subject to its jurisdiction who claim to be victims of a violation by a State Party of the provisions of the Convention. No communication shall be received by the Committee if it concerns a State Party which has not made such a declaration.

2. The Committee shall consider inadmissible any communication under this article which is anonymous or which it considers to be an abuse of the right of submission of such communications or to be incompatible with the provisions of this Convention.

3. Subject to the provisions of paragraph 2, the Committee shall bring any communications submitted to it under this article to the attention of the State Party of this Convention which has made a declaration under paragraph 1 and is alleged to be violating any provisions of the Convention. Within six months, the receiving State shall submit to the Committee written explanations or

statements clarifying the matter and the remedy, if any, that may have been taken by that State.

4. The Committee shall consider communications received under this article in the light of all information made available to it by or on behalf of the individual and by the State Party concerned.

5. The Committee shall not consider any communications from an individual under this article unless it has ascertained that:

(*a*) The same matter has not been, and is not being, examined under another procedure of international investigation or settlement;

(*b*) The individual has exhausted all available domestic remedies; this shall not be the rule where the application of the remedies is unreasonably prolonged or is unlikely to bring effective relief to the person who is the victim of the violation of this Convention.

6. The Committee shall hold closed meetings when examining communications under this article.

7. The Committee shall forward its views to the State Party concerned and to the individual.

8. The provisions of this article shall come into force when five States Parties to this Convention have made declarations under paragraph 1 of this article. Such declarations shall be deposited by the States Parties with the Secretary-General of the United Nations, who shall transmit copies thereof to the other States Parties. A declaration may be withdrawn at any time by notification to the Secretary-General. Such a withdrawal shall not prejudice the consideration of any matter which is the subject of a communication already transmitted under this article; no further communication by or on behalf of an individual shall be received under this article after the notification of withdrawal of the declaration has been received by the Secretary-General, unless the State Party has made a new declaration.

Article 23

The members of the Committee and of the *ad hoc* conciliation commissions which may be appointed under article 21, paragraph 1(*e*), shall be entitled to the facilities, privileges and immunities of experts on mission for the United Nations as laid down in the relevant sections of the Convention on the Privileges and Immunities of the United Nations.

Article 24

The Committee shall submit an annual report on its activities under this Convention to the States Parties and to the General Assembly of the United Nations.

PART III

Article 25

1. This Convention is open for signature by all States.

2. This Convention is subject to ratification. Instruments of ratification shall be deposited with the Secretary-General of the United Nations.

Article 26

This Convention is open to accession by all States. Accession shall be effected by the deposit of an instrument of accession with the Secretary-General of the United Nations.

Article 27

1. This Convention shall enter into force on the thirtieth day after the date of the deposit with the Secretary-General of the United Nations of the twentieth instrument of ratification or accession.

2. For each State ratifying this Convention or acceding to it after the deposit of the twentieth instrument of ratification or accession, the Convention shall enter into force on the thirtieth day after the date of the deposit of its own instrument of ratification or accession.

Article 28

1. Each State may, at the time of signature or ratification of this Convention or accession thereto, declare that it does not recognize the competence of the Committee provided for in article 20.

2. Any State Party having made a reservation in accordance with paragraph 1 of this article may, at any time, withdraw this reservation by notification to the Secretary-General of the United Nations.

Article 29

1. Any State Party to this Convention may propose an amendment and file it with the Secretary-General of the United Nations. The Secretary-General shall thereupon communicate the proposed amendment to the States Parties with a request that they notify him whether they favour a conference of States Parties for the purpose of considering and voting upon the proposal. In the event that within four months from the date of such communication at least one third of the States Parties favours such a conference, the Secretary-General shall convene the conference under the auspices of the United Nations. Any amendment adopted by a majority of the States Parties present and voting at the conference shall be submitted by the Secretary-General to all the States Parties for acceptance.

2. An amendment adopted in accordance with paragraph 1 of this article shall enter into force when two thirds of the States Parties to this Convention have notified the Secretary-General of the United Nations that they have accepted it in accordance with their respective constitutional processes.

3. When amendments enter into force, they shall be binding on those States Parties which have accepted them, other States Parties still being bound by the provisions of this Convention and any earlier amendments which they have accepted.

Article 30

1. Any dispute between two or more States Parties concerning the interpretation or application of this Convention which cannot be settled through negotiation shall, at the request of one of them, be submitted to arbitration. If within six months from the date of the request for arbitration the Parties are unable to agree on the organization of the arbitration, any one of those Parties may refer the dispute to the International Court of Justice by request in conformity with the Statute of the Court.

2. Each State may, at the time of signature or ratification of this Convention or accession thereto, declare that it does not consider itself bound by paragraph 1 of this article. The other States Parties shall not be bound by paragraph 1 of this article with respect to any State Party having made such a reservation.

3. Any State Party having made a reservation in accordance with paragraph 2 of this article may at any time withdraw this reservation by notification to the Secretary-General of the United Nations.

Article 31

1. A State Party may denounce this Convention by written notification to the Secretary-General of the United Nations. Denunciation becomes effective one year after the date of receipt of the notification by the Secretary-General.

2. Such a denunciation shall not have the effect of releasing the State Party from its obligations under this Convention in regard to any act or omission which occurs prior to the date at which the denunciation becomes effective, nor shall denunciation prejudice in any way the continued consideration of any matter which is already under consideration by the Committee prior to the date at which the denunciation becomes effective.

3. Following the date at which the denunciation of a State Party becomes effective, the Committee shall not commence consideration of any new matter regarding that State.

Article 32

The Secretary–General of the United Nations shall inform all States Members of the United Nations and all States which have signed this Convention or acceded to it of the following:

(*a*) Signatures, ratifications and accessions under articles 25 and 26;

(*b*) The date of entry into force of this Convention under article 27 and the date of the entry into force of any amendments under article 29;

(*c*) Denunciations under article 31.

Article 33

1. This Convention, of which the Arabic, Chinese, English, French, Russian and Spanish texts are equally authentic, shall be deposited with the Secretary-General of the United Nations.

2. The Secretary-General of the United Nations shall transmit certified copies of this Convention to all States.

APPENDIX 2

Declaration on the Protection of All Persons from Being Subjected to Torture and Other Cruel, Inhuman or Degrading Treatment or Punishment

Adopted by the United Nations General Assembly on 9 December 1975 (resolution 3452(XXX))

The General Assembly,

Considering that, in accordance with the principles proclaimed in the Charter of the United Nations, recognition of the inherent dignity and of the equal and inalienable rights of all members of the human family is the foundation of freedom, justice and peace in the world,

Considering that these rights derive from the inherent dignity of the human person,

Considering also the obligation of States under the Charter, in particular Article 55, to promote universal respect for, and observance of, human rights and fundamental freedoms,

Having regard to article 5 of the Universal Declaration of Human Rights and article 7 of the International Covenant on Civil and Political Rights, both of which provide that no one may be subjected to torture or to cruel, inhuman or degrading treatment or punishment,

Adopts the Declaration on the Protection of All Persons from Being Subjected to Torture and Other Cruel, Inhuman or Degrading Treatment or Punishment, the text of which is annexed to the present resolution, as a guideline for all States and other entities exercising effective power.

ANNEX

DECLARATION ON THE PROTECTION OF ALL PERSONS FROM BEING SUBJECTED TO TORTURE AND OTHER CRUEL, INHUMAN OR DEGRADING TREATMENT OR PUNISHMENT

Article 1

1. For the purpose of this Declaration, torture means any act by which severe pain or suffering, whether physical or mental, is intentionally inflicted by or at the instigation of a public official on a person for such purposes as obtaining from him or a third person information or confession, punishing him for an act he has committed or is suspected of having committed, or intimidating him or other persons. It does not include pain or suffering arising only from, inherent in or incidental to, lawful sanctions to the extent consistent with the Standard Minimum Rules for the Treatment of Prisoners.

2. Torture constitutes an aggravated and deliberate form of cruel, inhuman or degrading treatment or punishment.

Article 2

Any act of torture or other cruel, inhuman or degrading treatment or punishment is an offence to human dignity and shall be condemned as a denial of the purposes of the Charter of the United Nations and as a violation of the human rights and fundamental freedoms proclaimed in the Universal Declaration of Human Rights.

Article 3

No State may permit or tolerate torture or other cruel, inhuman or degrading treatment or punishment. Exceptional circumstances such as a state of war or a threat of war, internal political instability or any other public emergency may not be invoked as a justification of torture or other cruel, inhuman or degrading treatment or punishment.

Article 4

Each State shall, in accordance with the provisions of this Declaration, take effective measures to prevent torture and other cruel, inhuman or degrading treatment or punishment from being practised within its jurisdiction.

Article 5

The training of law enforcement personnel and of other public officials who may be responsible for persons deprived of their liberty shall ensure that full account is taken of the prohibition against torture and other cruel, inhuman or degrading treatment or punishment. This prohibition shall also, where appropriate, be included in such general rules or instructions as are issued in regard to the duties and functions of anyone who may be involved in the custody or treatment of such persons.

Article 6

Each State shall keep under systematic review interrogation methods and practices as well as arrangements for the custody and treatment of persons deprived of their liberty in its territory, with a view to preventing any cases of torture or other cruel, inhuman or degrading treatment or punishment.

Article 7

Each State shall ensure that all acts of torture as defined in article 1 are offences under its criminal law. The same shall apply in regard to acts which constitute participation in, complicity in, incitement to or an attempt to commit torture.

Article 8

Any person who alleges that he has been subjected to torture or other cruel, inhuman or degrading treatment or punishment by or at the instigation of a public official shall have the right to complain to, and to have his case impartially examined by, the competent authorities of the State concerned.

Article 9

Wherever there is reasonable ground to believe that an act of torture as defined in article 1 has been committed, the competent authorities of the State concerned shall promptly proceed to an impartial investigation even if there has been no formal complaint.

Article 10

If an investigation under article 8 or article 9 establishes that an act of torture as defined in article 1 appears to have been committed, criminal proceedings shall be instituted against the alleged offender or offenders in accordance with national law. If an allegation of other forms of cruel, inhuman or degrading treatment of punishment is considered to be well founded, the alleged offender or offenders shall be subject to criminal, disciplinary or other appropriate proceedings.

Article 11

Where it is proved that an act of torture or other cruel, inhuman or degrading treatment or punishment has been committed by or at the instigation of a public official, the victim shall be afforded redress and compensation in accordance with national law.

Article 12

Any statement which is established to have been made as a result of torture or other cruel, inhuman or degrading treatment or punishment may not be invoked as evidence against the person concerned or against any other person in any proceedings.

APPENDIX 3

Second resolution on torture and other cruel, inhuman or degrading treatment or punishment, adopted by the United Nations General Assembly on 9 December 1975 (resolution 3453(XXX))

The General Assembly,

Reaffirming the rejection, in its resolutions 3059 (XXVIII) of 2 November 1973 and 3218 (XXIX) of 6 November 1974, of any form of torture and other cruel, inhuman or degrading treatment or punishment,

Reiterating its conviction expressed in resolution 3318 (XXIX) that, because of the increase in the number of alarming reports on torture, further and sustained efforts are necessary to protect under all circumstances the basic human right to be free from torture and other cruel, inhuman or degrading treatment or punishment,

Welcoming resolution 4 (XXVIII) of 10 September 1975, adopted by the Sub-Commission on Prevention of Discrimination and Protection of Minorities,

Having considered the report of the Secretary-General containing an analytical summary of the information received under paragraph 1 of resolution 3218 (XXIX),

Recalling its request to the Fifth United Nations Congress on the Prevention of Crime and the Treatment of Offenders that it consider steps to be taken for the protection of all persons subjected to any form of detention or imprisonment against torture and other cruel, inhuman or degrading treatment or punishment, and to report thereon to the General Assembly at its thirtieth session,

Noting the working paper, entitled "Health aspects of avoidable maltreatment of prisoners and detainees", submitted by the World Health Organization to the Fifth United Nations Congress on the Prevention of Crime and the Treatment of Offenders.

Noting with appreciation the report of the Secretary-General prepared under paragraph 4 of resolution 3218 (XXIX),

Taking into account that the Fifth United Nations Congress on the Prevention of Crime and the Treatment of Offenders expressed the opinion that, on the matter of elaborating an International Code of Police Ethics, there should be further expert consideration,

Having adopted the Declaration on the Protection of All Persons from Being Subjected to Torture and Other Cruel, Inhuman or Degrading Treatment or Punishment, annexed to resolution 3452 (XXX) of 9 December 1975,

Believing that further international efforts are needed to ensure adequate protection for all against torture and other cruel, inhuman or degrading treatment or punishment,

1. *Expresses its appreciation* to the Fifth United Nations Congress on the Prevention of Crime and the Treatment of Offenders for the elaboration of the Declaration on the Protection of All Persons from Being Subjected to Torture and Other Cruel, Inhuman or Degrading Treatment or Punishment;

2. *Requests* the Commission on Human Rights at its thirty-second session to study the question of torture and any necessary steps for:

(*a*) Ensuring the effective observance of the Declaration on the Protection of All Persons from Being Subjected to Torture and Other Cruel, Inhuman or Degrading Treatment or Punishment;

(*b*) The formulation of a body of principles for the protection of all persons under any form of detention or imprisonment, on the basis of the *Study of the Right of Everyone to be Free from Arbitrary Arrest, Detention and Exile* and the draft principles on freedom from arbitrary arrest and detention contained therein;

3. *Requests* the Committee on Crime Prevention and Control to elaborate, on the basis of, *inter alia*, the proposals presented to and conclusions arrived at by the Fifth United Nations Congress on the Prevention of Crime and the Treatment of Offenders, a draft code of conduct for law enforcement officials and to submit this draft code to the General Assembly at its thirty-second session, through the Commission for Social Development and the Economic and Social Council;

4. *Invites* the World Health Organization to give further attention to the study and elaboration of principles of medical ethics relevant to the protection of persons subjected to any form of detention or imprisonment against torture and other cruel, inhuman or degrading treatment or punishment;

5. *Decides* to include in the provisional agenda of its thirty-first session an item entitled "Torture and other cruel, inhuman or degrading treatment or punishment" for the purpose of reviewing the progress achieved in accordance with the present resolution.

APPENDIX 4

Resolution concerning a draft convention against torture and other cruel, inhuman or degrading treatment or punishment, adopted by the United Nations General Assembly on 8 December 1977 (resolution 32/62)

The General Assembly,

Having regard to article 5 of the Universal Declaration of Human Rights and article 7 of the International Covenant on Civil and Political Rights, both of which provide that no one may be subjected to torture or to cruel, inhuman or degrading treatment or punishment,

Recalling the Declaration on the Protection of All Persons from Being Subjected to Torture and Other Cruel, Inhuman or Degrading Treatment or Punishment, contained in the annex to its resolution 3452 (XXX) of 9 December 1975,

Believing that further international efforts are needed to ensure adequate protection for all against torture and other cruel, inhuman or degrading treatment or punishment,

Welcoming in that regard the work that has been done, or is being done, on the basis of General Assembly resolution 3453 (XXX) of 9 December 1975,

Considering that a further significant step would be the adoption of an international convention against torture and other cruel, inhuman or degrading treatment or punishment,

1. *Requests* the Commission on Human Rights to draw up a draft convention against torture and other cruel, inhuman or degrading treatment or punishment, in the light of the principles embodied in the Declaration on the Protection of All Persons from Being Subjected to Torture and Other Cruel, Inhuman or Degrading Treatment or Punishment;

2. *Further requests* the Commission on Human Rights to submit a progress report on its work to the General Assembly at its thirty-third session;

3. *Decides* to include in the provisional agenda of its thirty-third session the item entitled "Torture and other cruel, inhuman or degrading treatment or punishment" for the purpose of reviewing the progress achieved in accordance with the present resolution.

APPENDIX 5

Draft Convention for the Prevention and Suppression of Torture, submitted by the International Association of Penal Law on 15 January 1978

(Document E/CN. 4/NGO/213)

The Parties to this Convention hereby agree as hereinafter provided:

Article I

(Torture as an international crime)

Torture is a crime under international law.

Article II

(Definition of torture)

For the purposes of this Convention, torture is any conduct by which severe pain or suffering, whether physical or mental, is intentionally inflicted on a person by or at the instigation of a public official or for which a public official is responsible under Article III, in order:

(a) to obtain from that person or another person information or a statement or confession; or

(b) to intimidate, discredit or humiliate that person or another person; or

(c) to inflict punishment on that person or another person, save where such conduct is in a proper execution of a lawful sanction not constituting cruel, inhuman or degrading treatment or punishment.

Article III

(Responsibility)

A person is responsible for committing or instigating torture when that person:

(a) personally engages in or participates in such conduct; or

(b) assists, incites, solicits, commands or conspires with others to commit torture; or

(c) being a public official, fails to take appropriate measures to prevent or suppress torture when such person has knowledge or reasonable belief that torture has been or is being committed and has the authority or is in a position to take such measures.

Article IV

(National measures for the prevention and suppression of torture)

The Contracting Parties undertake to adopt legislative, judicial, administrative and other measures necessary to give effect to this convention to prevent and suppress torture, and in particular, to ensure that:

(a) any act of torture is punishable under its laws as a grave crime;

(b) their public officials do not practice or permit any form of torture;

(c) all complaints of torture or any circumstances which give reasonable grounds to believe that torture has been committed shall be investigated speedily and effectively and that complainants shall not be exposed to any sanction by reason of their complaints, unless they have been shown to have been made falsely and maliciously;

(d) persons believed to be responsible for acts of torture are prosecuted and when found guilty, punished and disciplined in accordance with their laws;

(e) any victim of torture is afforded adequate and proper redress and compensation;

(f) no person is expelled or extradited to a State where there are reasonable grounds to believe that that person may be in danger of being tortured; and

(g) the text of this convention is widely disseminated and its contents made known to all persons arrested and detained.

Article V

(Superior orders)

The fact that a person was acting in obedience to superior orders shall not be a defence to a charge of torture.

Article VI

(Non-derogation)

Torture can in no circumstances be justified or excused by a state or threat of war or armed conflict, a state of siege, emergency or other exceptional circumstances, or by any necessity or any urgency of obtaining information, or by any other reason.

Article VII

(Evidentiary effect)

Any oral or written statement or confession obtained by means of torture or any other evidence derived therefrom shall have no legal effect whatever and shall not be invoked in any judicial or administrative proceedings, except against a person accused of obtaining it by torture.

Article VIII

(Period of limitation)

No prosecution or punishment of torture shall be barred by the application of a period of limitation of lesser duration than that applicable to the most serious offence in the laws of the Contracting Parties.

Article IX

(Jurisdiction)

1. Jurisdiction for the prosecution and punishment of the international crime of torture shall vest in the following order in:

(a) the Contracting Party in whose territory the act occurred;

(b) any Contracting Party of which the accused is a national;

(c) any Contracting Party of which the victim is a national;

(d) any other Contracting Party within whose territory the accused may be found.

2. Nothing in this Article shall be construed as affecting the jurisdiction of any competent international criminal court.

Article X

(Extradition)

1. Where a Contracting Party receives a request for extradition from a Contracting Party having prior or concurrent jurisdiction, it shall grant extradition of persons accused of torture in accordance with its laws and treaties in force and subject to the provisions of this Convention.

2. In the absence of a treaty of extradition with a requesting Contracting Party, the Contracting Parties undertake to extradite on the basis of this Convention.

3. Contracting Parties which do not make extradition conditional on the existence of a treaty shall recognize torture as an extraditable offence.

Article XI

(Co-operation)

The Contracting Parties shall afford one another the greatest measure of judicial and other co-operation in connexion with criminal proceedings brought in implementation of this Convention.

Article XII

(Torture not a political offence)

For the purposes of this Convention, torture shall not be deemed a political offence.

Article XIII

(International measures of implementation)

1. The Contracting Parties undertake to submit to the Human Rights Committee established under the International Covenant on Civil and Political Rights periodic reports on the legislative, judicial, administrative and other measures they have adopted to implement this Convention.

2. The first report of a Contracting Party shall be submitted within one (1) year of the entry into force of the Convention and thereafter a report shall be submitted every two (2) years.

3. The Chairman of the Human Rights Committee shall, after consulting the other members of the Committee, appoint a Special Committee on the Prevention of Torture, consisting of five (5) members of the Human Rights Committee who are also nationals of the Contracting Parties to this Convention to consider reports submitted by Contracting Parties in accordance with this Article.

4. If, among the members of the Human Rights Committee, there are no nationals of Contracting Parties to this Convention or if there are fewer than five such nationals, the Secretary-General of the United Nations shall, after consulting all Contracting Parties to this Convention, designate a national of the Contracting Party or nationals of the Contracting Parties which are not members of the Human Rights Committee to take part in the work of the Special Committee established in accordance with paragraph 3 of this Article, until such time as sufficient nationals of the Contracting Parties to this Convention are elected to the Human Rights Committee.

5. The Special Committee on the Prevention of Torture shall meet not less than once a year for a period of not more than five days, either before the opening or after the closing of sessions of the Human Rights Committee and shall issue an annual report of its findings.

Article XIV

(Settlement of disputes)

Any dispute by Contracting Parties arising out of the interpretation, application or implementation of this Convention which has not been settled by negotiation, arbitration or referral to an independent and impartial body shall, at the request of any party to the dispute, be brought before the International Court of Justice.

Article XV

(Signature and accessions)

1. This Convention is open for signature by all States.

2. Any State which does not sign this Convention before its entry into force may accede to it thereafter.

Article XVI

(Reservations)

No reservations may be made to Article VI of this Convention. The pertinent provisions of the Vienna Convention on the Law of Treaties shall apply with respect to any other reservations.

Article XVII

(Depositing instruments of ratification)

This Convention is subject to ratification. Instruments of ratification shall be deposited with the Secretary-General of the United Nations.

Article XVIII

(Accession)

Accession shall be effected by the deposit of an instrument of accession with the Secretary-General of the United Nations.

Article XIX

(Entry into force)

1. This Convention shall enter into force on the thirtieth day after the deposit of the tenth instrument of ratification or accession.

2. For each State ratifying this Convention or acceding to it after the deposit of the tenth instrument of ratification or accession, the Convention shall enter into force on the thirtieth day after the date of the deposit of its own instrument of ratification or accession.

Article XX

(Revision)

1. A request for the revision of this Convention may be made at any time by any Contracting Party by means of a notification in writing addressed to the Secretary-General of the United Nations.

2. The General Assembly of the United Nations shall decide upon the steps, if any, to be taken in respect to such a request.

Article XXI

(Notification)

The Secretary-General of the United Nations shall inform all States of the following particulars:

(1) Signatures, ratifications, accessions and reservations under Articles XV-XVIII of this Convention;

(2) The date of entry into force of the present Convention;

(3) Notification under Article XX of the present Convention.

Article XXII

(Official languages)

This Convention, of which the Arabic, Chinese, English, French, Russian and Spanish texts are equally authentic, shall be deposited in the archives of the United Nations.

Article XXIII

(Transmittal)

The Secretary-General of the United Nations shall transmit certified copies of this Convention to all Contracting Parties.

APPENDIX 6

Draft International Convention against Torture and Other Cruel, Inhuman or Degrading Treatment or Punishment, submitted by Sweden on 18 January 1978

(Document E/CN.4/1285)

(Preamble to be elaborated)

Article 1

1. For the purpose of the present Convention, torture means any act by which severe pain or suffering, whether physical or mental, is intentionally inflicted by or at the instigation of a public official on a person for such purposes as obtaining from him or a third person information or confession, punishing him for an act he has committed or is suspected of having committed, or intimidating him or other persons. It does not include pain or suffering arising only from, inherent in or incidental to, lawful sanctions to the extent consistent with the Standard Minimum Rules for the Treatment of Prisoners.

2. Torture constitutes an aggravated and deliberate form of cruel, inhuman or degrading treatment or punishment.

Article 2

1. Each State Party undertakes to ensure that torture or other cruel, inhuman or degrading treatment or punishment does not take place within its jurisdiction. Under no circumstances shall any State Party permit or tolerate torture or other cruel, inhuman or degrading treatment or punishment.

2. No exceptional circumstances whatsoever, whether a state of war or a threat of war, internal political instability or any other public emergency, may be invoked as a justification of torture or other cruel, inhuman or degrading treatment or punishment.

3. An order from a superior officer or a public authority may not be invoked as a justification of torture or other cruel, inhuman or degrading treatment or punishment.

Article 3

Each State Party shall, in accordance with the provisions of the present Convention, take legislative, administrative, judicial and other measures to prevent torture and other cruel, inhuman or degrading treatment or punishment from being practised within its jurisdiction.

Article 4

No State Party may expel or extradite a person to a State where there are reasonable grounds to believe that he may be in danger of being subjected to torture or other cruel, inhuman or degrading treatment or punishment.

Article 5

1. Each State Party shall ensure that education and information regarding the prohibition against torture and other cruel, inhuman or degrading treatment or punishment are fully included in the curricula of the training of law enforcement personnel and of other public officials as well as medical personnel who may be responsible for persons deprived of their liberty.

2. Each State Party shall include this prohibition in the general rules or instructions issued in regard to the duties and functions of anyone who may be involved in the custody or treatment of persons deprived of their liberty.

Article 6

Each State Party shall keep under systematic review interrogation methods and practices as well as arrangements for the custody and treatment of persons deprived of their liberty in its territory, with a view to preventing any cases of torture or other cruel, inhuman or degrading treatment or punishment.

Article 7

1. Each State Party shall ensure that all acts of torture as defined in article 1 are offences under its criminal law. The same shall apply in regard to acts which constitute participation in, complicity in, incitement to or an attempt to commit torture.

2. Each State Party undertakes to make the offences referred to in paragraph 1 of this article punishable by severe penalties.

Article 8

1. Each State Party shall take such measures as may be necessary to establish its jurisdiction over the offences referred to in article 7 in the following cases:

(a) when the offences are committed in the territory of that State or on board a ship or aircraft registered in that State;

(b) when the alleged offender is a national of that State;

(c) when the victim is a national of that State.

2. Each State Party shall likewise take such measures as may be necessary to establish its jurisdiction over these offences in cases where the alleged

offender is present in its territory and it does not extradite him pursuant to article 14 to any of the States mentioned in paragraph 1 of this article.

3. This Convention does not exclude any criminal jurisdiction exercised in accordance with internal law.

Article 9

Each State Party shall guarantee to any individual who alleges to have been subjected within its jurisdiction to torture or other cruel, inhuman or degrading treatment or punishment by or at the instigation of its public officials, the right to complain to and to have his case impartially examined by its competent authorities without threat of further torture or other cruel, inhuman or degrading treatment or punishment.

Article 10

Each State Party shall ensure that, even if there has been no formal complaint, its competent authorities proceed to an impartial, speedy and effective investigation, wherever there is reasonable ground to believe that an act of torture or other cruel, inhuman or degrading treatment or punishment has been committed within its jurisdiction.

Article 11

1. Each State Party shall, except in the cases referred to in article 14, ensure that criminal proceedings are instituted in accordance with its national law against an alleged offender who is present in its territory, if its competent authorities establish that an act of torture as defined in article 1 appears to have been committed and if that State Party has jurisdiction over the offence in accordance with article 8.

2. Each State Party shall ensure that an alleged offender is subject to criminal, disciplinary or other appropriate proceedings, when an allegation of other forms of cruel, inhuman or degrading treatment or punishment within its jurisdiction is considered to be well founded.

Article 12

Each State Party shall guarantee an enforceable right to compensation to the victim of an act of torture or other cruel, inhuman or degrading treatment or punishment committed by or at the instigation of its public officials. In the event of the death of the victim, his relatives or other successors shall be entitled to enforce this right to compensation.

Article 13

Each State Party shall ensure that any statement which is established to have been made as a result of torture or other cruel, inhuman or degrading treatment or punishment shall not be invoked as evidence against the person concerned or against any other person in any proceedings.

Article 14

Instead of instituting criminal proceedings in accordance with paragraph 1 of article 11, a State Party may, if requested, extradite the alleged offender to another State Party which has jurisdiction over the offence in accordance with article 8.

Article 15

1. States Parties shall afford one another the greatest measure of assistance in connection with proceedings referred to in article 11, including the supply of all evidence at their disposal necessary for the proceedings.

2. The provisions of paragraph 1 of this article shall not affect obligations concerning mutual judicial assistance embodied in any other treaty.

Article 16

States Parties undertake to submit to the Secretary-General of the United Nations, when so requested by the Human Rights Committee established in accordance with article 28 of the International Covenant on Civil and Political Rights (hereafter referred to in the present Convention as the Human Rights Committee), reports or other information on measures taken to suppress and punish torture and other cruel, inhuman or degrading treatment or punishment. Such reports or information shall be considered by the Human Rights Committee in accordance with the procedures set out in the International Covenant on Civil and Political Rights and in the Rules of Procedure of the Human Rights Committee.

Article 17

If the Human Rights Committee receives information that torture is being systematically practised in a certain State Party, the Committee may designate one or more of its members to carry out an inquiry and to report to the Committee urgently. The inquiry may include a visit to the State concerned, provided that the Government of that State gives its consent.

Article 18

1. A State Party may at any time declare under this article that it recognizes the competence of the Human Rights Committee to receive and consider communications to the effect that a State Party claims that another State Party is not fulfilling its obligations under the present Convention. Communications under this article may be received and considered only if submitted by a State Party which has made a declaration recognizing in regard to itself the competence of the Human Rights Committee. No communication shall be

received by the Human Rights Committee if it concerns a State Party which has not made such a declaration.

2. Communications received under this article shall be dealt with in accordance with the procedure provided for in article 41 of the International Covenant on Civil and Political Rights and in the Rules of Procedure of the Human Rights Committee.

Article 19

If a matter referred to the Human Rights Committee in accordance with article 18 is not resolved to the satisfaction of the States Parties concerned, the Committee may, with the prior consent of the States Parties concerned, appoint an *ad hoc* Conciliation Commission. The procedures governing this Commission shall be the same as those provided for in article 42 of the International Covenant on Civil and Political Rights and in the Rules of Procedure of the Human Rights Committee.

Article 20

1. A State Party may at any time declare under this article that it recognizes the competence of the Committee to receive and consider communications from individuals subject to its jurisdiction who claim to have been subjected to torture or other cruel, inhuman or degrading treatment or punishment in contravention of the obligations of that State Party under the present Convention. No communication shall be received by the Committee if it concerns a State Party which has not made such a declaration.

2. Communications received under this article shall be dealt with in accordance with the procedure provided for in the Optional Protocol to the International Covenant on Civil and Political Rights and in the Rules of Procedure of the Human Rights Committee.

Article 21

The Human Rights Committee shall include in its annual report to the General Assembly a summary of its activities under articles 16, 17, 18, 19 and 20 of the present Convention.

(Final clauses to be elaborated)

APPENDIX 7

Revised text of the substantive parts of the Draft Convention against Torture and Other Cruel, Inhuman or Degrading Treatment or Punishment, submitted by Sweden on 19 February 1979

(Document E/CN.4/WG.1/WP.1)

Article 1

1. For the purposes of this Convention, torture means any act by which severe pain or suffering, whether physical or mental, is intentionally inflicted on a person for such purposes as obtaining from him or a third person information or a confession, punishing him for an act he or a third person has committed or is suspected of having committed, or intimidating or coercing him or a third person, or for any reason based on discrimination of any kind, when such pain or suffering is inflicted by or at the instigation of or with the consent or acquiescence of a public official or other person acting in an official capacity. It does not include pain or suffering arising only from, inherent in or incidental to lawful sanctions.

[2. Torture is an aggravated and deliberate form of cruel, inhuman or degrading treatment or punishment.]

3. This Article is without prejudice to any international instrument or national legislation which does or may contain provisions of wider application relating to the subject matter of this Convention.

Article 2

1. Each State party shall take effective legislative, administrative, judicial or other measures to prevent acts of torture in any territory under its jurisdiction.

2. No exceptional circumstances whatsoever, whether a state of war or a threat of war, internal political instability or any other public emergency, may be invoked as a justification of torture.

3. An order from a superior officer or a public authority may not be invoked as a justification of torture; [however, this may be considered a ground for mitigation of punishment, if justice so requires.]

Article 3

No State Party shall expel, return ("refouler") or extradite a person where there are substantial grounds for believing that he would be in danger of being subjected to torture.

(Remark to be included in the Commission's report:

"Some delegations indicated that their States might wish, at the time of signature or ratification of the Convention or accession thereto, to declare that they did not consider themselves bound by Article 3 of the Convention, in so far as that Article might not be compatible with obligations towards States not Party to the Convention under extradition treaties concluded before the date of the signature of the Convention.")

Article 4

1. Each State Party shall ensure that all acts of torture are offences under its criminal law. The same shall apply to an attempt to commit torture and to an act by any person which constitutes complicity or participation in torture.

2. Each State Party shall make these offences punishable by appropriate penalties which take into account their grave nature.

Article 5

1. Each State Party shall take such measures as may be necessary to establish its jurisdiction over the offences referred to in Article 4 in the following cases:

(a) when the offences are committed in any territory under its jurisdiction;

(b) when the alleged offender is a national of that State;

[(c) when the victim is a national of that State.]

2. Each State Party shall likewise take such measures as may be necessary to establish its jurisdiction over such offences in cases where the alleged offender is present in any territory under its jurisdiction and it does not extradite him pursuant to Article 8 to any of the States mentioned in paragraph 1 of this Article.

3. This Convention does not exclude any criminal jurisdiction exercised in accordance with internal law.

Article 6

1. Upon being satisfied that the circumstances so warrant, any State Party in territory under whose jurisdiction a person alleged to have committed any offence referred to in Article 4 is present, shall take him into custody or take other measures to ensure his presence. The custody and other measures shall be as provided in the law of that State but may be continued only for such time as is necessary to enable any criminal or extradition proceedings to be instituted.

2. Such State shall immediately make a preliminary enquiry into the facts.

3. Any person in custody pursuant to paragraph 1 of this Article shall be assisted in communicating immediately with the nearest appropriate representative of the State of which he is a national.

4. When a State, pursuant to this Article, has taken a person into custody, it shall immediately notify the States referred to in Article 5, paragraph 1, of the fact that such person is in custody and of the circumstances which warrent his detention. The State which makes the preliminary enquiry contemplated in paragraph 2 of this Article shall promptly report its findings to the said States and shall indicate whether it intends to exercise jurisdiction.

5. Any person regarding whom proceedings are being carried out in connection with any of the offences referred to in Article 4 shall be guaranteed fair treatment at all stages of the proceedings.

Article 7

The State Party in territory under whose jurisdiction a person alleged to have committed any offence referred to in Article 4 is found shall, if it does not extradite him, be obliged, without exception whatsoever and whether or not the offence was committed in any territory under its jurisdiction, to submit the case to its competent authorities for the purpose of prosecution. Those authorities shall take their decision in the same manner as in the case of any offence of a serious nature under the law of that State.

Article 8

1. The offences referred to in Article 4 shall be deemed to be included as extraditable offences in any extradition treaty existing between States Parties. States Parties undertake to include such offences as extraditable offences in every extradition treaty to be concluded between them.

2. If a State Party which makes extradition conditional on the existence of a treaty receives a request for extradition from another State Party with which it has no extradition treaty, it [may] [shall] consider this Convention as the legal basis for extradition in respect of such offences. Extradition shall be subject to the other conditions provided by the law of the requested State.

3. States Parties which do not make extradition conditional on the existence of a treaty shall recognize such offences as extraditable offences between themselves subject to the conditions provided by the law of the requested State.

4. Such offences shall be treated, for the purpose of extradition between States Parties, as if they had been committed not only in the place in which they occurred but also in the territories of the States required to establish their jurisdiction in accordance with Article 5, paragraph 1.

Article 9

1. States Parties shall afford one another the greatest measure of assistance in connection with criminal proceedings brought in respect of any of the offences referred to in Article 4, including the supply of all evidence at their disposal necessary for the proceedings.

2. The provisions of paragraph 1 of this Article shall not affect obligations under any other treaty, bilateral or multilateral, which governs or will govern, in whole or in part, mutual assistance in criminal matters.

Article 10

1. Each State Party shall ensure that education and information regarding the prohibition against torture are fully included in the training of law enforcement personnel, civil or military, medical personnel, public officials and other persons who may be involved in the custody, interrogation or treatment of any individual subjected to any form of arrest, detention or imprisonment.

2. Each State Party shall include this prohibition in the rules or instructions issued in regard to the duties and functions of any such persons.

Article 11

Each State Party shall keep under systematic review interrogation methods and practices as well as arrangements for the custody and treatment of persons subjected to any form of arrest, detention or imprisonment in any territory under its jurisdiction, with a view to preventing any cases of torture.

Article 12

Each State Party shall ensure that any individual who alleges he has been subjected to torture in any territory under its jurisdiction has the right to complain to and to have his case promptly and impartially examined by its competent authorities. Steps shall be taken to ensure that the complainant is protected against ill-treatment in consequence of his complaint.

Article 13

Each State Party shall ensure that, even if there has been no formal complaint, its competent authorities proceed to a prompt and impartial investigation, wherever there is reasonable ground to believe that an act of torture has been committed in any territory under its jurisdiction.

Article 14

1. Each State Party shall ensure that the victim of an act of torture has an enforceable right to compensation. In the event of the death of the victim as a result of an act of torture, his dependents shall be entitled to compensation.

2. Nothing in this Article shall affect any other right to compensation which may exist under national law.

Article 15

Each State Party shall ensure that any statement which is established to have been made as a result of torture shall not be invoked as evidence in any proceedings except against a person accused of obtaining that statement by torture.

Article 16

This Convention shall be without prejudice to any provisions in other international instruments or in national law which prohibit cruel, inhuman and degrading treatment and punishment.

APPENDIX 8

Draft Optional Protocol to the Draft International Convention against Torture and Other Cruel, Inhuman or Degrading Treatment or Punishment, submitted by Costa Rica on 6 March 1980

(Document E/CN.4/1409)

The States Parties to the present Protocol,

Considering that in order further to achieve the purpose of the International Convention against Torture and other Cruel, Inhuman or Degrading Treatment or Punishment (hereinafter referred to as the Convention) and the implementation of its provisions, it would be appropriate to establish an independent International Committee authorised to arrange visits to places of detention of all kinds under the jurisdiction of the States Parties to the present Protocol and to report thereon with recommendations to the governments concerned,

Have agreed as follows:

Article 1

1. A State Party to the Convention that becomes a party to the present Protocol agrees to permit visits in accordance with the terms of the present Protocol to any place (hereinafter referred to as a place of detention) subject to the jurisdiction of a State Party where persons are held who have been deprived of their liberty for any reason, including persons under investigation by the law enforcement authorities, civil or military, persons in preventive, administrative or re-educative detention, persons who are being prosecuted or punished for any offence and persons in custody for medical reasons.

2. A place of detention within the meaning of this Article shall not include any place which representatives or delegates of a Protecting Power or of the International Committee of the Red Cross are entitled to visit and do visit pursuant to the Geneva Conventions of 1949 and their additional protocols of 1977.

Article 2

Exceptional circumstances, such as a state of war, state of siege, state of emergency or the passing of emergency legislation shall not suspend the application of the present Protocol.

Article 3

1. The States Parties to the present Protocol shall meet in Assembly once a year. They shall be convened by the Government of ... or such other Government as may accept their request to do so.

2. The Assembly shall elect the members of an International Committee responsible for the application of the present Protocol (hereinafter referred to as the Committee), shall adopt the budget for implementing the present Protocol, shall consider the general reports of the Committee and any other matters relating to the present Protocol and its application, and shall give general directions to the Committee.

Article 4

1. The Committee shall be composed of 10 members until such time as there are not less than 25 States Parties to the present Protocol. Thereafter the Committee shall be composed of 18 members.

2. The members of the Committee shall be persons of high moral character and recognised competence in the field of human rights and in the matters dealt with in the Convention and the present Protocol.

3. The members of the Committee shall be elected and shall serve in their personal capacity.

Article 5

1. The members of the Committee shall be elected by secret ballot from a list of persons possessing the qualifications prescribed in Article 4 and nominated for the purpose by the States Parties to the present Protocol.

2. Each State Party may nominate not more than four persons or, where there are not less than 25 States Parties, not more than two persons. These persons shall be nationals of the nominating State.

3. A person shall be eligible for renomination.

Article 6

1. The members of the Committee shall be elected for a term of four years. However, at the first election half of the members shall be elected for two years. Thereafter, elections shall be held every two years for half of the members of the Committee.

2. Initially the Committee shall not include more than two members from the same State. When there are more than 10 States Parties to the present Protocol, the Committee shall not include more than one member from the same State, save that members elected while there were ten States Parties or less shall continue to serve for the unexpired portion of their term.

3. In the election of the Committee, consideration shall be given to equitable geographical distribution of membership and to the representation of the different forms of civilisation and of the different legal systems.

Article 7

1. The Committee shall meet for regular sessions twice a year, and for special sessions at the initiative of its Chairman or at the request of not less than one third of its members.

2. The Committee shall adopt its own rules of procedure. Its decisions shall be taken by a majority of its members present and voting.

3. Half of the members shall constitute a quorum.

Article 8

1. The Committee shall be responsible for arranging visits to places of detention subject to the jurisdiction of the States Parties to the present Convention.

2. The Committee shall establish a programme of regular visits to each of the said States Parties and shall arrange such further visits as may appear necessary from time to time.

Article 9

1. The Committee may nominate as its delegates to carry out such visits one or more persons being members of the Committee or members of a panel of qualified persons chosen by the Committee from among the nationals of the States Parties to the present Protocol.

2. Members of the said panel shall be nominated for periods of three years. Their names shall be communicated to the States Parties to the present Protocol.

3. A State Party may exceptionally and for confidential reasons given confidentially to the Committee declare that a particular delegate will not be acceptable as a visitor to its territory.

Article 10

1. Subject to the provisions of Article 9, paragraph 3, when the Government of a State Party to the present Protocol has been informed of a mission assigned to one or more delegate(s), the latter shall be authorised to visit in all circumstances and without previous notice any place of detention within the jurisdiction of the State Party.

2. The delegates shall receive from the State Party concerned all facilities for the accomplishment of their task. They may, in particular, obtain all information about the places where there are persons deprived of their liberty and interview them there without witnesses and at leisure.

3. Delegates may enter into contact with the families, friends and lawyers of persons deprived of their liberty.

4. During each visit, the delegates shall verify that persons deprived of their liberty are being treated in conformity with the provisions of the Convention.

5. If appropriate, they shall at once submit observations and recommendations to the competent authorities of the State Party concerned.

6. They shall submit a full report on their mission, with their observations and recommendations, to the Committee.

Article 11

1. The Committee, after considering a report of its delegates, shall inform the State Party concerned in confidence of its findings and, if necessary, make recommendations. It may initiate consultations with the State Party with a view to furthering the protection of persons deprived of their liberty.

2. With the consent of the State Party concerned the Committee may publish its findings and recommendations in whole or in part.

3. In the event of a disagreement between the State Party concerned and the Committee as to the Committee's findings or as to the implementation of its recommendations, the Committee may at its discretion publish its findings or recommendations or both in whole or in part.

4. The Committee shall submit to the annual Assembly a general report which shall be made public.

Article 12

1. The Committee shall appoint a Secretary-General and one or more assistants.

2. Under the authority of the Committee the Secretary-General shall carry out the tasks assigned to him by the Committee and shall be responsible for the day to day administration in the implementation of the present Protocol. He shall appoint the members of the secretariat.

3. He shall collect information from all available sources pertaining to the treatment of persons deprived of their liberty within the jurisdiction of the States Parties. He shall not communicate the source of any such information to the State Party concerned without the consent of the informant.

4. Between sessions of the Committee, if it appears to the Secretary-General that an urgent mission is required to one or more places of detention within the jurisdiction of a State Party, the Secretary-General may, with the agreement of the Chairman of the Committee, organise a mission to the State Party concerned and such mission shall be entitled to the same rights and facilities as a mission authorised by the Committee.

Article 13

1. Each State Party shall contribute to the expenditure incurred in the implementation of the present Protocol on the basis of the scale used by the United Nations Organization.

2. The draft annual budget, after approval by the Committee, shall be submitted by the Secretary-General to the annual Assembly of the States Parties.

Article 14

1. The present Protocol is open for signature by any State which has signed the Convention.

2. The present Protocol is subject to ratification or accession by any State which has ratified or acceded to the Convention. Instruments of ratification or accession shall be deposited with the Secretary-General of the United Nations.

3. The Secretary-General of the United Nations shall inform all States which have signed the present Protocol or acceded to it of the deposit of each instrument of ratification or accession.

Article 15

1. Subject to the entry into force of the Convention, the present Protocol shall enter into force three months after the deposit of the fifth instrument of ratification or accession.

2. For each State ratifying the present Protocol or acceding to it after the deposit of the fifth instrument of ratification or instrument of accession the present Protocol shall enter into force three months after the date of the deposit of its own instrument of ratification or instrument of accession.

Article 16

Any State Party may denounce the present Protocol at any time by written notification addressed to the Secretary-General of the United Nations, who shall inform the other States Parties and the Committee. Denunciation shall take effect one year after the date of receipt of the notification. Denunciation shall not affect the execution of measures authorised prior to it.

APPENDIX 9

Proposals for the preamble and the final provisions of the Draft Convention, submitted by Sweden on 2 December 1980

(Document E/CN.4/1427)

PREAMBLE

The States Parties to the present Convention,

Considering that, in accordance with the principles proclaimed in the Charter of the United Nations, recognition of the inherent dignity and of the equal and inalienable rights of all members of the human family is the foundation of freedom, justice and peace in the world,

Recognizing that these rights derive from the inherent dignity of the human person,

Considering the obligation of States under the Charter of the United Nations to promote universal respect for, and observance of, human rights and fundamental freedoms,

Having regard to article 5 of the Universal Declaration of Human Rights and article 7 of the International Covenant on Civil and Political Rights, both of which provide that no one may be subjected to torture or to cruel, inhuman or degrading treatment or punishment,

Having regard also to the Declaration on the Protection of All Persons from Being Subjected to Torture and Other Cruel, Inhuman or Degrading Treatment or Punishment, adopted by the General Assembly on 9 December 1975 (resolution 3452 (XXX)),

Desiring to convert the principles of the Declaration into binding treaty obligations and to adopt a system for their effective implementation,

Have agreed as follows:

……

FINAL PROVISIONS

Article A

1. The present Convention is open for signature by all States at United Nations Headquarters in New York.

2. Any State which does not sign the Convention before its entry into force may accede to it.

Article B

1. The present Convention is subject to ratification. Instruments of ratification shall be deposited with the Secretary-General of the United Nations.

2. Accession shall be effected by the deposit of an instrument of accession with the Secretary-General of the United Nations.

Article C

1. The present Convention shall enter into force on the thirtieth day after the date of the deposit with the Secretary-General of the United Nations of the tenth instrument of ratification or accession.

2. For each State ratifying the present Convention or acceding to it after the deposit of the tenth instrument of ratification or accession, the Convention shall enter into force on the thirtieth day after the date of the deposit of its own instrument of ratification or accession.

Article D

1. A request for the revision of the present Convention may be made at any time by any State Party by means of a notification in writing addressed to the Secretary-General of the United Nations.

2. The General Assembly of the United Nations shall decide upon the steps, if any, to be taken in respect of such a request.

Article E

The Secretary-General of the United Nations shall inform all States of the following particulars:

(a) Signatures, ratifications and accessions under articles A and B;

(b) The date of entry into force of the present Convention under article C;

(c) Notifications under article D.

Article F

1. The present Convention, of which the Arabic, Chinese, English, French,

Russian and Spanish texts are equally authentic, shall be deposited in the archives of the United Nations.

2. The Secretary-General of the United Nations shall transmit certified copies of the present Convention to all States.

APPENDIX 10

New proposals for the implementation provisions of the Draft Convention, submitted by Sweden on 22 December 1981

(Document E/CN.4/1493)

Article 17

1. There shall be established a Committee against Torture (hereinafter referred to as the Committee). It shall consist of nine members and shall carry out the functions hereinafter provided.

2. The Committee shall be composed of nationals of the States Parties to the present Convention and, so far as possible, of persons who are also members of the Human Rights Committee established in accordance with Article 28 of the International Covenant on Civil and Political Rights. The members of the Committee shall be persons of high moral character and recognized competence in the field of human rights, consideration being given to the usefulness of the participation of some persons having legal experience.

3. The members of the Committee shall be elected and shall serve in their personal capacity.

Article 18

1. The members of the Committee shall be elected by secret ballot from a list of persons possessing the qualifications prescribed in article 17 and nominated for the purpose by the States Parties to the present Convention.

2. Each State Party to the present Convention may nominate not more than two persons. These persons shall be nationals of the nominating State.

3. A person shall be eligible for renomination.

Article 19

1. The initial election to the Committee shall be held no later than six months after the date of the entry into force of the present Convention.

2. At least four months before the date of each election to the Committee, other than an election to fill a vacancy in accordance with article 23, the Secretary-General of the United Nations shall address a written invitation to the States Parties to the present Convention to submit their nominations for membership of the Committee within three months.

3. The Secretary-General of the United Nations shall prepare a list in alphabetical order of all the persons thus nominated, with an indication of the States Parties which have nominated them, and shall submit it to the States Parties to the present Convention no later than one month before the date of each election.

4. Elections of the members of the Committee shall be held at a meeting of the States Parties to the present Convention convened by the Secretary-General of the United Nations at the Headquarters of the United Nations or at the United Nations Office at Geneva. At that meeting, for which two thirds of the States Parties to the present Convention shall constitute a quorum, the persons elected to the Committee shall be those nominees who obtain the largest number of votes and an absolute majority of the votes of the representatives of the States Parties present and voting.

Article 20

1. The Committee may not include more than one national of the same State.

2. In the election of the Committee, consideration shall be given to equitable geographical distribution of membership and to the representation of the different forms of civilization and of the principal legal systems.

Article 21

1. The members of the Committee shall be elected for a term of four years. They shall be eligible for re-election if renominated.

2. Elections at the expiry of office shall be held in accordance with the preceding articles of the present Convention.

Article 22

1. If, in the unanimous opinion of the other members, a member of the Committee has ceased to carry out his functions for any cause other than absence of a temporary character, the Chairman of the Committee shall notify the Secretary-General of the United Nations, who shall then declare the seat of that member to be vacant.

2. In the event of the death or the resignation of a member of the Committee, the Chairman shall immediately notify the Secretary-General of the United Nations, who shall declare the seat vacant from the date of death or the date on which the resignation takes effect.

Article 23

1. When a vacancy is declared in accordance with article 22 and if the term of office of the member to be replaced does not expire within six months of the declaration of the vacancy, the Secretary-General of the United Nations

shall notify each of the States Parties to the present Convention, which may within two months submit nominations in accordance with article 18 for the purpose of filling the vacancy.

2. The Secretary-General of the United Nations shall prepare a list in alphabetical order of the persons thus nominated and shall submit it to the States Parties to the present Convention. The election to fill the vacancy shall then take place in accordance with the relevant provisions of the present Convention.

3. A member of the Committee elected to fill a vacancy declared in accordance with article 22 shall hold office for the remainder of the term of the member who vacated the seat on the Committee under the provisions of that article.

Article 24

The States Parties to the present Convention shall be responsible, in the same proportions as their contributions to the general budget of the United Nations, for the expenses of the members of the Committee while they are in performance of Committee duties.

Article 25

The Secretary-General of the United Nations shall provide the necessary staff and facilities for the effective performance of the functions of the Committee under the present Convention.

Article 26

1. The Secretary-General of the United Nations shall convene the initial meeting of the Committee at the Headquarters of the United Nations or at the United Nations Office at Geneva.

2. After this initial meeting, the Committee shall meet at such times as shall be provided in its rules of procedure.

3. The Committee shall normally meet at the Headquarters of the United Nations or at the United Nations Office at Geneva.

Article 27

Every member of the Committee shall, before taking up his duties, make a solemn declaration in open committee that he will perform his functions impartially and conscientiously.

Article 28

1. The Committee shall elect its officers for a term of two years. They may be re-elected.

2. The Committee shall establish its own rules of procedure, but these rules shall provide, *inter alia*, that:

(a) six members shall constitute a quorum;

(b) decisions of the Committee shall be made by a majority vote of the members present.

Article 29

1. The States Parties to the present Convention undertake to submit to the Secretary-General of the United Nations

(a) within one year of the entry into force of the Convention for the States Parties concerned, reports on measures they have taken to give effect to their undertakings under the Convention; and

(b) subsequently, when so requested by the Committee, reports or other information relating to the application of the Convention.

2. Such reports or other information shall be considered by the Committee, which shall transmit such comments or suggestions relating to them as it may consider appropriate to the States Parties. The Committee may also transmit such comments or suggestions to the Economic and Social Council along with copies of the reports it has received from the States Parties.

3. The States Parties may submit to the Committee observations on any comments or suggestions that may be made in accordance with paragraph 2 of this article.

Article 30

1. If the Committee receives reliably attested information from any source indicating that torture is being systematically practised in the territory of a State Party to the present Convention, the Committee, after giving that State Party the opportunity to state its views on the situation, may designate one or more of its members to make a confidential enquiry and to report to the Committee urgently.

2. An enquiry made in accordance with paragraph 1 of this article may include a visit to the territory of the State Party concerned, unless the Government of that State Party refuses to give its consent.

Article 31

1. A State Party to the present Convention may at any time declare under this

article that it recognizes the competence of the Committee to receive and consider communications to the effect that a State Party claims that another State Party is not fulfilling its obligations under the present Convention. Such communications may be received and considered according to the procedures laid down in this article only if submitted by a State Party which has made a declaration recognizing in regard to itself the competence of the Committee. No communication shall be dealt with by the Committee under this article if it concerns a State Party which has not made such a declaration. Communications received under this article shall be dealt with in accordance with the following procedure:

(a) If a State Party considers that another State Party is not giving effect to the provisions of the present Convention, it may, by written communication, bring the matter to the attention of that State Party. Within three months after the receipt of the communication the receiving State shall afford the State which sent the communication an explanation, or any other statement in writing clarifying the matter which should include, to the extent possible and pertinent, reference to domestic procedures and remedies taken, pending, or available in the matter.

(b) If the matter is not adjusted to the satisfaction of both States Parties concerned within six months after the receipt by the receiving State of the initial communication, either State shall have the right to refer the matter to the Committee, by notice given to the Committee and to the other State.

(c) The Committee shall deal with a matter referred to it under this article only after it has ascertained that all domestic remedies have been invoked and exhausted in the matter, in conformity with the generally recognized principles of international law. This shall not be the rule where the application of the remedies is unreasonably prolonged or is unlikely to bring effective relief to the person who is the victim of the violation of the present Convention.

(d) The Committee shall hold closed meetings when examining communications under this article.

(e) Subject to the provisions of subparagraph (c), the Committee shall make available its good offices to the States Parties concerned with a view to a friendly solution of the matter on the basis of respect for the obligations provided for in the present Convention. For this purpose, the Committee may, when appropriate, set up an *ad hoc* conciliation commission.

(f) In any matter referred to it under this article, the Committee may call upon the States Parties concerned, referred to in subparagraph (b), to supply any relevant information.

(g) The States Parties concerned, referred to in subparagraph (b), shall have the right to be represented when the matter is being considered by the Committee and to make submissions orally and/or in writing.

(h) The Committee shall, within 12 months after the date of receipt of notice under subparagraph (b), submit a report:

(i) If a solution within the terms of subparagraph (e) is reached, the Committee shall confine its report to a brief statement of the facts and of the solution reached.
(ii) If a solution within the terms of subparagraph (e) is not reached, the Committee shall confine its report to a brief statement of the facts; the written submissions and record of the oral submissions made by the States Parties concerned shall be attached to the report.

In every matter, the report shall be communicated to the States Parties concerned.

2. The provisions of this article shall come into force when five States Parties to the present Convention have made declarations under paragraph 1 of this article. Such declarations shall be deposited by the States Parties with the Secretary-General of the United Nations, who shall transmit copies thereof to the other States Parties. A declaration may be withdrawn at any time by notification to the Secretary-General. Such a withdrawal shall not prejudice the consideration of any matter which is the subject of a communication already transmitted under this article; no further communication by any State Party shall be received under this article after the notification of withdrawal of the declaration has been received by the Secretary-General, unless the State Party concerned has made a new declaration.

Article 32

1. A State Party to the present Convention may at any time declare under this article that it recognizes the competence of the Committee to receive and consider communications from or on behalf of individuals subject to its jurisdiction who claim to be victims of a violation by a State Party of the provisions of the Convention. No communication shall be received by the Committee if it concerns a State Party to the Convention which has not made such a declaration.

2. The Committee shall consider inadmissible any communication under this article which is anonymous, or which it considers to be an abuse of the right of submission of such communications or to be incompatible with the provisions of the present Convention.

3. Subject to the provisions of paragraph 2, the Committee shall bring any communications submitted to it under this article to the attention of the State Party to the present Convention which has made a declaration under paragraph 1 and is alleged to be violating any provisions of the Convention. Within six months, the receiving State shall submit to the Committee written explan-

ations or statements clarifying the matter and the remedy, if any, that may have been taken by that State.

4. The Committee shall consider communications received under this article in the light of all information made available to it by or on behalf of the individual and by the State Party concerned.

5. The Committee shall not consider any communications from an individual under this article unless it has ascertained that

(a) the same matter has not been, and is not being, examined under another procedure of international investigation or settlement;

(b) the individual has exhausted all available domestic remedies; this shall not be the rule where the application of the remedies is unreasonably prolonged or is unlikely to bring effective relief to the person who is the victim of the violation of the present Convention.

6. The Committee shall hold closed meetings when examining communications under this article.

7. The Committee shall forward its views to the State Party concerned and to the individual.

8. The provisions of this article shall come into force when five States Parties to the present Convention have made declarations under paragraph 1 of this article. Such declarations shall be deposited by the States Parties with the Secretary-General of the United Nations, who shall transmit copies thereof to the other States Parties. A declaration may be withdrawn at any time by notification to the Secretary-General. Such a withdrawal shall not prejudice the consideration of any matter which is the subject of a communication already transmitted under this article; no further communication by or on behalf of an individual shall be received under this article after the notification of withdrawal of the declaration has been received by the Secretary-General, unless the State Party concerned has made a new declaration.

Article 33

The members of the Committee, and of the *ad hoc* conciliation commissions which may be appointed under article 31, paragraph 1 (e), shall be entitled to the facilities, privileges and immunities of experts on mission for the United Nations as laid down in the relevant sections of the Convention on the Privileges and Immunities of the United Nations.

Article 34

The Committee shall submit to the General Assembly of the United Nations, through the Economic and Social Council, an annual report on its activities.

APPENDIX 11

Draft implementation provisions, submitted by the Chairman-Rapporteur of the Working Group on 1 February 1982 as a possible alternative to the new Swedish proposals

(Document E/CN.4/1982/WG.2/WP.6)

Article 17

1. For the performance of the functions described in articles 18 and 19 there shall be established a group consisting of five persons of recognized competence in the field of human rights, consideration being given to the usefulness of the participation of some persons having legal experience.

2. The Chairman of the Commission on Human Rights shall appoint the members of the group from among representatives to the Commission on Human Rights who are nationals of States Parties to the Convention. If fewer than five States Parties to the Convention are members of the Commission on Human Rights, the Secretary-General of the United Nations shall, after consulting with all States Parties to the Convention, designate one or more nationals of States Parties which are not members of the Commission to take part in the work of the group until the next session of the Commission on Human Rights.

3. The members of the group established in accordance with the preceding paragraphs shall serve in their personal capacity.

4. The Secretary-General of the United Nations shall provide the necessary staff and facilities for the effective performance of the functions of the group established in accordance with paragraphs 1 and 2.

5. The group established in accordance with paragraphs 1 and 2 shall forward an annual report on its performance of the functions described in articles 18 and 19 to the States Parties to the Convention. It shall forward a copy of this report to the Commission on Human Rights.

Article 18

1. The States Parties to the Convention undertake to submit to the Secretary-General of the United Nations reports on the measures they have taken to give effect to their undertakings under the Convention:

(a) within one year of the entry into force of the Convention for the States Parties concerned; and

(b) whenever any new measures have been taken; and

(c) when the group established in accordance with article 17 so requests.

2. Such reports shall be considered by the group established in accordance with article 17, which shall transmit them with such comments and suggestions as it may consider appropriate to the States Parties. The group may also transmit such comments or suggestions to the Commission on Human Rights along with copies of the reports it has received from the States Parties.

3. The States Parties may submit to the group established in accordance with article 17 observations on any comments or suggestions that may be made in accordance with paragraph 2 of the present article.

Article 19

1. If the group established in accordance with article 17 receives information from any source which in its view appears to indicate that torture is being systematically practised in the territory of a State Party to the Convention, the group shall invite that State Party to submit observations with regard to the information concerned.

2. On the basis of all relevant information available to the group, including any observations which may have been submitted by the State Party concerned, the group may, if it decides that this is warranted, designate one or more of its members to make a confidential enquiry and to report to the group urgently.

3. An enquiry made in accordance with paragraph 2 of this article may include a visit to the territory of the State Party concerned, unless the Government of that State Party when informed of the intended visit, does not give its consent.

4. After examining the report of its member or members submitted in accordance with paragraph 2 of this article, the group may transmit to the State Party concerned any comments or suggestions which seem appropriate in view of the situation.

5. All the proceedings of the group under this article shall be confidential.

Article 20

1. The States Parties to the Convention shall seek a solution to any dispute that may arise between them concerning the interpretation or application of the Convention through the means indicated in article 33 of the Charter of the United Nations.

2. The existence of a dispute shall particularly be recognized when one State Party to the Convention has addressed to another State Party a written communication alleging that this other State Party has failed to fulfil one of its obligations under the Convention and the State Party to whom the communication has been addressed denies the allegation or fails to reply within 45 days.

3. If after the expiry of a period of 45 days after the existence of the dispute is recognized the States Parties concerned have not agreed on another method of settlement, any of them may set in motion the procedure of conciliation specified in the Annex to the present Convention, through a request made to the Secretary-General of the United Nations.

ANNEX

1. A list of conciliators consisting of persons of high moral character and recognized competence in the field of human rights shall be maintained by the Secretary-General of the United Nations. To this end, every State Party to the Convention shall be invited to nominate two conciliators, and the names of the persons so nominated shall constitute the list. The term of a conciliator, including that of any conciliator nominated to fill a vacancy, shall be five years and may be renewed. A conciliator whose term expires shall continue to fulfil any function for which he shall have been chosen under the following paragraphs.

2. When a request has been made to the Secretary-General in accordance with article 20, paragraph 3, of the Convention, the Secretary-General shall bring the dispute before a Conciliation Commission constituted as follows.

The State or States constituting one of the parties to the dispute shall appoint:

(a) one conciliator of the nationality of that State or one of those States, who may or may not be chosen from the list referred to in paragraph 1, and

(b) one conciliator not of the nationality of that State or of any of those States, who shall be chosen from the list.

The State or States constituting the other party to the dispute shall appoint two conciliators in the same way. The four conciliators chosen by the parties to the dispute shall be appointed within 45 days following the date on which the Secretary-General receives the request.

The four conciliators shall, within 45 days following the appointment of the last of them, appoint a fifth conciliator from the list, who shall be the chairman of the Conciliation Commission.

If the appointment of the chairman or of any of the other conciliators has not been made within the period prescribed above for such appointments, it shall be made by the Secretary-General within 45 days following the expiry of that period. Any of the periods within which appointments must be made may be extended by agreement between the parties to the dispute.

Any vacancy shall be filled in the manner prescribed for the initial appointment.

3. The Conciliation Commission shall decide its own procedure. Decisions

and recommendations of the Commission shall be made by a majority vote of the five members.

4. The Commission shall hear the parties to the dispute and examine the claims and objections. It may make recommendations at any time and shall present a Final Report within 180 days after its constitution. The Report, and any recommendations made by the Commission, shall not be binding upon the parties and shall have no other character than that of recommendations submitted for consideration to the parties.

5. The Secretary-General shall provide the Commission with such assistance and facilities as it may require for the performance of its function. The expenses of the Commission shall be borne by the United Nations.

APPENDIX 12

Four draft articles on implementation, with an explanatory note, submitted by the Chairman-Rapporteur on 24 December 1982

(Document E/CN.4/1983/WG.2/2)

DRAFT ARTICLES

Article 17

1. There shall be established a Committee against Torture (hereinafter referred to as the Committee) which shall carry out the functions hereinafter provided. The Committee shall consist of nine experts of high moral standing and recognized competence in the field of human rights, who shall serve in their personal capacity. The experts shall be elected by the States Parties, consideration being given to equitable geographical distribution and to the usefulness of the participation of some persons having legal experience.

2. The members of the Committee shall be elected by secret ballot from a list of persons nominated by States Parties. Each State Party may nominate one person from among its own nationals. States Parties shall bear in mind the usefulness of nominating persons who are also members of the Human Rights Committee established under the International Covenant on Civil and Political Rights and are willing to serve on the Committee against Torture.

3. Elections of the members of the Committee shall be held at biennial meetings of States Parties convened by the Secretary-General of the United Nations. At those meetings, for which two thirds of the States Parties shall constitute a quorum, the persons elected to the Committee shall be those who obtain the largest number of votes and an absolute majority of the votes of the representatives of States Parties present and voting.

4. The initial election shall be held no later than six months after the date of the entry into force of this Convention. At least four months before the date of each election the Secretary-General of the United Nations shall address a letter to the States Parties inviting them to submit their nominations within three months. The Secretary-General shall prepare a list in alphabetical order of all persons thus nominated, indicating the States Parties which have nominated them, and shall submit it to the States Parties.

5. The members of the Committee shall be elected for a term of four years. They shall be eligible for re-election if renominated. However, the term of four of the members elected at the first election shall expire at the end of two years; immediately after the first election the names of these four members shall be chosen by lot by the chairman of the meeting referred to in paragraph 3.

6. For the filling of casual vacancies, the State Party whose expert has ceased to function as a member of the Committee shall appoint another expert from among its nationals, subject to the approval of the Committee.

7. The members of the Committee shall receive emoluments as well as compensation for their expenses while they are in performance of Committee functions, on such terms and conditions as the biennial meetings of States Parties may decide. The States Parties shall be responsible for these emoluments and expenses in the same proportions as their contributions to the general budget of the United Nations.

Article 18

1. The Committee shall elect its officers for a term of two years. They may be re-elected.

2. The Committee shall establish its own rules of procedure, but these rules shall provide, *inter alia*, that:

(a) five members shall constitute a quorum;

(b) decisions of the Committee shall be made by a majority vote of the members present.

3. The Secretary-General of the United Nations shall provide the necessary staff and facilities for the effective performance of the functions of the Committee under this Convention.

4. The Secretary-General of the United Nations shall convene the initial meeting of the Committee. After its initial meeting, the Committee shall meet at such times as shall be provided in its rules of procedure.

Article 19

1. The States Parties undertake to submit to the Secretary-General of the United Nations reports on the measures they have taken to give effect to their undertakings under this Convention:

(a) within one year of the entry into force of this Convention for the State Party concerned; and

(b) whenever any new measures have been taken; and

(c) when the Committee so requests.

2. Such reports shall be considered by the Committee, which shall transmit them with such comments or suggestions as it may consider appropriate to the States Parties. The Committee may also transmit such comments or suggestions to the United Nations Commission on Human Rights along with copies of the reports it has received from the States Parties.

3. The States Parties may submit to the Committee observations on any comments or suggestions that may be made in accordance with paragraph 2.

Article 20

1. If the Committee receives information from any source which in its view appears to indicate that torture is being systematically practised in the territory of a State Party, the Committee shall invite that State Party to submit observations with regard to the information concerned.

2. On the basis of all relevant information available to the Committee, including any observations which may have been submitted by the State Party concerned, the Committee may, if it decides that this is warranted, designate one or more of its members to make a confidential enquiry and to report to the Committee urgently.

3. An enquiry made in accordance with paragraph 2 may include a visit to the territory of the State Party concerned, unless the Government of that State Party when informed of the intended visit, does not give its consent.

4. After examining the report of its member or members submitted in accordance with paragraph 2, the Committee may transmit to the State Party concerned any comments or suggestions which seem appropriate in view of the situation.

5. All the proceedings of the Committee under this article shall be confidential.

EXPLANATORY NOTE

On the recommendation of the Commission on Human Rights in its resolution 1982/44 of 11 March 1982, the Economic and Social Council, by its resolution 1982/38 of 7 May 1982, authorized the meeting of an open-ended Working Group for a period of one week prior to the thirty-ninth session of the Commission in order to complete the work on a draft convention against torture and other cruel, inhuman or degrading treatment or punishment. The issues to be dealt with by the Working Group are: the preamble, the material provisions, the implementation provisions, and the final clauses of the draft convention.

With regard to the preamble and the final clauses, the Working Group will have before it the proposals submitted by Sweden, contained in document E/CN.4/1427 of 2 December 1980. With regard to the material provisions of the draft convention, the Working Group will have before it the text of the draft articles 1-16, partially adopted and partially not yet adopted, contained in annex I to the report of the 1982 Working Group, document E/CN.4/1982/30/Add. 1, pages 19-23. With regard to the implementation provisions, the Working Group will have before it the draft articles 17-34 proposed by Sweden, contained in document E/CN.4/1493 of 31 December

1981 as well as in annex II to the report of the 1982 Working Group, pages 24-29.

As to the implementation issue, it may be recalled that the 1982 Working Group discussed extensively both the question of measures of international implementation and the question of the nature and composition of the implementation organ.

In considering the first question, the discussion concentrated on the draft articles 29 and 30 proposed by Sweden. With regard to each of these articles, several changes were suggested in the course of the discussion. The Working Group's report, however, does not contain the full text of these articles in the version which takes account of all suggestions that were accepted by the Swedish delegation. The Chairman-Rapporteur of the 1982 Working Group thinks that the work of the 1983 Working Group may be facilitated if it has this version of the draft articles before it.

As to the second question, many ideas were put forward in respect of the nature and composition of the implementation organ. *Inter alia*, some delegations considered the provisions proposed by Sweden too lengthy and complicated in proportion to the material provisions of the draft convention. A number of delegations expressed their preference, with varying emphasis, for the following basic elements: election of the implementation organ by the States parties, a requirement that all or part of the members should also belong to the Human Rights Committee and that the term of office should be carried out in a personal capacity. Other delegations spoke in favour of the establishment of an entirely new organ. The Chairman-Rapporteur of the 1982 Working Group thinks that it may be useful for the 1983 Working Group to have before it a revised set of provisions which endeavours to take into account the comments just referred to. He has, therefore, drafted such a revised set of provisions, taking into consideration the provisions on implementation organs contained in the 1965 International Convention on the Elimination of All Forms of Racial Discrimination and the 1979 Convention on the Elimination of All Forms of Discrimination against Women.

Accordingly, an informal draft of four articles on implementation is submitted with this explanatory note.

The draft articles 17 and 18 contain the above-mentioned revised set of provisions concerning the nature and the composition of the implementation organ.

The draft articles 19 and 20 reflect the outcome of the discussions that have taken place in the 1982 Working Group concerning articles 29 and 30 of the Swedish draft.

In order to avoid any misunderstanding it should be pointed out that these draft articles do not cover the implementation issue in its entirety. The Working Group will also proceed with the discussion of complaint and/or settlement-of-disputes provisions as well as of a provision on annual reporting by the Committee.

APPENDIX 13

Draft Convention, preceded by an explanatory note, as contained in the Annex to the report submitted by the Working Group in 1983

Document E/CN.4/1983/63

EXPLANATORY NOTE

The Annex contains a compilation of draft provisions adopted during working group sessions in 1979, 1980, 1981, 1982 and 1983, draft provisions proposed by Sweden which have not yet been adopted, and draft provisions as they emerged from the discussions and which the Working Group decided to include in the Annex as a basis for further consideration. All provisions which were not formally adopted have been placed between square brackets.

The Annex does not give a complete inventory of all proposals that have been tabled in the Working Group concerning the text of the draft convention. As to such proposals tabled in 1983, reference is made to paragraphs 12, 22, 23, 33, 45, 49, 56, 70 and 71 of the Report.

In respect of the different parts of the draft convention reproduced in the Annex, the following can be observed.

The preambular part contains seven preambular clauses adopted by the Working Group in 1983.

Part I contains sixteen substantive articles as they emerged from earlier discussions. Most of these provisions have already been adopted. Decisions are still pending with regard to the draft articles 3, 5, 6, 7 and 16.

Part II contains eight articles relating to implementation of the convention. The draft articles 17, 18, 19, 20 and 24 are based on proposals submitted by the Chairman-Rapporteur in 1983, adapted in the light of the discussions thereon. The draft articles 21, 22 and 23 are identical with the draft articles 31, 32 and 33 proposed by Sweden in 1981 (document E/CN.4/1493).

Part III contains seven final clauses. The draft articles 25, 26, 27, 28, 29 and 30 are based on proposals submitted by the Chairman-Rapporteur in 1983. Draft article 31 is identical with draft article F proposed by Sweden in 1980 (document E/CN.4/1427).

DRAFT CONVENTION AGAINST TORTURE AND OTHER CRUEL, INHUMAN OR DEGRADING TREATMENT OR PUNISHMENT

The States Parties to the present Convention,

Considering that, in accordance with the principles proclaimed in the Charter of the United Nations, recognition of the equal and inalienable rights of all members of the human family is the foundation of freedom, justice and peace in the world,

Recognizing that those rights derive from the inherent dignity of the human person,

Considering the obligation of States under the Charter, in particular Article 55, to promote universal respect for, and observance of, human rights and fundamental freedoms,

Having regard to article 5 of the Universal Declaration of Human Rights and article 7 of the International Covenant on Civil and Political Rights, both of which provide that no one may be subjected to torture or to cruel, inhuman or degrading treatment or punishment,

Having regard also to the Declaration on the Protection of All persons from Being subjected to Torture and Other Cruel, Inhuman or Degrading Treatment or Punishment, adopted by the General Assembly on 9 December 1975 (resolution 3452 (XXX)),

Desiring to make more effective the struggle against torture and other cruel, inhuman or degrading treatment or punishment throughout the world,

Have agreed as follows:

PART I

Article I

1. For the purposes of this Convention, torture means any act by which severe pain or suffering, whether physical or mental, is intentionally inflicted on a person for such purposes as obtaining from him or a third person information or a confession, punishing him for an act he or a third person has committed or is suspected of having committed, or intimidating or coercing him or a third person, or for any reason based on discrimination of any kind, when such pain or suffering is inflicted by or at the instigation of or with the consent or acquiescence of a public official or other person acting in an official capacity. It does not include pain or suffering arising only from, inherent in or incidental to lawful sanctions.

2. This article is without prejudice to any international instrument or national legislation which does or may contain provisions of wider application.

Article 2

1. Each State Party shall take effective legislative, administrative, judicial or other measures to prevent acts of torture in any territory under its jurisdiction.

2. No exceptional circumstances whatsoever, whether a state of war or a threat of war, internal political instability or any other public emergency, may be invoked as a justification of torture.

3. An order from a superior officer or a public authority may not be invoked as a justification of torture.

Article 3

1. No State Party shall expel, return ("*refouler*") or extradite a person to another State where there are substantial grounds for believing that he would be in danger of being subjected to torture.

2. [For the purpose of determining whether there are such grounds all relevant considerations shall be taken into account including, where applicable, the existence in the State concerned of a consistent pattern of gross violations of human rights, such as those resulting from a State policy of *apartheid*, racial discrimination or genocide, colonialism or neo-colonialism, the suppression of national liberation movements or the occupation of foreign territory.]

"Remark: Some delegations indicated that their States might wish, at the time of signature or ratification of the Convention or accession thereto, to declare that they did not consider themselves bound by article 3 of the Convention, in so far as that article might not be compatible with obligations towards States not Party to the convention under extradition treaties concluded before the date of the signature of the Convention."

Article 4

1. Each State Party shall ensure that all acts of torture are offences under its criminal law. The same shall apply to an attempt to commit torture and to an act by any person which constitutes complicity or participation in torture.*

2. Each State Party shall make these offences punishable by appropriate penalties which take into acount their grave nature.

---

* The term "complicity" includes "*encubrimiento*" in the Spanish text.

In the Spanish text

[Add at the end of para. 1: "*o encubrimiento de la tortura*".]

In the French text

[Add a foot-note reading: "le terme 'complicité' comprend '*encubrimiento*' dans le texte espagnol".]

Article 5

1. Each State Party shall take such measures as may be necessary to establish its jurisdiction over the offences referred to in article 4 in the following cases:

(a) When the offences are committed in any territory under its jurisdiction or on board a ship or aircraft registered in that State;

(b) When the alleged offender is a national of that State;

(c) When the victim is a national of that State if that State considers it appropriate.

[2. Each State Party shall likewise take such measures as may be necessary to establish its jurisdiction over such offences in cases where the alleged offender is present in any territory under its jurisdiction and it does not extradite him pursuant to article 8 to any of the States mentioned in paragraph 1 of this article.]

3. This Convention does not exclude any criminal jurisdiction exercised in accordance with internal law.

Article 6

1. Upon being satisfied, after an examination of information available to it, that the circumstances so warrant, any State Party in whose territory a person alleged to have committed any offence referred to in article 4 is present, shall take him into custody or take other legal measures to ensure his presence. The custody and other legal measures shall be as provided in the law of that State but may be continued only for such time as is necessary to enable any criminal or extradition proceedings to be instituted.

2. Such State shall immediately make a preliminary inquiry into the facts.

3. Any person in custody pursuant to paragraph 1 of this article shall be assisted in communicating immediately with the nearest appropriate representative of the State of which he is a national, or, if he is a stateless person, with the representative of the State where he usually resides.

[4. When a State, pursuant to this article, has taken a person into custody, it shall immediately notify the States referred to in article 5, paragraph 1, of the fact that such person is in custody and of the circumstances which warrant his detention. The State which makes the preliminary inquiry contemplated in paragraph 2 of this article shall promptly report its findings to the said States and shall indicate whether it intends to exercise jurisdiction.]

Article 7

[1. The State Party in territory under whose jurisdiction a person alleged to have committed any offence referred to in article 4 is found, shall in the cases contemplated in article 5, if it does not extradite him, submit the case to its competent authorities for the purpose of prosecution.

2. These authorities shall take their decision in the same manner as in the case of any ordinary offence of a serious nature under the law of that State. In the cases referred to in article 5, paragraph 2, the standards of evidence required for prosecution and conviction shall in no way be less stringent than those which apply in the cases referred to in article 5, paragraph 1.

3. Any person regarding whom proceedings are brought in connection with any of the offences referred to in article 4 shall be guaranteed fair treatment at all stages of the proceedings.]

Article 8

1. The offences referred to in article 4 shall be deemed to be included as extraditable offences in any extradition treaty existing between States Parties. States Parties undertake to include such offences as extraditable offences in every extradition treaty to be concluded between them.

2. If a State Party which makes extradition conditional on the existence of a treaty receives a request for extradition from another State Party with which it has no extradition treaty, it may consider this Convention as the legal basis for extradition in respect of such offences. Extradition shall be subject to the other conditions provided by the law of the requested State.

3. States Parties which do not make extradition conditional on the existence of a treaty shall recognize such offences as extraditable offences between themselves subject to the conditions provided by the law of the requested State.

4. Such offences shall be treated, for the purpose of extradition between States Parties, as if they had been committed not only in the place in which they occurred but also in the territories of the States required to establish their jurisdiction in accordance with article 5, paragraph 1.

Article 9

1. States Parties shall afford one another the greatest measure of assistance in connection with criminal proceedings brought in respect of any of the offences referred to in article 4, including the supply of all evidence at their disposal necessary for the proceedings.

2. States Parties shall carry out their obligations under paragraph 1 of this article in conformity with any treaties on mutual judicial assistance that may exist between them.

Article 10

1. Each State Party shall ensure that education and information regarding the prohibition against torture are fully included in the training of law enforcement personnel, civil or military, medical personnel, public officials and other persons who may be involved in the custody, interrogation or treatment of any individual subjected to any form of arrest, detention or imprisonment.

2. Each State Party shall include this prohibition in the rules or instructions issued in regard to the duties and functions of any such persons.

Article 11

Each State Party shall keep under systematic review interrogation rules, instructions, methods and practices as well as arrangements for the custody and treatment of persons subjected to any form of arrest, detention or imprisonment in any territory under its jurisdiction, with a view to preventing any cases of torture.

Article 12

Each State Party shall ensure that its competent authorities proceed to a prompt and impartial investigation, wherever there is reasonable ground to believe that an act of torture has been committed in any territory under its jurisdiction.

Article 13

Each State Party shall ensure that any individual who alleges he has been subjected to torture in any territory under its jurisdiction has the right to complain to and to have his case promptly and impartially examined by its competent authorities. Steps shall be taken to ensure that the complainant and witnesses are protected against all ill-treatment or intimidation as a consequence of his complaint or any evidence given.

Article 14

1. Each State Party shall ensure in its legal system that the victim of an act of torture be redressed and have an enforceable right to fair and adequate compensation including the means for as full rehabilitation as possible. In the event of the death of the victim as a result of an act of torture, his dependants shall be entitled to compensation.

2. Nothing in this article shall affect any right of the victim or other persons to compensation which may exist under national law.

Article 15

Each State Party shall ensure that any statement which is established to have been made as a result of torture shall not be invoked as evidence in any proceedings, except against a person accused of torture as evidence that the statement was made.

Article 16

1. Each State Party shall undertake to prevent in any territory under its jurisdiction other acts of cruel, inhuman or degrading treatment or punishment which do not amount to torture as defined in article 1, when such acts are committed by or at the instigation of or with the consent or acquiescence of a public official or other person acting in an official capacity. In particular, the obligations contained in articles 10, 11, 12, 13 and [14] shall apply with the substitution for references to torture of references to other forms of cruel, inhuman or degrading treatment or punishment.

2. The provisions of this Convention are without prejudice to the provisions of any other international instrument or national law which prohibit cruel, inhuman or degrading treatment or punishment or which relate to extradition or expulsion.

PART II

Article 17

[1. There shall be established a Committee against Torture (hereinafter referred to as the Committee) which shall carry out the functions hereinafter provided. The Committee shall consist of nine experts of high moral standing and recognized competence in the field of human rights, who shall serve in their personal capacity. The experts shall be elected by the States parties, consideration being given to equitable geographical distribution and to the usefulness of the participation of some persons having legal experience.

2. The members of the Committee shall be elected by secret ballot from a list of persons nominated by States parties. Each State party may nominate one person from among its own nationals. States parties shall bear in mind the usefulness of nominating persons who are also members of the Human Rights Committee established under the International Covenant on Civil and Political Rights and are willing to serve on the Committee against Torture.

3. Elections of the members of the Committee shall be held at biennial meetings of States parties convened by the Secretary-General of the United Nations. At those meetings, for which two thirds of the States parties shall constitute a quorum, the persons elected to the Committee shall be those who

obtain the largest number of votes and an absolute majoity of the votes of the representatives of States parties present and voting.

4. The initial election shall be held no later than six months after the date of the entry into force of this Convention. At least four months before the date of each election, the Secretary-General of the United Nations shall address a letter to the States parties inviting them to submit their nominations within three months. The Secretary-General shall prepare a list in alphabetical order of all persons thus nominated, indicating the States parties which have nominated them, and shall submit it to the States parties.

5. The members of the Committee shall be elected for a term of four years. They shall be eligible for re-election if renominated. However, the term of four of the members elected at the first election shall expire at the end of two years; immediately after the first election the names of these four members shall be chosen by lot by the chairman of the meeting referred to in paragraph 3.

6. If a member of the Committee dies or resigns or for any other cause can no longer perform his Committee duties, the State party which nominated him shall appoint another expert from among its nationals to serve for the remainder of his term, subject to the approval of the majority of the States parties. The approval shall be considered given unless half or more of the States parties respond negatively within six weeks after having been informed by the Secretary-General of the United Nations of the proposed appointment.

7. States parties shall be responsible for the expenses of the members of the Committee while they are in performance of Committee duties.]

Article 18

[1. The Committee shall elect its officers for a term of two years. They may be re-elected.

2. The committee shall establish its own rules of procedure, but these rules shall provide, *inter alia*, that:

(a) six members shall constitute a quorum;

(b) decisions of the Committee shall be made by a majority vote of the members present.

3. The Secretary-General of the United Nations shall provide the necessary staff and facilities for the effective performance of the functions of the Committee under this Convention.

4. The Secretary-General of the United Nations shall convene the initial meeting of the Committee. After its initial meeting, the Committee shall meet at such times as shall be provided in its rules of procedure.]

Article 19

[1. The States parties shall submit to the Committee, through the Secretary-General of the United Nations, reports on the measures they have taken to give effect to their undertakings under this Convention, within one year after the entry into force of this Convention for the State party concerned. Thereafter the States parties shall submit supplementary reports every four years on any new measures taken, and such other reports as the committee may request.

2. The Secretary-General shall transmit the reports to all States parties.

3. Each report shall be considered by the Committee which may make such comments or suggestions on the report as it may consider appropriate, and shall forward these to the State party concerned. That State party may respond with any observations it chooses to the Committee.

4. The Committee may, at its discretion, decide to include any comments or suggestions made by it in accordance with paragraph 3, together with the observations thereon received from the State party concerned, in its annual report made in accordance with article 24.]

Article 20

[1. If the Committee receives information which appears to it to contain reliable indications that torture is being systematically practised in the territory of a State party, the Committee shall invite that State party to submit observations with regard to the information concerned.

2. Taking into account any observations which may have been submitted by the State party concerned as well as any other relevant information available to it, the Committee may, if it decides that this is warranted, designate one or more of its members to make a confidential inquiry and to report to the Committee urgently.

3. If an inquiry is made in accordance with paragraph 2, the Committee shall seek the co-operation of the State party concerned. In agreement with that State party, such an inquiry may include a visit to its territory.

4. After examining the findings of its member or members submitted in accordance with paragraph 2, the Committee shall transmit these findings to the State party concerned together with any comments or suggestions which seem appropriate in view of the situation.

5. All the proceedings of the Committee referred to in the paragraphs 1-4 shall be confidential. After such proceedings have been completed with regard to an inquiry made in accordance with paragraph 2, the Committee may, at its

discretion, decide to include a summary account of the results of the proceedings in its annual report made in accordance with article 24.]

Article 21

[1. A State party to the present Convention may at any time declare under this article that it recognizes the competence of the Committee to receive and consider communications to the effect that a State party claims that another State party is not fulfilling its obligations under the present Convention. Such communications may be received and considered according to the procedures laid down in this article only if submitted by a State party which has made a declaration recognizing in regard to itself the competence of the Committee. No communication shall be dealt with by the Committee under this article if it concerns a State party which has not made such a declaration. Communications received under this article shall be dealt with in accordance with the following procedure:

(a) If a State party considers that another State party is not giving effect to the provisions of the present Convention, it may, by written communication, bring the matter to the attention of that State party. Within three months after the receipt of the communication the receiving State shall afford the State which sent the communication an explanation or any other statement in writing clarifying the matter which should include, to the extent possible and pertinent, reference to domestic procedures and remedies taken, pending, or available in the matter.

(b) If the matter is not adjusted to the satisfaction of both States parties concerned within six months after the receipt by the receiving State of the initial communication, either State shall have the right to refer the matter to the Committee, by notice given to the Committee and to the other State.

(c) The Committee shall deal with a matter referred to it under this article only after it has ascertained that all domestic remedies have been invoked and exhausted in the matter, in conformity with the generally recognized principles of international law. This shall not be the rule where the application of the remedies is unreasonably prolonged or is unlikely to bring effective relief to the person who is the victim of the violation of the present Convention.

(d) The Committee shall hold closed meetings when examining communications under this article.

(e) Subject to the provisions of subparagraph (c), the Committee shall make available its good offices to the States parties concerned with a view to a friendly solution of the matter on the basis of respect for the obligations provided for in the present Convention. For this purpose, the Committee may, when appropriate, set up an *ad hoc* conciliation commission.

(f) In any matter referred to it under this article, the Committee may call upon the States parties concerned, referred to in subparagraph (b), to supply any relevant information.

(g) The States parties concerned, referred to in subparagraph (b), shall have the right to be represented when the matter is being considered by the Committee and to make submissions orally and/or in writing.

(h) The Committee shall, within 12 months after the date of receipt of notice under subparagraph (b), submit a report:

(i) If a solution within the terms of subparagraph (e) is reached, the Committee shall confine its report to a brief statement of the facts and of the solution reached.

(ii) If a solution within the terms of subparagraph (e) is not reached, the Committee shall confine its report to a brief statement of the facts; the written submissions and record of the oral submissions made by the States parties concerned shall be attached to the report.

In every matter, the report shall be communicated to the States parties concerned.

2. The provisions of this article shall come into force when five States parties to the present Convention have made declarations under paragraph 1 of this article. Such declarations shall be deposited by the States parties with the Secretary-General of the United Nations, who shall transmit copies thereof to the other States parties. A declaration may be withdrawn at any time by notification to the Secretary-General. Such a withdrawal shall not prejudice the consideration of any matter which is the subject of a communication already transmitted under this article; no further communication by any State party shall be received under this article after the notification of withdrawal of the declaration has been received by the Secretary-General, unless the State party concerned has made a new declaration.]

Article 22

[1. A State party to the present Convention may at any time declare under this article that it recognizes the competence of the Committee to receive and consider communications from or on behalf of individuals subject to its jurisdiction who claim to be victims of a violation by a State party of the provisions of the Convention. No communication shall be received by the Committee if it concerns a State party to the Convention which has not made such a declaration.

2. The Committee shall consider inadmissible any communication under this article which is anonymous, or which it considers to be an abuse of the right

of submission of such communications or to be incompatible with the provisions of the present Convention.

3. Subject to the provisions of paragraph 2, the Committee shall bring any communications submitted to it under this article to the attention of the State party to the present Convention which has made a declaration under paragraph 1 and is alleged to be violating any provisions of the Convention. Within six months, the receiving State shall submit to the Committee written explanations or statements clarifying the matter and the remedy, if any, that may have been taken by that State.

4. The Committee shall consider communications received under this article in the light of all information made available to it by or on behalf of the individual and by the State party concerned.

5. The Committee shall not consider any communications from an individual under this article unless it has ascertained that

(a) the same matter has not been, and is not being, examined under another procedure of international investigation or settlement;

(b) the individual has exhausted all available domestic remedies; this shall not be the rule where the application of the remedies is unreasonably prolonged or is unlikely to bring effective relief to the person who is the victim of the violation of the present Convention.

6. The Committee shall hold closed meetings when examining communications under this article.

7. The Committee shall forward its views to the State party concerned and to the individual.

8. The provisions of this article shall come into force when five States parties to the present Convention have made declarations under paragraph 1 of this article. Such declarations shall be deposited by the States parties with the Secretary-General of the United Nations, who shall transmit copies thereof to the other States parties. A declaration may be withdrawn at any time by notification to the Secretary-General. Such a withdrawal shall not prejudice the consideration of any matter which is the subject of a communicaton already transmitted under this article; no further communication by or on behalf of an individual shall be received under this article after the notification of withdrawal of the declaration has been received by the Secretary-General, unless the State party concerned has made a new declaration.]

Article 23

[The members of the Committee, and of the *ad hoc* conciliation commissions which may be appointed under article 21, paragraph 1 (e), shall be entitled to the facilities, privileges and immunities of experts on mission for the United Nations as laid down in the relevant sections of the Convention on the Privileges and Immunities of the United Nations.]

Article 24

[The Committee shall submit an annual report on its activities under this Convention to the States parties and to the General Assembly of the United Nations.]

PART III

Article 25

[1. This Convention is open for signature by all States.

2. This Convention is subject to ratification. Instruments of ratification shall be deposited with the Secretary-General of the United Nations.]

Article 26

[This Convention is open to accession by all States. Accession shall be effected by the deposit of an instrument of accession with the Secretary-General of the United Nations.]

Article 27

[1. This Convention shall enter into force on the thirtieth day after the date of the deposit with the Secretary-General of the United Nations of the [twentieth] instrument of ratification or accession.

2. For each State ratifying this Convention or acceding to it after the deposit of the [twentieth] instrument of ratification or accession, the Convention shall enter into force on the thirtieth day after the date of the deposit of its own instrument of ratification or accession.]

Article 28

[1. Any State Party to this Convention may propose an amendment and file it with the Secretary-General of the United Nations. The Secretary-General shall thereupon communicate the proposed amendment to the States Parties to this Convention with a request that they notify him whether they favour a conference of States Parties for the purpose of considering and voting upon the proposal. In the event that at least one third of the States Parties favours such a conference, the Secretary-General shall convene the conference under the auspices of the United Nations. Any amendment adopted by a majority of the States Parties present and voting at the conference shall be submitted by the Secretary-General to all the States Parties for acceptance.

2. An amendment adopted in accordance with paragraph 1 shall enter into force when two thirds of the States Parties to this Convention have notified the Secretary-General of the United Nations that they have accepted it in accordance with their respective constitutional processes.

3. When amendments enter into force, they shall be binding on those States Parties which have accepted them, other States Parties still being bound by the provisions of this Convention and any earlier amendments which they have accepted.]

Article 29

[A State Party may denounce this Convention by written notification to the Secretary-General of the United Nations. Denunciation shall take effect one year after the date of receipt of the notification by the Secretary-General.]

Article 30

[The Secretary-General of the United Nations shall inform all members of the United Nations and all States which have signed this Convention or acceded to it, of the following particulars:

(a) Signatures, ratifications and accessions under articles 25 and 26;

(b) The date of entry into force of this Convention under article 27 and the date of the entry into force of any amendments under article 28;

(c) Denunciations under article 29.]

Article 31

[1. The present Convention, of which the Arabic, Chinese, English, French, Russian and Spanish texts are equally authentic, shall be deposited in the archives of the United Nations.

2. The Secretary-General of the United Nations shall transmit certified copies of the present Convention to all States.]

APPENDIX 14

Resolution concerning the Convention against Torture and Other Cruel, Inhuman or Degrading Treatment or Punishment, adopted by the United Nations General Assembly on 10 December 1984 (resolution 39/46)

The General Assembly,

Recalling the Declaration on the Protection of All Persons from Being Subjected to Torture and Other Cruel, Inhuman or Degrading Treatment or Punishment, adopted by the General Assembly in its resolution 3452 (XXX) of 9 December 1975,

Recalling also its resolution 32/62 of 8 December 1977, in which it requested the Commission on Human Rights to draw up a draft convention against torture and other cruel, inhuman or degrading treatment or punishment, in the light of the principles embodied in the Declaration,

Recalling further that, in its resolution 38/119 of 16 December 1983, it requested the Commission on Human Rights to complete, at its fortieth session, as a matter of highest priority, the drafting of such a convention, with a view to submitting a draft, including provisions for the effective implementation of the future convention, to the General Assembly at its thirty-ninth session,

Noting with satisfaction Commission on Human Rights resolution 1984/21 of 6 March 1984, by which the Commission decided to transmit the text of a draft convention against torture and other cruel, inhuman or degrading treatment or punishment, contained in the annex to the report of the Working Group, to the General Assembly for its consideration,

Desirous of achieving a more effective implementation of the existing prohibition under international and national law of the practice of torture and other cruel, inhuman or degrading treatment or punishment,

1. *Expresses its appreciation* for the work achieved by the Commission on Human Rights in preparing the text of a draft convention against torture and other cruel, inhuman or degrading treatment or punishment;

2. *Adopts* and opens for signature, ratification and accession the Convention against Torture and Other Cruel, Inhuman or Degrading Treatment or Punishment contained in the annex to the present resolution;[1]

3. *Calls upon* all Governments to consider signing and ratifying the Convention as a matter of priority.

---

[1] The text of the annex is not reproduced here because it is practically identical with the text reproduced in Appendix 1. After the adoption of this resolution the Secretariat of the United Nations made a few purely editorial alterations in Part III of the text of the Convention that was prepared for signature.

APPENDIX 15

Articles 31, 32, 33 and 34 of the Standard Minimum Rules for the Treatment of Prisoners

Adopted by the First United Nations Congress on the Prevention of Crime and the Treatment of Offenders on 30 August 1955 and approved by the United Nations Economic and Social Council on 31 July 1957

31. Corporal punishment, punishment by placing in a dark cell, and all cruel, inhuman or degrading punishments shall be completely prohibited as punishments for disciplinary offences.

32. (1) Punishment by close confinement or reduction of diet shall never be inflicted unless the medical officer has examined the prisoner and certified in writing that he is fit to sustain it.

(2) The same shall apply to any other punishment that may be prejudicial to the physical or mental health of a prisoner. In no case may such punishment be contrary to or depart from the principle stated in rule 31.

(3) The medical officer shall visit daily prisoners undergoing such punishments and shall advise the director if he considers the termination or alteration of the punishment necessary on grounds of physical or mental health.

33. Instruments of restraint, such as handcuffs, chains, irons and straitjackets, shall never be applied as a punishment. Furthermore, chains or irons shall not be used as restraints. Other instruments of restraint shall not be used except in the following circumstances:

(*a*) As a precaution against escape during a transfer, provided that they shall be removed when the prisoner appears before a judicial or administrative authority;

(*b*) On medical grounds by direction of the medical officer;

(*c*) By order of the director, if other methods of control fail, in order to prevent a prisoner from injuring himself or others or from damaging property; in such instances the director shall at once consult the medical officer and report to the higher administrative authority.

34. The patterns and manner of use of instruments of restraint shall be decided by the central prison administration. Such instruments must not be applied for any longer time than is strictly necessary.

APPENDIX 16

Article 5 of the Code of Conduct for Law Enforcement Officials

Adopted by the United Nations General Assembly on 17 December 1979 (resolution 34/169)

Article 5

No law enforcement official may inflict, instigate or tolerate any act of torture or other cruel, inhuman or degrading treatment or punishment, nor may any law enforcement official invoke superior orders or exceptional circumstances such as a state of war or a threat of war, a threat to national security, internal political instability or any other public emergency as a justification of torture or other cruel, inhuman of degrading treatment or punishment.

Commentary:

(a) This prohibition derives from the Declaration on the Protection of All Persons from Being Subjected to Torture and Other Cruel, Inhuman or Degrading Treatment or Punishment, adopted by the General Assembly, according to which:

"[Such an act is] an offence to human dignity and shall be condemned as a denial of the purposes of the Charter of the United Nations and as a violation of the human rights and fundamental freedoms proclaimed in the Universal Declaration of Human Rights [and other international human rights instruments]."

(b) The Declaration defines torture as follows:

"... torture means any act by which severe pain or suffering, whether physical or mental, is intentionally inflicted by or at the instigation of a public official on a person for such purposes as obtaining from him or a third person information or confession, punishing him for an act he has committed or is suspected of having committed, or intimidating him or other persons. It does not include pain or suffering arising only from, inherent in or incidental to, lawful sanctions to the extent consistent with the Standard Minimum Rules for the Treatment of Prisoners."

(c) The term "cruel, inhuman or degrading treatment or punishment" has not been defined by the General Assembly but should be interpreted so as to extend the widest possible protection against abuses, whether physical or mental.

APPENDIX 17

Principles of Medical Ethics relevant to the Role of Health Personnel, particularly Physicians, in the Protection of Prisoners and Detainees against Torture and Other Cruel, Inhuman or Degrading Treatment or Punishment

Adopted by the United Nations General Assembly on 18 December 1982 (resolution 37/194)

The General Assembly,

Recalling its resolution 31/85 of 13 December 1976, in which it invited the World Health Organization to prepare a draft code of medical ethics relevant to the protection of persons subjected to any form of detention or imprisonment against torture and other cruel, inhuman or degrading treatment or punishment,

Expressing once again its appreciation to the Executive Board of the World Health Organization which, at its sixty-third session in January 1979, decided to endorse the principles set forth in a report entitled "Development of codes of medical ethics" containing, in an annex, a draft body of principles prepared by the Council for International Organizations of Medical Sciences and entitled "Principles of medical ethics relevant to the role of health personnel in the protection of persons against torture and other cruel, inhuman or degrading treatment or punishment",

Bearing in mind Economic and Social Council resolution 1981/27 of 6 May 1981, in which the Council recommended that the General Assembly should take measures to finalize the draft Principles of Medical Ethics at its thirty-sixth session,

Recalling its resolution 36/61 of 25 November 1981, in which it decided to consider the draft Principles of Medical Ethics at its thirty-seventh session with a view to adopting them,

Alarmed that not infrequently members of the medical profession or other health personnel are engaged in activities which are difficult to reconcile with medical ethics,

Recognizing that throughout the world significant medical activities are being performed increasingly by health personnel not licensed or trained as physicians, such as physician-assistants, paramedics, physical therapists and nurse practitioners,

Recalling with appreciation the Declaration of Tokyo of the World Medical Association, containing the Guidelines for Medical Doctors concerning Torture and other Cruel, Inhuman or Degrading Treatment or Punishment in relation to Detention and Imprisonment, adopted by the twenty-ninth World

Medical Assembly, held at Tokyo in October 1975,

Noting that in accordance with the Declaration of Tokyo measures should be taken by States and by professional associations and other bodies, as appropriate, against any attempt to subject health personnel or members of their families to threats or reprisals resulting from a refusal by such personnel to condone the use of torture or other forms of cruel, inhuman or degrading treatment,

Reaffirming the Declaration on the Protection of All Persons from Being Subjected to Torture and Other Cruel, Inhuman or Degrading Treatment or Punishment, unanimously adopted by the General Assembly in its resolution 3452 (XXX) of 9 December 1975, in which it declared any act of torture or other cruel, inhuman or degrading treatment or punishment an offence to human dignity, a denial of the purposes of the Charter of the United Nations and a violation of the Universal Declaration of Human Rights,

Recalling that, in accordance with article 7 of the Declaration adopted in resolution 3452 (XXX), each State shall ensure that the commission of all acts of torture, as defined in article 1 of that Declaration, or participation in, complicity in, incitement to or attempt to commit torture, are offences under its criminal law,

Convinced that under no circumstances should a person be punished for carrying out medical activities compatible with medical ethics regardless of the person benefiting therefrom, or be compelled to perform acts or to carry out work in contravention of medical ethics, but that, at the same time, contravention of medical ethics for which health personnel, particularly physicians, can be held responsible should entail accountability,

Desirous of setting further standards in this field which ought to be implemented by health personnel, particularly physicians, and by Government officials,

1. *Adopts* the Principles of Medical Ethics relevant to the role of health personnel, particularly physicians, in the protection of prisoners and detainees against torture and other cruel, inhuman or degrading treatment or punishment set forth in the annex to the present resolution;

2. *Calls upon* all Governments to give the Principles of Medical Ethics, together with the present resolution, the widest possible distribution, in particular among medical and paramedical associations and institutions of detention or imprisonment in an official language of the State;

3. *Invites* all relevant intergovernmental organizations, in particular the World Health Organization, and nongovernmental organizations concerned to bring the Principles of Medical Ethics to the attention of the widest possible group of individuals, especially those active in the medical and paramedical field.

Annex

PRINCIPLES OF MEDICAL ETHICS RELEVANT TO THE ROLE OF HEALTH PERSONNEL, PARTICULARLY PHYSICIANS, IN THE PROTECTION OF PRISONERS AND DETAINEES AGAINST TORTURE AND OTHER CRUEL, INHUMAN OR DEGRADING TREATMENT OR PUNISHMENT

Principle 1

Health personnel, particularly physicians, charged with the medical care of prisoners and detainees have a duty to provide them with protection of their physical and mental health and treatment of disease of the same quality and standard as is afforded to those who are not imprisoned or detained.

Principle 2

It is a gross contravention of medical ethics, as well as an offence under applicable international instruments, for health personnel, particularly physicians, to engage, actively or passively, in acts which constitute participation in, complicity in, incitement to or attempts to commit torture or other cruel, inhuman or degrading treatment or punishment.

Principle 3

It is a contravention of medical ethics for health personnel, particularly physicians, to be involved in any professional relationship with prisoners or detainees the purpose of which is not solely to evaluate, protect or improve their physical and mental health.

Principle 4

It is a contravention of medical ethics for health personnel, particularly physicians:

(a) To apply their knowledge and skills in order to assist in the interrogation of prisoners and detainees in a manner that may adversely affect the physical or mental health or condition of such prisoners or detainees and which is not in accordance with the relevant international instruments;

(b) To certify, or to participate in the certification of, the fitness of prisoners or detaineees for any form of treatment or punishment that may adversely affect their physical or mental health and which is not in accordance with the relevant international instruments, or to participate in any way in the infliction of any such treatment or punishment which is not in accordance with the relevant international instruments.

Principle 5

It is a contravention of medical ethics for health personnel, particularly physicians, to participate in any procedure for restraining a prisoner or detainee unless such a procedure is determined in accordance with purely medical criteria as being necessary for the protection of the physical or mental health or the safety of the prisoner or detainee himself, of his fellow prisoners or detainees, or of his guardians, and presents no hazard to his physical or mental health.

Principle 6

There may be no derogation from the foregoing principles on any ground whatsoever, including public emergency.

APPENDIX 18

Inter-American Convention to Prevent and Punish Torture

Signed at Cartagena de Indias, Colombia, on 9 December 1985 at the Fifteenth Regular Session of the General Assembly of the Organization of American States

The American States signatory to the present Convention,

Aware of the provision of the American Convention on Human Rights that no one shall be subjected to torture or to cruel, inhuman, or degrading punishment or treatment;

Reaffirming that all acts of torture or any other cruel, inhuman, or degrading treatment or punishment constitute an offense against human dignity and a denial of the principles set forth in the Charter of the Organization of American States and in the Charter of the United Nations and are violations of the fundamental human rights and freedoms proclaimed in the American Declaration of the Rights and Duties of Man and the Universal Declaration of Human Rights;

Noting that, in order for the pertinent rules contained in the aforementioned global and regional instruments to take effect, it is necessary to draft an Inter-American Convention that prevents and punishes torture;

Reaffirming their purpose of consolidating in this hemisphere the conditions that make for recognition of and respect for the inherent dignity of man, and ensure the full exercise of his fundamental rights and freedoms,

Have agreed upon the following:

Article 1

The States Parties undertake to prevent and punish torture in accordance with the terms of this Convention.

Article 2

For the purposes of this Convention, torture shall be understood to be any act intentionally performed whereby physical or mental pain or suffering is inflicted on a person for purposes of criminal investigation, as a means of intimidation, as personal punishment, as a preventive measure, as a penalty, or for any other purpose. Torture shall also be understood to be the use of methods upon a person intended to obliterate the personality of the victim or to diminish his physical or mental capacities, even if they do not cause physical pain or mental anguish.

The concept of torture shall not include physical or mental pain or suffering that is inherent in or solely the consequence of lawful measures, provided that they do not include the performance of the acts or use of the methods referred to in this article.

Article 3

The following shall be held guilty of the crime of torture:

a. A public servant or employee who acting in that capacity orders, instigates or induces the use of torture, or who directly commits it or who, being able to prevent it, fails to do so.

b. A person who at the instigation of a public servant or employee mentioned in subparagraph (a) orders, instigates or induces the use of torture, directly commits it or is an accomplice thereto.

Article 4

The fact of having acted under orders of a superior shall not provide exemption from the corresponding criminal liability.

Article 5

The existence of circumstances such as a state of war, threat of war, state of siege or of emergency, domestic disturbance or strife, suspension of constitutional guarantees, domestic political instability, or other public emergencies or disasters shall not be invoked or admitted as justification for the crime of torture.

Neither the dangerous character of the detainee or prisoner, nor the lack of security of the prison establishment or penitentiary shall justify torture.

Article 6

In accordance with the terms of Article 1, the States Parties shall take effective measures to prevent and punish torture within their jurisdiction.

The States Parties shall ensure that all acts of torture and attempts to commit torture are offenses under their criminal law and shall make such acts punishable by severe penalties that take into account their serious nature.

The States Parties likewise shall take effective measures to prevent and punish other cruel, inhuman, or degrading treatment or punishment within their jurisdiction.

Article 7

The States Parties shall take measures so that, in the training of police officers and other public officials responsible for the custody of persons temporarily or definitively deprived of their freedom, special emphasis shall be put on the prohibition of the use of torture in interrogation, detention, or arrest.

The States Parties likewise shall take similar measures to prevent other cruel, inhuman, or degrading treatment or punishment.

Article 8

The States Parties shall guarantee that any person making an accusation of having been subjected to torture within their jurisdiction shall have the right to an impartial examination of this case.

Likewise, if there is an accusation or well-grounded reason to believe that an act of torture has been committed within their jurisdiction, the States Parties shall guarantee that their respective authorities will proceed properly and immediately to conduct an investigation into the case and to initiate, whenever appropriate, the corresponding criminal process.

After all the domestic legal procedures of the respective State and the corresponding appeals have been exhausted, the case may be submitted to the international fora whose competence has been recognized by that State.

Article 9

The States Parties undertake to incorporate into their national laws regulations guaranteeing suitable compensation for victims of torture.

None of the provisions of this article shall affect the right to receive compensation that the victim or other persons may have by virtue of existing national legislation.

Article 10

No statement that is verified as having been obtained through torture shall be admissible as evidence in a legal proceeding, except in a legal action taken against a person or persons accused of having elicited it through acts of torture, and only as evidence that the accused obtained such statement by such means.

Article 11

The States Parties shall take the necessary steps to extradite anyone accused of having committed the crime of torture or sentenced for commission of that crime, in accordance with their respective national laws on extradition and their international commitments on this matter.

Article 12

Every State Party shall take the necessary measures to establish its jurisdiction over the crime described in this Convention in the following cases:

a. When torture has been committed within its jurisdiction;

b. When the alleged criminal is a national of that State; or

c. When the victim is a national of that State and it so deems appropriate.

Every State Party shall also take the necessary measures to establish its jurisdiction over the crime described in this Convention when the alleged criminal is within the area under its jurisdiction and it is not appropriate to extradite him in accordance with Article 11.

This Convention does not exclude criminal jurisdiction exercised in accordance with domestic law.

Article 13

The crime referred to in Article 2 shall be deemed to be included among the extraditable crimes in every extradition treaty entered into between States Parties. The States Parties undertake to include the crime of torture as an extraditable offence in every extradition treaty to be concluded between them.

Every State Party that makes extradition conditional on the existence of a treaty may, if it receives a request for extradition from another State Party with which it has no extradition treaty, consider this Convention as the legal basis for extradition in respect of the crime of torture. Extradition shall be subject to the other conditions that may be required by the law of the requested State.

States Parties which do not make extradition conditional on the existence of a treaty shall recognize such crimes as extraditable offences between themselves, subject to the conditions required by the law of the requested State.

Extradition shall not be granted nor shall the person sought be returned when there are grounds to believe that his life is in danger, that he will be subjected to torture or to cruel, inhuman or degrading treatment, or that he will be tried by special or *ad hoc* courts in the requesting State.

Article 14

When a State Party does not grant the extradition, the case shall be submitted to its competent authorities as if the crime had been committed within its jurisdiction, for the purposes of investigation, and when appropriate, for criminal action, in accordance with its national law. Any decision adopted by these authorities shall be communicated to the State that has requested the extradition.

Article 15

No provision of this Convention may be interpreted as limiting the right of asylum, when appropriate, nor as altering the obligations of the States Parties in the matter of extradition.

Article 16

This Convention shall not limit the provisions of the American Convention on Human Rights, other conventions on the subject, or the Statutes of the Inter-American Commission on Human Rights, with respect to the crime of torture.

Article 17

The States Parties undertake to inform the Inter-American Commission on Human Rights of any legislative, judicial, administrative, or other measures they adopt in application of this Convention.

In keeping with its duties and responsibilities, the Inter-American Commission on Human Rights will endeavor in its annual report to analyze the existing situation in the member states of the Organization of American States in regard to the prevention and elimination of torture.

Article 18

This Convention is open to signature by the member states of the Organization of American States.

Article 19

This Convention is subject to ratification. The instruments of ratification shall be deposited with the General Secretariat of the Organization of American States.

Article 20

This Convention is open to accession by any other American state. The instruments of accession shall be deposited with the General Secretariat of the Organization of American States.

Article 21

The States Parties may, at the time of approval, signature, ratification, or accession, make reservations to this Convention, provided that such reservations are not incompatible with the object and purpose of the Convention and concern one or more specific provisions.

Article 22

This Convention shall enter into force on the thirtieth day following the date on which the second instrument of ratification is deposited. For each State ratifying or acceding to the Convention after the second instrument of ratification has been deposited, the Convention shall enter into force on the thirtieth day following the date on which that State deposits its instrument of ratification or accession.

Article 23

This Convention shall remain in force indefinitely, but may be denounced by any State Party. The instrument of denunciation shall be deposited with the General Secretariat of the Organization of American States. After one year from the date of deposit of the instrument of denunciation, this Convention shall cease to be in effect for the denouncing State but shall remain in force for the remaining States Parties.

Article 24

The original instrument of this Convention, the English, French, Portuguese, and Spanish texts of which are equally authentic, shall be deposited with the General Secretariat of the Organization of American States, which shall send a certified copy to the Secretariat of the United Nations for registration and publication, in accordance with the provisions of Article 102 of the United Nations Charter. The General Secretariat of the Organization of American States shall notify the member states of the Organization and the states that have acceded to the Convention of signatures and of deposits of instruments of ratification, accession, and denunciation, as well as reservations, if any.

APPENDIX 19

European Convention for the Prevention of Torture and Inhuman or Degrading Treatment or Punishment

Adopted by the Committee of Ministers of the Council of Europe on 26 June 1987 and opened for signature at Strasbourg on 26 November 1987

The member States of the Council of Europe, signatory hereto,

Having regard to the provisions of the Convention for the Protection of Human Rights and Fundamental Freedoms,

Recalling that, under Article 3 of the same Convention, "no one shall be subjected to torture or to inhuman or degrading treatment or punishment";

Noting that the machinery provided for in that Convention operates in relation to persons who allege that they are victims of violations of Article 3;

Convinced that the protection of persons deprived of their liberty against torture and inhuman or degrading treatment or punishment could be strengthened by non-judicial means of a preventive character based on visits,

Have agreed as follows:

CHAPTER I

Article 1

There shall be established a European Committee for the Prevention of Torture and Inhuman or Degrading Treatment or Punishment (hereinafter referred to as "the Committee"). The Committee shall, by means of visits, examine the treatment of persons deprived of their liberty with a view to strengthening, if necessary, the protection of such persons from torture and from inhuman or degrading treatment or punishment.

Article 2

Each Party shall permit visits, in accordance with this Convention, to any place within its jurisdiction where persons are deprived of their liberty by a public authority.

Article 3

In the application of this Convention, the Committee and the competent national authorities of the Party concerned shall co-operate with each other.

CHAPTER II

Article 4

1. The Committee shall consist of a number of members equal to that of the Parties.

2. The members of the Committee shall be chosen from among persons of high moral character, known for their competence in the field of human rights or having professional experience in the areas covered by this Convention.

3. No two members of the Committee may be nationals of the same State.

4. The members shall serve in their individual capacity, shall be independent and impartial, and shall be available to serve the Committee effectively.

Article 5

1. The members of the Committee shall be elected by the Committee of Ministers of the Council of Europe by an absolute majority of votes, from a list of names drawn up by the Bureau of the Consultative Assembly of the Council of Europe; each national delegation of the Parties in the Consultative Assembly shall put forward three candidates, of whom two at least shall be its nationals.

2. The same procedure shall be followed in filling casual vacancies.

3. The members of the Committee shall be elected for a period of four years. They may only be re-elected once. However, among the members elected at the first election, the terms of three members shall expire at the end of two years. The members whose terms are to expire at the end of the initial period of two years shall be chosen by lot by the Secretary General of the Council of Europe immediately after the first election has been completed.

Article 6

1. The Committee shall meet in camera. A quorum shall be equal to the majority of its members. The decisions of the Committee shall be taken by a majority of the members present, subject to Article 10, paragraph 2.

2. The Committee shall draw up its own rules of procedure.

3. The Secretariat of the Committee shall be provided by the Secretary General of the Council of Europe.

CHAPTER III

Article 7

1. The Committee shall organise visits to places referred to in Article 2. Apart from periodic visits, the Committee may organise such other visits as appear to it to be required in the circumstances.

2. As a general rule, the visits shall be carried out by at least two members of the Committee. The Committee may, if it considers it necessary, be assisted by experts and interpreters.

Article 8

1. The Committee shall notify the Government of the Party concerned of its intention to carry out a visit. After such notification, it may at any time visit any place referred to in Article 2.

2. A Party shall provide the Committee with the following facilities to carry out its task:

a. access to its territory and the right to travel without restriction;

b. full information on the places where persons deprived of their liberty are being held;

c. unlimited access to any place where persons are deprived of their liberty, including the right to move inside such places without restriction;

d. other information available to the Party which is necessary for the Committee to carry out its task. In seeking such information, the Committee shall have regard to applicable rules of national law and professional ethics.

3. The Committee may interview in private persons deprived of their liberty.

4. The Committee may communicate freely with any person whom it believes can supply relevant information.

5. If necessary, the Committee may immediately communicate observations to the competent authorities of the Party concerned.

Article 9

1. In exceptional circumstances, the competent authorities of the Party concerned may make representations to the Committee against a visit at the time or to the particular place proposed by the Committee. Such representations may only be made on grounds of national defence, public safety, serious disorder in places where persons are deprived of their liberty, the medical

conditions of a person or that an urgent interrogation relating to a serious crime is in progress.

2. Following such representations, the Committee and the Party shall immediately enter into consultations in order to clarify the situation and seek agreement on arrangements to enable the Committee to exercise its functions expeditiously. Such arrangements may include the transfer to another place of any person whom the Committee proposed to visit. Until the visit takes place, the Party shall provide information to the Committee about any person concerned.

Article 10

1. After each visit, the Committee shall draw up a report on the facts found during the visit, taking account of any observations which may have been submitted by the Party concerned. It shall transmit to the latter its report containing any recommendations it considers necessary. The Committee may consult with the Party with a view to suggesting, if necessary, improvements in the protection of persons deprived of their liberty.

2. If the Party fails to co-operate or refuses to improve the situation in the light of the Committee's recommendations, the Committee may decide, after the Party has had an opportunity to make known its views, by a majority of two-thirds of its members to make a public statement on the matter.

Article 11

1. The information gathered by the Committee in relation to a visit, its report and its consultations with the Party concerned shall be confidential.

2. The Committee shall publish its report, together with any comments of the Party concerned, whenever requested to do so by that Party.

3. However, no personal data shall be published without the express consent of the person concerned.

Article 12

Subject to the rules of confidentiality in Article 11, the Committee shall every year submit to the Committee of Ministers a general report on its activities which shall be transmitted to the Consultative Assembly and made public.

Article 13

The members of the Committee, experts and other persons assisting the Committee are required, during and after their terms of office, to maintain the confidentiality of the facts or information of which they have become aware during the discharge of their functions.

Article 14

1. The names of persons assisting the Committee shall be specified in the notification under Article 8, paragraph 1.

2. Experts shall act on the instructions and under the authority of the Committee. They shall have particular knowledge and experience in the areas covered by this Convention and shall be bound by the same duties of independence, impartiality and availability as the members of the Committee.

3. A Party may exceptionally declare that an expert or other person assisting the Committee may not be allowed to take part in a visit to a place within its jurisdiction.

CHAPTER IV

Article 15

Each Party shall inform the Committee of the name and address of the authority competent to receive notifications to its Government, and of any liaison officer it may appoint.

Article 16

The Committee, its members and experts referred to in Article 7, paragraph 2 shall enjoy the privileges and immunities set out in the Annex to this Convention.

Article 17

1. This Convention shall not prejudice the provisions of domestic law or any international agreement which provide greater protection for persons deprived of their liberty.

2. Nothing in this Convention shall be construed as limiting or derogating from the competence of the organs of the European Convention on Human Rights or from the obligations assumed by the Parties under that Convention.

3. The Committee shall not visit places which representatives or delegates of Protecting Powers or the International Committee of the Red Cross effectively visit on a regular basis by virtue of the Geneva Conventions of 12 August 1949 and the Additional Protocols of 8 June 1977 thereto.

CHAPTER V

Article 18

This Convention shall be open for signature by the member States of the Council of Europe. It is subject to ratification, acceptance or approval. Instruments of ratification, acceptance or approval shall be deposited with the Secretary General of the Council of Europe.

Article 19

1. This Convention shall enter into force on the first day of the month following the expiration of a period of three months after the date on which seven member States of the Council of Europe have expressed their consent to be bound by the Convention in accordance with the provisions of Article 18.

2. In respect of any member State which subsequently expresses its consent to be bound by it, the Convention shall enter into force on the first day of the month following the expiration of a period of three months after the date of the deposit of the instrument of ratification, acceptance or approval.

Article 20

1. Any State may at the time of signature or when depositing its instrument of ratification, acceptance or approval, specify the territory or territories to which this Convention shall apply.

2. Any State may at any later date, by a declaration addressed to the Secretary General of the Council of Europe, extend the application of this Convention to any other territory specified in the declaration. In respect of such territory the Convention shall enter into force on the first day of the month following the expiration of a period of three months after the date of receipt of such declaration by the Secretary General.

3. Any declaration made under the two preceding paragraphs may, in respect of any territory specified in such declaration, be withdrawn by a notification addressed to the Secretary General. The withdrawal shall become effective on the first day of the month following the expiration of a period of three months after the date of receipt of such notification by the Secretary General.

Article 21

No reservation may be made in respect of the provisions of this Convention.

Article 22

1. Any Party may, at any time, denounce this Convention by means of a notification addressed to the Secretary General of the Council of Europe.

2. Such denunciation shall become effective on the first day of the month following the expiration of a period of twelve months after the date of receipt of the notification by the Secretary General.

Article 23

The Secretary General of the Council of Europe shall notify the member States of the Council of Europe of:

a. any signature;

b. the deposit of any instrument of ratification, acceptance or approval;

c. any date of entry into force of this Convention in accordance with Articles 19 and 20;

d. any other act, notification or communication relating to this Convention, except for action taken in pursuance of Articles 8 and 10.

In witness whereof, the undersigned, being duly authorised thereto, have signed this Convention.

Done at Strasbourg, the 26th November 1987, in English and French, both texts being equally authentic, in a single copy which shall be deposited in the archives of the Council of Europe. The Secretary General of the Council of Europe shall transmit certified copies to each member State of the Council of Europe.

Annex

Privileges and immunities (Article 16)

1. For the purpose of this annex, references to members of the Committee shall be deemed to include references to experts mentioned in Article 7, paragraph 2.

2. The members of the Committee shall, while exercising their functions and during journeys made in the exercise of their functions, enjoy the following privileges and immunities:

a. immunity from personal arrest or detention and from seizure of their personal baggage and, in respect of words spoken or written and all acts done by them in their official capacity, immunity from legal process of every kind;

b. exemption from any restrictions on their freedom of movement on exit from and return to their country of residence, and entry into and exit from the country in which they exercise their functions, and from alien registration in the country which they are visiting or through which they are passing in the exercise of their functions.

3. In the course of journeys undertaken in the exercise of their functions, the members of the Committee shall, in the matter of customs and exchange control, be accorded:

a. by their own Government, the same facilities as those accorded to senior officials travelling abroad on temporary official duty;

b. by the Governments of other Parties, the same facilities as those accorded to representatives of foreign Governments on temporary official duty.

4. Documents and papers of the Committee, in so far as they relate to the business of the Committee, shall be inviolable.

The official correspondence and other official communications of the Committee may not be held up or subjected to censorship.

5. In order to secure for the members of the Committee complete freedom of speech and complete independence in the discharge of their duties, the immunity from legal process in respect of words spoken or written and all acts done by them in discharging their duties shall continue to be accorded, notwithstanding that the persons concerned are no longer engaged in the discharge of such duties.

6. Privileges and immunities are accorded to the members of the Committee, not for the personal benefit of the individuals themselves but in order to safeguard the independent exercise of their functions. The Committee alone shall be competent to waive the immunity of its members; it has not only the right, but is under a duty, to waive the immunity of one of its members in any case where, in its opinion, the immunity would impede the course of justice, and where it can be waived without prejudice to the purpose for which the immunity is accorded.